P
i

w

79 309 236 6

THE GARDEN IN THE CLOUDS

THE GARDEN IN THE CLOUDS

*From Derelict Smallholding to
Mountain Paradise*

———— ◆ ————

ANTONY WOODWARD

Harper
Press

HarperPress
An imprint of HarperCollinsPublishers
77–85 Fulham Palace Road
Hammersmith, London W6 8JB
www.harpercollins.co.uk

Visit our authors' blog: www.fifthestate.co.uk
Love this book? www.bookarmy.com

First published in Great Britain by HarperPress in 2010

1

A catalogue record for this book is
available from the British Library

ISBN 978-0-00-721651-2

Typeset in Adobe Garamond

Printed and bound in Great Britain by Clays Ltd, St Ives plc

Mixed Sources
Product group from well-managed
forests and other controlled sources
www.fsc.org Cert no. SW-COC-001806
© 1996 Forest Stewardship Council

FSC

To Vez

sine qua non

It is better to have your head in the clouds, and know where you are ... than to breathe the clearer atmosphere below them, and think that you are in paradise.

HENRY DAVID THOREAU

The link between imagination and place is no trivial matter.

The existential question, 'Where do I belong?' is addressed to the imagination. To inhabit a place physically, but to remain unaware of what it means or how it feels, is a deprivation more profound than deafness at a concert or blindness in an art gallery. Humans in this condition belong no *where*.

EUGENE WALTER, *Placeways*, 1988

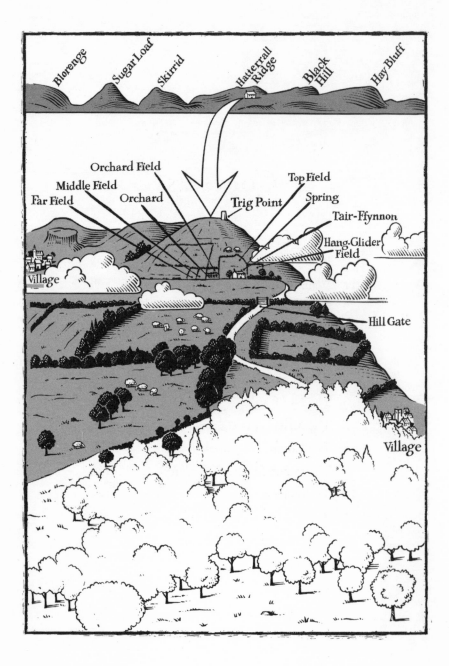

Contents

Prologue

Hell is all right. The human mind is inspired enough
when it comes to inventing horrors; it is when it tries to
invent a Heaven that it shows itself cloddish.

EVELYN WAUGH, *Put Out More Flags*, 1942

My first involvement with gardening was aged seven. I am sitting in
the back of my mother's car (Austin 1300 Countryman, cream, wood-
effect trim). She's at the wheel; my father's in the passenger seat, my
older brother Jonathan is in the back with me. We've pulled off a country road alongside some iron railings. Through the railings a garden can
be seen leading back, via a wide lawn, to a handsome stone-built villa.
Wiltshire probably; possibly Gloucestershire or Somerset.

'Antony'—my mother only used my full Christian name when she
was serious—'I won't ask you again. Get out of the car.'

'No.'

'Get—out—of—the—car.'

'Why? Why me?'

'The more you sit here arguing, the longer we're going to be.'

'Why can't Jonny do it?'

'You're smaller than he is. Anyway, it's your turn.'

'What if someone comes? What if the people come back?'

'They won't come back.'

'But what if they do?'

'I must say, I'm not sure this is wise,' says my father. 'It's breaking the law.'

'Don't be so feeble, Peter. How could anyone mind? If the child got on with it, we could all be on our way home by now.'

'Exactly. It's breaking the—'

'Be quiet, Antony.'

'What if someone does come?' says my father.

'He just runs for it, of course.' She turns to me. 'You can come back through the gate if you want. Look,' she adopts a more conciliatory tone, 'it won't take a second. You'll be back here before you know it, and I'll cook sausages for tea.'

'The fence is too high. I'll never get over.'

'It does look high, Liza. I really do think—' says my father.

'Fiddlesticks. Really Peter, you're as bad as the children.'

'It's not fair ... where's the bloody thing again?'

'Don't use bad language. It's the *helianthemum*. Over there under the wall, with the small white flowers. In that raised bed. On the left.'

From the car there is a view through the wrought-iron gate, down a short, flag-stoned path onto the lawn. Diagonally across this is the raised bed, about eighty yards away.

'The white thing by the big red bush?'

'Yes. Now get a move on. And remember: pull downwards so a piece of the stalk comes with it.'

It had recently rained and as I push through the shrubbery to the railings, every move brings a shower of water droplets down my neck and arms. Insects hum loudly, and beetles keep dropping onto me. Straddling the crossbar, trying to get my second leg over, one of my belt loops catches on an iron point. For a few seconds I'm helpless, exposed to both the house and anyone passing. Vigorous arm movements from the car indicate that my mother thinks I'm stalling. I wriggle free, drop back down into the laurels, crawling under their cover until I reach the lawn's edge. Then I sprint. By the raised bed, I grab at the plant, and a few moments later, breathless with adrenaline, I'm back at the gate. The latch is tight, lifting with a clang, the hinges screech deafeningly, but at last I'm back in the safety of the car.

'Quick, go,' I pant, pulling the car door shut.

'Let me see,' demands my mother.

I thrust the sprig of foliage into her hand.

'Come on. *Go.*'

'This isn't a *helianthemum*,' says my mother. 'This is *aubrietia*. You nincompoop, Ant. You've got the wrong plant.'

'*What?*'

'This is no use at all.'

'Well, I can't help it. You should have said.'

'No use at all,' repeats my mother. 'Why on earth would I ask for *aubrietia*? Quick—back you go.'

'*WHAT?*'

'Come on. We haven't got all day.'

'I'm not going back in there.'

'Of course you are. And this time, use your nous,' she adds, tapping her temple with her forefinger; 'it's an alpine. Come on. Get on with it.'

For the second time, I find myself ejected. 'Well make sure you switch the engine on …'

'Yes, yes, yes.'

The angry yell of a man's voice comes from the direction of the house just as my hand stretches out to the raised bed: 'Hey! You! What are you doing?'

I don't look, I just leg it across the lawn to the flagged path to the gate. This is my undoing. Following the rain, as soon as my feet touch the flags, I perform a graceless cartwheel, coming down agonisingly on my left thigh. Picking myself up, I fumble for the gate latch. A clang, a squeal of hinges, and I'm back in the car. 'Quick. Quick. Someone's coming. Quick. Go. Go, go, go.'

My mother hasn't started the engine. I dive behind the front seats as she fiddles unhurriedly with the ignition. As we at last pull away, I emerge to find my mother holding the cutting at arm's length (she's longsighted), appraising as she steers with one hand.

'Please keep your eyes on the road, Liza,' says my father.

'That should take alright,' she says. She starts to wrap the cutting in one of the numerous crumpled paper handkerchiefs that always surround her, the car swerving dangerously as she does so. 'See darling?' she says, turning to me. 'That couldn't have been easier, could it? All that fuss. You do make such a meal of everything.'

—◆—

This book is partly about an attempt to make a garden and partly an attempt to resolve my vexed relationship with the whole subject of gardening. The specific impulse was planted about twenty years ago, during a conversation with a friend whose party trick was hypnotising people. 'We all have a garden in our heads,' he happened to mention. Asked to close our eyes and imagine ourselves in our favourite garden, most people will find a special place, usually a childhood garden. Real or imaginary, once chosen, it'll always be the same place we visit, if requested to do so thereafter, again and again. This fact, he said, was indispensable to hypnotists, who need to make their subject feel secure, contented, fulfilled, calm and relaxed—in short, highly susceptible to whatever humiliating routines he had planned for them—in a hurry. 'Just get them into the garden,' he finished cheerfully. 'Then you've got 'em.'

'What if they don't have a favourite garden?'

'Everyone has a favourite garden.'

Somehow, this idea stuck in my head. The genius of it was its individuality. The instant he said it, I knew I had just such a place. It was the house where my grandmother lived when I was little: a gabled, Elizabethan Cotswold farmhouse with outbuildings, down a long drive, above a valley of hanging beech woods. The house was built of that honey-coloured limestone that seems to absorb the sunshine then radiate it back so even on grey days it still felt warm. The roof was of mossy stone tiles, the windows mullioned. The south-facing garden side was framed by two trees: a vast and ancient Irish yew and a flowering cherry whose white blossom indicated spring had arrived. A stream ran across the lawn in front of the house, feeding a natural swimming pool hewn out of the rock. Inside the dark interior, there were beams and oak panelling and a smell of wood smoke and beeswax. A trap door under the sitting-room carpet led to the cellar. Even the name was charmed: Rookwoods-on-the-Holy-Brook.

Rookwoods was sold in 1968, when I was five and my brother Jonny was seven. 'It was far too remote for an old woman in winter,' my mother would declare matter-of-factly when, later, we demanded to know why. 'It only took a frost for her to be cut off.' It was the only criticism of Rookwoods I ever heard. The sense of loss, the mounting resentment, the indignant accusations, they followed gradually. As we grew up, vignettes of our Cotswold idyll would drift back, until, by our teens, mere mention of the name was enough to trigger outraged nostalgia. My brother and I would compete for whose imagination had the greater claim on the place, trumping each other's memories in an area in which my brother, with a two-and-a-half-year head start, had an irksome advantage.

When Granny died, decades later, we inherited two Rookwoods heirlooms. One was a bird table made by Cyril, the gardener. Architecturally, it was little different to most bird tables—a platform on a post beneath a pitched roof—but it was clearly handmade. The pitched roof was of beaten tin. Whittled oak pegs served as perches. The supporting pole had an irregular section where Cyril had taken the corners off with a draw knife. Erected in its new home, our garden, the bits gradually fell off: first the roof, then the supporting pillars, then the perches and the lip to stop the food blowing off. But, because it was oak, the rest, the pole and the platform, lasted: a daily presence outside the kitchen, gently reminding us of its charmed provenance.

The other heirloom was a picture. Before selling Rookwoods, Granny commissioned a painting of the house from a retired artist who lived nearby. The artist was Ernest Dinkel (the illustrator behind some of the classic 1930s underground posters) and he made a particularly good job of it. His watercolour, in its limed oak frame, moved with Granny to her next house. When she died it came to us, and when Jonny and I left home, it went to him, sparking a row so immense my father had a copy made for me.

———•◆•———

I once read that in loving relationships between adults, the relationship does not start the day two people meet, but in the childhood of each partner. That's when the template which governs adult behaviour, when it comes to love, is laid down. If that's the case, then why shouldn't much the same apply to our relationship with places? It's always fascinated me that if you ask someone where, if they could have one, their secret rural hideaway would be—by a stream, say, in the woods, by the sea or in the hills—they always seem to know immediately. How can this be?

When I started trying to make my own garden, I discovered the task had actually begun years earlier, before I'd even found the place where my garden was to be, and that I was embarking on a more involved adventure than I could possibly have guessed, one in which all kinds of unexpected influences came to bear. Careful, patient assessment of the garden in my head, no doubt, might have explained some of these things, while simultaneously revealing much about myself (to make your paradise, after all, you need to know yourself). I did no such thing. Instead, I blundered on, baffled but trying to stay loyal to my instincts, following inexplicable imperatives. Only gradually did some explanations begin to dawn. The result is a book that often strays beyond the garden gate to all kinds of peripheral things, from childhood and family to wood-chopping.

My hope is that, on the off chance that others, too, have a garden in their heads alongside the one that they're trying to make for real, my explorations will prompt them to reflect on theirs. After all, no-one can deny the sheer grandeur of ambition or romantic purity of the impulse behind Britain's greatest shared passion, to which anyone who's ever dropped into a garden centre of a Saturday morning, hauled resentfully on a mower pull-start, or opened a packet of seeds has, however unconsciously, already succumbed.

A. W.
Tair-Ffynnon, 2010

1

Walking country

Now and then we passed through winding valleys speckled with
farms that looked romantic and pretty from a distance, but bleak
and comfortless up close. Mostly they were smallholdings with
lots of rusted tin everywhere—tin sheds, tin hen huts, tin fences
—looking rickety and weatherbattered. We were entering one
of those weird zones, always a sign of remoteness from the known
world, where nothing is ever thrown away. Every farmyard was
cluttered with piles of cast-offs, as if the owner thought that one
day he might need 132 half-rotted fence-posts, a ton of broken
bricks and the shell of a 1964 Ford Zodiac.

BILL BRYSON, *Notes from a Small Island*, 1996

'What d'you want that old place for? You a farmer? You don't sound
like a farmer.'

Mr Games had the easy telephone manner of someone used to talking for a living and the cheery directness which I was beginning to associate with the Borderland brogue. It was late September and I'd been told there was nothing he didn't know about property in the Black Mountains of South Wales. If we needed someone to bid on our behalf, then, as a pillar of one of the old established local auctioneers, valuers and land agents, no-one was better for the task than Mr Games.

'I'm a writer.'

'Are you, bloody hell?'

'I was wondering, is there any chance—'

'If you're a writer, you'll know Oliver Goldsmith? I was thinking of him just now.'

'Oliver Goldsmith? No, I don't think—'

'*Her modest looks the cottage might adorn,/Sweet as the primrose peeps beneath the thorn;/Now lost to all; her friends, her virtue fled,/Near her betrayer's door she lays her head,/And, pinched with cold and shrinking from the shower,/With heavy heart deplores that luckless hour.*'

'That *is* lovely. No, I don't know that poem, but—'

'*The Deserted Village.* You must know that.'

'I must look it up. But I was wondering—?'

'What about Keats? *Adieu! adieu! thy plaintive anthem fades/Past the near meadows, over the still stream,/Up the hill-side; and now 'tis buried deep/In the next valley-glades:/Was it a vision, or a waking dream?/Fled is that music—do I wake or sleep?* How do they do it? That's the bloody question. It's in there you know, right from the start. Thomas, d'you read much of him? "And Death Shall Have No Dominion?"'

'I ... er ...'

'*No more may gulls cry at their ears/Or waves break loud on the seashores ...*'

Was everyone in Border Country like this, I wondered? Everyone we met seemed to love to talk.

'... He was nineteen. *Nineteen.* How can you know that stuff aged nineteen?'

'Amazing, isn't it? But I was wondering—'

'So why d'you want this house anyway? It's in the middle of bloody nowhere.'

'That's the point. I like—'

'D'you read Johnston? You must've read him? That time at the Giant's Causeway …'

And he was off again. Forty minutes later, with difficulty, I extricated myself ('Got to go, have you?')—though, as I put the phone down, I felt at least we now had a sound ally. I arranged to meet at his office the following Friday at twelve o'clock to run through the formalities before the afternoon's auction.

The call was the culmination of a decade of dreaming followed by a three-year wild-goose chase. I'd been looking for a rural hideaway for as long as I could remember. In my mind, I knew precisely what I was after. It would be a remote, whitewashed stone cottage with a sagging roof of mossy stone slates, up a long, rocky track. Inside would be a sitting room lined with books, and battered old leather armchairs, a threadbare carpet and a blazing log fire. The place would have elements of Gavin Maxwell's Camusfearna (his cottage on the West Coast of Scotland in *Ring of Bright Water*), Uncle Monty's Lake District retreat in the film *Withnail and I*, and Shackleton's hut at the South Pole, with its tin stove pipe, cosy bunks and (yes, let us not forget) plentiful wooden packing cases of canned lobster soup and vintage claret. It had to be somewhere properly wild: mountains or moorland—walking country—where the wind howled and the rain lashed, somewhere that would be cut off for weeks by snow in winter, as an antidote to the airless, Tupperware skies of London. In this place, after long walks in the hills (wearing sturdy, red-laced boots), worries could be soaked away in deep baths while sipping whisky (not that I liked whisky) while savouring the sound of the weather hammering the windows. It seemed a straightforward enough fantasy, yet finding it had proved anything but. Scotland, Snowdonia and the Lakes were too far. The Dales and High Peak were too expensive. Exmoor wasn't wild enough. Dartmoor wasn't mountainous enough.

And thus my late twenties passed into my thirties, with me no nearer, mentally or financially, to finding my rural hideaway. So, my forties on the horizon, I compromised. I bought an ancient Land Rover and parked it in the street as a daily reminder that one day that's where I was going.

Then I met Vez, who also worked in London, and thoughts of escape to remote rural hideaways seemed less urgent.

Until, out of the blue, my friend Mary called. She'd heard of a place in the Black Mountains, likely to be cheap, but we'd have to move fast. I'd not even heard of the Black Mountains, but spring was in the air and it felt like an adventure. So Vez and I dropped everything, called in sick to our respective offices, and next day drove down the M4 to Wales.

We met our mystery guide, Ian, in a pub. From the start a sense of intrigue and skulduggery pervaded the day, enough to make us feel, for once, we were on the inside track. In the pub, Ian spoke in whispers: 'Keep your voice down, these walls have ears.' Then he whisked us off in his car along a wide green valley of big fields, before turning up an unsigned lane, the sides of which narrowed and deepened as it began to climb until the car fitted it like a tube train. Up and up we went, the lane kinking and twisting past ancient tree trunks whose vast boles were sawn flush to allow just enough room for a car to squeeze by. Eventually the gradient eased and we emerged, blinking in the light, at a small crossroads. Ahead of us, framed through a gateway, rose a table-topped summit. 'Sugar Loaf,' said Ian.

He took a turning marked 'No Through Road'. A dark mountain-scape opened up on our left, completely different to the grassy valley where we'd started. A hairpin bend took us steeply uphill again. The hedges were getting scrappier now, and gateways revealed ever-more-dramatic panoramas of heathery hilltops above sheep-dotted fields. Up and up—my ears popped—until a quarter of a mile later the road ended at a gate between dry-stone walls. An embossed wooden sign read: 'No Cars on The Common. Private Access Only.' Beyond the gate a rocky track bordered by a stone wall continued upwards, curving tantalisingly out of sight between bracken-covered banks before disappearing into wispy fog. 'That's as far as we can go,' said Ian at that point. There were complications. The house was being sold by Court Order: a bitter divorce. There was no question of actually seeing the place. We wouldn't understand the niceties, he said, but he'd keep us posted.

And with that, we returned to London. But over the days and weeks that followed, phrases Ian had used kept drifting back. 'Over a thousand feet', 'National Park', 'Offa's Dyke', 'red kites', 'wild ponies', 'spring water' … Each alone was enough to send me into happy reveries. As it turned out, however, it didn't come to market. 'Don't give up,' said Ian. 'It'll happen.'

Our next attempt to see the place coincided with the height of the foot-and-mouth epidemic in 2001. With the grand obliviousness to rural affairs that only the truly urban can display, we'd booked a B&B, packed walking boots and maps and arrived in the Black Mountains astonished to find every road into the uplands ending in sinister roadblocks plastered with yellow warning notices: 'FOOT-AND-MOUTH DISEASE. BY ORDER, KEEP OUT.'

The effect of this was to make a place already enticingly elusive positively tantalising. What was this mysterious, out-of-reach farmstead like? By now I could think of little else. Sitting in London traffic, Vez got used to endless conversations prefaced: 'Just say we got the place in Wales …' Briefly, it looked as if it might really be coming to market. Ian sent us a small ad in the local paper formally announcing its sale, only to call, a few weeks later, telling us it had again been withdrawn. A third visit, six months later, prompted by a friend's wedding near Hay-on-Wye, found the Black Mountains open and accessible again. Festooned with binoculars and cameras we walked up Offa's Dyke footpath, looking forward to glimpsing for the first time the subject of so much discussion, only to find that due to a fold of the hill and some trees still in leaf, almost nothing could be made out except a collection of ramshackle outbuildings and tin barns clustered round a boxy house. Big dry-stone walls reached up the hill behind to claim green fields back from the gorse and bracken. To take too much interest, however, seemed like tempting fate. The place clearly wasn't coming to market, so after a few minutes, we walked briskly on.

Abandoning hope, we left our names with other agents. But every set of particulars that arrived—for derelict water mills in dank valleys, remote farms beyond the protective cocoon of the National Park, medieval farmhouses way beyond our price range—just seemed to confirm the essential rightness of 'our place'.

Then, unexpectedly, the day Vez went into hospital to have our first baby, particulars for 'our place' arrived. 'Tair-Ffynnon', we learnt it was called (formerly 'Hill Cottage'). It was described as 'occupying an outstanding rural location in the Brecon Beacons National Park, a good size, three-bedroom, detached, two-storey cottage in need of modernisation and improvement. The property occupies a spectacular position with outstanding views from its isolated location ... approached via a stone track across the common ... approximately 5 acres of sloping pasture ... private water supply from a natural spring ... For sale by public auction 3rd October.' There was a smudgy photograph of the house but, it was pleasingly awful, it conveyed no sense to anyone who didn't know the place of its remarkable setting.

And so, finally, with our daughter Maya just seven days old, we saw it properly. We drove through the hill gate, bumped up the track, and arrived, officially, to inspect my dream hideaway. Admittedly, to an impartial observer, the place's appeal might have seemed obscure. The yard was littered with derelict cars and bits of twisted metal, jostling with random lumber heaps, rubble and old tyres. Geese babbled and puttered in the mud. A wall-eyed sheepdog ambushed us as we got out of the car with a series of terrific lunges to the limit of a long chain. The assorted outbuildings all looked on the point of collapse. As for the house, it was hard to say which side was ugliest. It had received a full 1970s

makeover, burying all trace of the stone cottage it presumably replaced beneath breezeblock, render, concrete tiles and cavernous, flush-fitted windows. The fields around were so lumpy with anthills they appeared to have a kind of geomorphological acne, and ruckled up like bedclothes on the steep slope. There was a suggestion in the hulks of broken farm machinery that things had grown here, but it was hard to conceive what or when.

But I was not an impartial observer. I was in love. My only concern was that, with so much emotion invested, I might cock up the bidding. Which was why Ian had suggested Mr Games as our man.

———•◦•———

The Montague Harris office was exactly as I imagined an old established auctioneers and valuers ('offices Brecon and Abergavenny, serving the Usk Valley') in a rural market town should be. Its sash windows overlooked the cattle market, with (this not being market day) its metal sheds and steel sheep pens empty. A receptionist led us upstairs to Mr Games's office where, behind a panelled door, was a wide leather-topped desk, behind which was Mr Games himself. The floor sagged, perhaps from age, perhaps from the weight of the desk and the hundreds of calf-bound volumes and racing calendars that lined the shelves behind it. Mr Games, as he rose to greet us, contributed a considerable presence. His complexion was that of the pure-bred countryman, evoking the hills and the hunting field and dispersal sales held in all weathers, balanced and offset by his shoes, polished to a deep-hued patina somewhere between oxblood and mahogany. Those shoes were things of wonder: mighty, double-welted brogues against which the turn-ups of his heavy green tweed suit gently broke. 'You're the one wants that bloody place on the mountain.' He looked me up and down. His eyes narrowed: 'You don't look mad. Are you mad?'

His secretary was despatched to fetch a disclaimer form. On it there was a box for the highest bid we were prepared to make. The night before, I'd persuaded Vez that we must be prepared to pay what it cost, to remortgage ourselves for everything we had if necessary. We'd agreed on a figure that was absurdly high for a derelict smallholding in the hills; it would have required us both to sell our cars and probably our television too. I wrote in the amount. Mr Games took my arm and led me over to the other side of the room, out of Vez's earshot. He lowered his voice. 'You're bloody mad. It's not worth it. You might think it's alright now, in October, but get up there in the winter, in the mist and the rain and the snow and the mud. You don't want that place.' Evidently feeling he'd discharged his responsibilities as best he could, he watched as I signed the paper. Vez couldn't bring herself to sign. When I proffered the paper, she turned away, pretending not to know. 'Well, don't say I didn't tell you you're bloody mad,' said Mr Games.

In the end, it was neither as cheap as we hoped, nor, happily, anywhere near as much as I'd have paid. Mr Games sat silently through the bidding, before calmly rising to secure it with two perfectly timed movements of his hand.

And so, thirty days later, I got to drive my Land Rover to its new country home.

2

Tair-Ffynnon

I usually skip topographical details in novels. The more elaborate the description of the locality, the more confused does my mental impression become. You know the sort of thing:—*Jill stood looking out of the door of her cottage. To the North rose the vast peak of Snowdon. To the South swept the valley, dotted with fir trees. Beyond the main ridge of mountains a pleasant wooded country extended itself, but the nearer slopes were scarred and desolate. Miles below a thin ribbon of river wound towards the sea, which shone, like a distant shield, beyond the etc. etc.* By the time I have read a little of this sort of thing I feel dizzy. Is Snowdon in front or behind? Are the woods to the right or to the left? The mind makes frenzied efforts to carry it all, without success. It would be very much better if the novelist said 'Jill stood on the top of a hill, and looked down into the valley below.' And left it at that.

BEVERLEY NICHOLS, *Down the Garden Path*, 1932

An obligatory requirement for any house in interesting country is a wall-map. Having made the satisfying discovery that Tair-Ffynnon was not only marked on the Black Mountains map, but mentioned by name—we were, literally, 'on the map'—I wasted no time in pasting one up by the stairs. The map of the Black Mountains is a particularly pleasing one. The many contours make up the shape of a bony old hand, a left hand placed palm down by someone sitting opposite you. Four parallel ridges form the fingers, with the peaks of Mynydd Troed and Mynydd Llangorse constituting the joints of the thumb. At the joint between the second and third fingers is the Grwyne Fawr reservoir, up a long no through road. Between the third and fourth knuckles is the one through route, a mountain road that passes up the Llanthony Valley, past the abbey and Capel-y-Fin ('the chapel at the end') and up over the Gospel Pass (at 1,880 feet the highest road pass in Wales), before switchbacking down to Hay-on-Wye.

Hay, at the northern end, with its castle and bookshops and spring literary festival, is one of the three towns that skirt the Black Mountains. Crickhowell is to the south-west, beneath its flat-topped 'Table Mountain' ('Crug Hywel', from which the town takes its name). With its medieval bridge, antique shops and hint of gentility, Crickhowell is to the Black Mountains what Burford is to the Cotswolds. To the south-east, Abergavenny is the town with the least pretensions of the three, sitting beneath the great bulk of Blorenge (one of the few words in the English language to rhyme with 'orange') as Wengen sits beneath the Eiger. Central to our new universe was the Skirrid Mountain Garage, a name which conjured (to me, at least) wind-flayed and hail-battered petrol pumps huddled beneath a high pass, but which, in reality, was a homely establishment facing the mountain, selling everything the rural dweller could need, from chicken feed to home-made cakes.

Until some basic building work allowed us to move properly—installing central heating, replacing missing windows and slates, moving the bathroom upstairs—we were still only visiting Tair-Ffynnon at

weekends, armed with drills and paint brushes. Our
first night on the hill, after weeks of B&Bs down in
the valley, felt as remote and exciting as bivouacking
on Mount Everest, especially when we woke to find a
hard, blue-skied frost had turned everything white and
brought five Welsh Mountain ponies with
romantically trailing manes and tails to drink
at the bathtub where the spring emerged. The same day
we spotted our first pair of red kites, easily distinguishable from the
ubiquitous buzzards by their forked tails, elegant flight and mournful,
whistled cries: *pweee-ooo ee oo ee oo ee oo, pweee-ooo ee oo ee oo ee oo.*

Between DIY efforts, we explored. No-one who hasn't moved to a
new area can understand the excitement that almost every modest outing
brings, be it merely trying out a pub or seeking a recommended shop,
and the incidental discoveries the journey brings in the form of new
views, a charming farm or enticing-looking walk for some future date.
Much of our delight came just from being somewhere we'd chosen to
be, as opposed to somewhere foisted upon us by our work or childhood.
From growing up in Somerset I knew it was possible to live in a place
without feeling the slightest connection with it, and the experience had
left me hungry for knowledge of our new locality. Skirrid, Sugar Loaf
and Blorenge, as the three triangulation points visible from most places,
had to be climbed. The Black Hill and Golden Valley had to be
inspected to see if they lived up to their names. Expeditions had to
be mounted to walk Offa's Dyke, and to drive the upland roads where
Top Gear tested their supercars, to check out Cwmyoy church's crooked
tower and Kilpeck church's saucy gargoyles of peeing women. And
when we heard that a cult porn classic had been filmed in 1992
exclusively around a particular local farm, naturally we hurried off to see
that too. *The Revenge of Billy the Kid** (plot: farmer shags goat;

---

* According to *Halliwell's Film Guide*, a 'grotesque and disgusting low-budget horror
comedy. A credit for "Flatulence Artists" sets the tone.'

monstrous half-goat-half-man progeny returns to kill his family) may not rank directly alongside Kilvert's *Diaries*, Chatwin's *On the Black Hill*, or Eric Gill's sculptures (not that Gill's extra-curricular activities were so far removed) but it still supplied local colour.

After the auction, when I'd shaken hands with the vendor's solicitor, he'd said: 'If you'll be wanting a builder up there, I can recommend a tidy one. Very tidy.' Any impartial recommendation of a local trades-man was plainly useful, given our newcomer status. And I could see that the notion of a tidy builder—the phrase, after all, was practically an oxymoron—was praiseworthy. But even if the one he was recom-mending was exceptionally orderly, even if he dusted every finished surface and ran the Hoover round before leaving, was this feature, in itself, sufficient justification for recommendation? Surely the foremost qualities for a builder must be workmanship, diligence, reliability, integrity, value for money, and so on, all before the undoubted bonus of tidy-mindedness?

Having, nevertheless, taken up his recommendation, over the suc-ceeding weeks we heard mention of tidy jobs, tidy places, tidy machines, and it dawned that 'tidy', of course, didn't really mean tidy at all, but was local vernacular for 'good' or 'excellent'. As, in due course, we learnt that 'ground' was the term for 'land', *cwtsh* (pronounced 'cutch' as in 'butch') for cuddle, trow for 'trough', 'by here' for 'here' and so on, my favourite being the localised version of good-bye, the delightful 'bye now', as if parting were a mere trifling interruption, that resumption of contact was taken for granted. Phones, too, were generally answered with a joyful ''Alloooo', as if you caught the recipient moments after his lottery win. The accent's combination of Herefordshire and a hint of West Country, with a sing-song Welsh lilt, made communication easy on the ear, if periodically incomprehensible.

It also highlighted we were not just in a different place but in a different country, with a different language. 'ARAF' painted on roads at junctions meant 'Slow', while the word 'HEDDLU' appeared on the side of police cars. Signposts to bigger villages carried place names in both English and Welsh, however similar. The sign into our local village was large to accommodate (for absolute clarity) both 'Llanfihangel Crucornau' and 'Llanvihangel Crucorney'. Cash machines offered Welsh instructions. Station and Post Office announcements were in Welsh as well as English. All official council, government or civil service documentation was bi-lingual, more than doubling its length. Names of smaller villages and individual properties tended to be in Welsh. In fact such a bewildering profusion of the same words kept cropping up again and again, of Pentwyns and Bettwses and Llanfihangels and Cwm-Thises and Nanty-Thats, that we bought a Welsh dictionary for the car. A new world emerged. In combination with words for 'big', 'little', 'over', 'under', 'near' or numbers, a poetic topography of landform sprang out.* Yet, despite this, and despite a general allegiance to Wales

---

* Tair-Ffynnon meant Four Springs (though we could only find one, emerging icy cold, delicious and, as it turned out, laced with *E. coli* from a bracken-filled bowl in the field above the house). Other words commonly combined into names included:

Aber- mouth of	Cefn- ridge	Llyn- pool or lake
Allt wooded slope	Cilfynydd mountain	Maen stone or rock
Blaenau- uplands, source	nook	Maes- field
or head waters	Coed- wood	Mynydd- mountain
Bryn- small rounded hill	Cwm- valley	Nanty- stream
Builth- cow pasture	-fan peak	Pant hollow
Bwlch pass, hence Dan Y	-ffrydd moorland or	Pentwyn top of the
Bwlch ('under the	upland pasture	hillock
pass')	Foel- bare hill	Rhos- moorland
Caer- fort	-glaes stream	Rhyd- ford
Carn- cairn	Graig rock	Troed- foot
Carrog- swift flowing	-Hendre winter dwelling	Ty'n- croft
stream or torrent	Llan church of	-wern yew tree

(especially evident during televised rugby finals), we soon discovered next to no-one spoke or even understood Welsh.

The area seemed to be in the grip of a benign, easygoing, low-level identity crisis. Keen to learn a few basics, I spent an afternoon in the local reference library. The three classic guidebooks, A. G. Bradley's *In the March and Borderland of Wales* (1905) and P. Thoresby Jones's *Welsh Border Country* (1938) and H. J. Massingham's *The Southern Marches* (1952), devoted pages simply trying to define where they were talking about. Everywhere there were signs of Welshness, or Englishness, or of a confusion between the two. Despite the unambiguous geophysical boundary of the ten-mile Hatterrall Ridge, the actual border with England ran only part of the way along its length, before descending to make various arbitrary and unpredictable kinks and turns, with the result that a short drive 'round the mountain' to Hereford or Hay crisscrossed the border repeatedly. So, not surprisingly, at least as many people seemed to be called Powell and Jones and Davies in neighbouring Herefordshire as in Monmouthshire. It was similarly interesting, if a little bewildering, to be given the option in every newsagent, however small, of nine local papers: the *Abergavenny Chronicle, Monmouthshire Beacon, Abergavenny Free Press, Hereford Times, Brecon and Radnorshire Express, Western Mail, Western Free Press, Gwent Gazette* and the *South Wales Argus*. For leisure moments, these were supplemented by the magazines *Wye Valley Life, Usk Valley Life, Monmouthshire Life* and *Herefordshire Life*, plus, for the macro view, *Welsh Life*. Whole sections of most newsagents were set aside for this remarkable array of verbiage. Even Abergavenny's slogan—'Markets, Mountains and More'—on signs hanging off lampposts and on its literature, suggested a certain doubt about exactly what it was the place stood for.

This uncertainty was echoed by the physical landscape. Upland or lowland? Sheep or cattle grazing? Hedge country or stone wall country? On the last question, most fields seemed to be a mixture, as if, halfway through walling, the waller had thought: 'Sod this. Why don't we just plant a hedge?' Then, fifty years later when the hedges weren't doing so well, another generation had said: 'Hedges here? What were they thinking of? This should be a bloody wall.' Even the birds seemed confused. At Tair-Ffynnon there were few trees but we had several fat green woodpeckers feeding off ants from the anthills, along with treecreepers and nuthatches. We had mountain birds like red kites and ravens, and moorland ones like red grouse and merlins. Yet we also had farmland birds like redstarts and fieldfares, water birds like yellow wagtails and herons, and garden birds: tits, chaffinches and blackbirds (though no songthrushes, strangely).

It was Border Country alright. Monmouthshire, a county in-between. But tidy, nevertheless.

———◆———

My father and brother Jonny came to inspect the place. 'D'you think my car will recover?' said my father, parking his Fiesta after picking his way up the track. He looked well, but then he always did. Now in his eighties, he hardly seemed to have changed in the time I'd known him. Largely bald with white Professor Calculus-style hair, he'd looked old when he was young, but as his contemporaries aged, he'd just stayed the same. I bent down to kiss him, giving Jonny the usual curt nod. 'Wonderful view. What a hideous house,' said my father, fastidiously surveying the yard, taking in the scrap metal and the junk, as I helped him out of the car. 'And what an appalling mess. What possessed you to buy this place, darling?'

I'd known my father wouldn't like it. He loathed disorder, crudeness, ugliness. His relationship with the countryside was one of suspicion bordering on revulsion, and I guessed this counted as extreme countryside. I was impressed, frankly, given how bad the track was, he'd attempted it at all.

Although, technically, we'd all grown up in the country, in as much as our house was located in rural Somerset, ours wasn't a rural existence. My father would vastly have preferred to live in the town. We were there entirely on my mother's account, because she was obsessed with horses. Although dedicated to his garden, his interest was in abstract, strictly non-productive gardening. Most day-to-day aspects of rural living my father cordially detested. The getting stuck behind tractors and milk lorries. The smell of muck-spreading. The filth and slime with which the lanes steadily filled from December to March. It was a point almost of pride that he possessed not a solitary item of the default green country wear sold by shops with 'country' in their name. He was repelled by traditional rural activities such as hunting, shooting and fishing and would not have dreamt of attending an event such as the Badminton Horse Trials, had the latter not been forced upon him by my mother. Visiting churches, distinguished gardens and occasional walks up Crook's Peak were the extent of his rural ambitions. We kept no animals, other than horses, and grew no fruit or vegetables. He wished for no contact with country people and did not enjoy having it foisted upon him (such as when he answered the door to find Ken, the farmer at the top of our lane, following one of the periodic shoots through the adjacent wood, bearing the unwelcome gift of a brace of pheasants). He made no secret of the fact that he was in the country on sufferance and would have preferred to occupy a terraced house in Bristol or Bath. Maybe it was from him that I acquired the sense of rural root-lessness that had driven me up a Welsh mountain.*

Jonny, on the other hand, was in heaven, as he methodically inspected every inch of the place, shed by shed, rusty wreck by rusty wreck. For fifteen years, Jonny's day job had been as a Formula One motor-racing

---

* My own relationship being perfectly summed up by Siegfried Sassoon: 'I was conscious of having no genuine connection with the countryside. Other people owned estates, or rented farms, or did something countrified; but I only walked along the roads or took furtive short cuts across the fields of persons who might easily have bawled at me if they had caught sight of me. And I felt shy and "out of it" among the local landowners—most of whose conversation was about shooting. So I went mooning, more and more moodily, about the looming landscape.' From *Memoirs of a Fox-Hunting Man,* 1928.

mechanic, at one time ending up as head of Ayrton Senna's car—thus maintaining the Woodward tradition of having a job sufficiently specialised to be utterly meaningless to other members of the family. He was so shy, with us at least, he'd never, under any circumstances, contemplate leaving answerphone messages. Yet his spiky handwriting, indenting at least three sheets of paper beneath the one he was writing on, hinted at his determination once he'd set his mind on something. In recent years we'd bonded, bizarrely, over an affection for old farm machinery; the key difference between us being that he was a mechanical genius. Machines in his hands sprang back to life, as plants did in my mother's, and as they died in my own.

'Pick-up cylinder off an International B74 baler … radiator off a David Brown … top link arm … link box flap … hitch and footplates off a Super Major. Did you know your hay trailer's the converted chassis of a Bedford Army Four-tonner?'

I could tell Jonny was as approving as it was possible for him to be.

'However do you know this stuff, darling?' said my father.

'I just do,' said Jonny.

We went into the house for lunch. 'What's going there?' asked Jonny, indicating the empty space left for the Aga.

'An Aga.'

'An Aga? How *awful*,' said my father.

'Oh, I don't know. I rather like an Aga,' said my brother. 'What colour are you getting?'

'Cream.'

'Thank goodness for that.'

After lunch, Jonny returned to his inspection outside, exactly where he'd left off.

'This hay rake's been converted. Look, you can see where it used to be horse-drawn and they've welded a tractor hitch on. See, just there. Bamford's side delivery rake … mmm, nice.'

'What's this called?' We were standing next to a particularly eccentric-looking appliance which consisted of four huge metal wheels in an offset row, each spoked with sprung metal tines. From seeing it in the fields as a child, I knew it had been used for turning hay.

'A Vicon Lily Acrobat.' He enunciated the syllables slowly, ironically. We all smiled.

'How *do* you know this stuff?' said my father.

'You've got three Ferguson ploughs, so whoever was here before you obviously had a Fergie. And a lot of this other kit's for a Fergie too: the potato ridger, the spring tine cultivator. You can see it all used to be painted grey. Hmm,' said Jonny, surveying it all. 'Looks as if you'd better get yourself a tractor.'

———— ·•·•· ————

Gradually, we began to meet our neighbours. Key amongst them was Ness, darkly beautiful, gypsy-like, striding the hill with a long-legged gait and her sheepdog Molly. She lived in a cottage behind a hedge on the lane and talked with a force and speed I have yet to encounter in another human being, as if life were too short to leave gaps between words. She was also, it soon emerged, a kind of self-appointed guardian of our corner of the National Park, waging a lone battle against what she regarded—aptly, in many people's view—as mediocrity, idleness, bad taste, stupidity or the general failure of officialdom to discharge its duties adequately. Gratuitous street-lighting, crass development, over-signage—all fell within her remit as unofficial custodian. Early on I'd had the privilege of hearing her in action when I'd dropped in for something. Some ominous big 'C's had recently appeared in yellow paint on the trunks and branches of various trees on the lane up the hill, including one on the bole of a mighty, spreading oak. I found her pacing the room with a phone hooked under her chin. 'So, are we quite clear on this Mr—? If anything—*anything*—happens to that tree following this conversation…I have your name here so I know *exactly* who to come back to.'

It was clear from her tone that her blood was up, that she'd been fobbed off by one jobsworth too many claiming he or she didn't know what the markings meant, or that they were there in the name of health and safety. I watched agog as, with hurricane-force indefatigability, she worked her way up the hierarchy of plainly shell-shocked and unprepared officials until, when she decided she'd got far enough, she delivered her pièce de résistance: 'Is that clear? For your information I have been tape recording this conversation, so, as I say, I will be holding you *personally responsible*. Thank you very much.' She put the phone down. 'That should stir them up a bit,' she said cheerfully, lighting a Silk Cut from a lighter marked 'BUY YOUR OWN FUCKING LIGHTER'. 'Now, can I offer you a cup of coffee or d' you want something stronger? Glad you've called in because I've been meaning to ask you …'

I need hardly add that the sentenced oak still stands, wearing its yellow death warrant like a badge of honour, a daily reminder that battles with mindless bureaucracy can be won.

Ness became a vital source of information from the start, issuing us with contact sheets of trusted local artisans, sources and suppliers, each accompanied by comprehensive briefing notes. Another was Les the Post. We enjoyed what must be one of the best-value mail services in the British Isles, with Les frequently negotiating two gates and a mile of rough track simply to deliver a flyer promising 'Anglia Double Glazing now in your area'. He was regularly to be seen chivvying stray sheep back into their fields (being familiar with every local farmer's markings) where we would just push uncertainly by, often herding them ever further from home. Start a conversation with Les, however, and, as he switched his engine off, you knew it was unlikely to last less than twenty minutes.

In February, we encountered our most exotic and colourful visitors to the hill. We'd had intimations of their presence, in the form of folded five pound notes wedged into cracks of the porch, or neat piles of coins left by the door, which we'd discover on Saturday mornings when we emerged, blinking, into the daylight. On this occasion, a car with long overhanging bundles on its roof-rack came racing up the track. It swept into the yard, and, without slowing, splashed through the muddy gateway to the field. Two figures leapt out and started untying the long bundles. After that, cars started arriving in a more or less steady stream. The wind was in the east. The hang-gliders and paragliders had arrived.

We'd already heard a lot about them. Within moments of getting Tair-Ffynnon at the auction, a man had introduced himself, congratulated us on our success, and explained he'd been the under-bidder, representing a consortium of hang and paraglider flyers. Were we aware, he said, that Tair-Ffynnon was one of the finest paragliding sites in the country? Apparently the Hatterrall Ridge was the first significant geological barrier to east-flowing air after the Urals on the far side of the Russian steppes two and a half thousand miles away. The previous owner had allowed, even encouraged, parking in her field: would we consider doing the same? I mumbled something about being sure we could work something out, only to discover I'd entered a minefield. The site was popular because the combination of the track and parking meant pilots could drive their heavy gear all the way to the take-off point, something few sites allowed. But permitting parking encouraged greater use of the site, sending Ness, for one, crazy from cars driving up and down past her house all day. We decided the best course for the time being was to do nothing.

There's no doubt they were a dramatic spectacle in the late winter haze. The brightly coloured canopies of the paragliders stood out against the bracken and lichen-covered stone walls, and across the hill drifted the murmur of voices punctuated by the crackles and soft *wumphs* of air pockets inflating and deflating. We counted thirty in the air simultaneously that day. They brought a note of glamour and contemporaneity to the ancient hillside.

———

By the third week of February, the Aga still wasn't installed. We'd ordered one secondhand and it was supposed to have been delivered and fitted by Christmas. After the delivery driver had failed to find Tair-Ffynnon on his first attempt, then declared the track too rough on his second, his third attempt coincided with a hard frost, converting the wet lane into an impassable sheet of ice. A fourth attempt was finally successful, but unfortunately by this time we'd missed our slot with the fitter. The disembowelled cooker was heaped in the lean-to pending his return from his January break. When he finally arrived, fresh and recuperated, he informed us the parts were from Agas of different dates and incompatible. As we'd torn out the existing Rayburn to make way for the Aga, the house was distinctly chilly and unwelcoming without either, so after that Vez declared we should not return to Tair-Ffynnon until the correct Aga parts were ready for assembly.

Then the forecast promised snow in the south of England. During weekdays away from Tair-Ffynnon a curious imaginative process had started taking place. The less we were there, the more romantically unreal the place began to seem. Stuck in London, enduring yet another mild, drearily overcast day, what I wanted to know was: what was it like on the hill, in the high, clear, cold air there? I had no difficulty imagining that a place less than two hundred miles to the west of the capital and a thousand-odd feet higher could be experiencing an entirely different climate. I was convinced a frost in London must mean feet of snow on the hill. Indeed, it would have been but a step for me to believe woolly mammoths bestrode the ridge. I got sidetracked for almost a morning researching what kind of generator would be most suitable for the inevitable power cuts and how much snow chains would be for the car. So when genuine snow was promised—well, that could not be missed.

Thus it was against Vez's better judgement that we descended off the elevated section of the Westway out of London that Friday afternoon, the car's temperature gauge hovering at a disappointing +1°C. (I had become a compulsive watcher of the car's temperature gauge, which routinely indicated a two-, three-, even four-degree difference between the bottom of the hill up to Tair-Ffynnon and the top.) By Reading, however, the digital display showed 0°C and big flakes started coming at us out of the night. Larger and larger, they made a soft, unfamiliar *pffffff* … *pffffff* … *pffffff* … *pffffff* … as they settled on the windscreen. The temperature started to drop promisingly … –1°C, –1.5°C, –2°C. 'This is mad. We'll never get up the hill. We should go back,' said Vez.

'Don't be silly. What's the point of having the place? Of course we'll get up the hill. And if we can't, I'll get the Land Rover.' The Land Rover now lived proudly in one of the sheds at Tair-Ffynnon.

'We've got a four-month-old baby in the car and no supplies.'

'We'll be fine.'

By the time we turned off the main road, the countryside was white and so was the tarmac. At the bottom of the hill the temperature gauge showed a satisfying –4°C. As we turned up the unsigned lane it was hard to tell how deep the snow was, but there was enough on the ground to soften the edges between the road and the hedgerow banks. The lane led directly through the yard of a farm and we were about to join the road out the other side when the front wheels began to spin. We lost traction. I reversed back to try and gain momentum, but the wheels spun again. I tried a longer run-up, reversing all the way back to the turning. I could get no further. We were, indubitably, stuck.

Strapping on a backpack, and glowing with manly virtue, I crunched and squeaked my way up the hill through pristine powder snow. The clouds had cleared by this time, revealing a moonlit snowscape beneath an absurdly starry sky. Unfortunately, having reached the Land Rover, I found I had forgotten the keys, necessitating a slightly less satisfying trudge back down the hill to fetch Vez and Maya on foot. At length, however, we were installed in the house.

Next day I got the Land Rover out of its shed, but by then more snow had fallen and it was too deep for us to go anywhere. There wasn't much to do except pass most of the weekend huddled in bed to keep warm. 'I hope it was worth it,' said Vez, a little uncharitably on Sunday, as we crouched over our fourth meal of canned soup, cooked on the old electric cooker, facing the space where the Aga was supposed to be.

Eventually we trudged back down the hill to the car and returned to London.

The Aga in which we'd planned to cook our Christmas turkey was eventually installed and working in time for Easter and the spring.

3

The Yellow Book

Even when German bombing signalled the start of
the Battle of Britain and fear of invasion spread, the
Gardens Scheme carried on …

A Nurturing Nature:
The Story of the National Gardens Scheme, 2002

I could now think of little besides Tair-Ffynnon. All other matters
seemed an annoying distraction. I'd taken to carrying a camera whenever out of town, snapping odd things—ferns on an old chimney-stack,
yellow lichen on a slate roof, rusting machines in corners of farmyards.
I'd also begun tearing pictures out of magazines and newspapers, images
of lonely crofter's cottages, Icelandic turf-roofed churches, old tin
frontier buildings. Lots of new things had become interesting, from old
farm buildings and dry-stone walls to trees and wild flowers. I edited

these cuttings into a scrapbook, which I could spend almost indefinite periods leafing through, daydreaming contentedly, shoving it guiltily away like porn if I heard footsteps approaching the door.

So I suppose I was searching for an excuse to immerse myself in the place. The garden idea came about partly because of that. But it was partly, too, that we'd had it up to here with remarks masquerading as polite interest ('How did you stumble on this place?', 'I can see it has great potential') that we were perfectly aware translated as 'What a dump!' My father had made no secret of his bafflement, and Vez's mum had watched with mortification as her daughter exchanged a successful career and a warm, clean house in London for a derelict shack up a mountain. True, some people 'got' it instantly, but many more did not. Why couldn't they see it? Were its charms really so obscure? I'd recently visited Derek Jarman's garden in Dungeness and been deeply impressed by the way he'd seen the beauty of that place, hitherto an isolated, little-known shingle headland in the shadow of a nuclear power station. Through his minute garden, hardly bigger than the fishing hut it adjoined, he'd shown that beauty to others too. It seemed to absorb its surrounding seascape and play it back in distilled form. Why couldn't we try something similar at Tair-Ffynnon?

The idea was no doubt encouraged, as April turned to May, by the first tentative signs of spring's arrival on the hill, in the form of a dishevelled swallow resting on the telephone wire. The following week, two dozen more had joined it, and the place had come alive with flitting, wheeling, diving, skimming birds playing tag around the house as they noisily nested in the barns. Our home, it seemed, was others' too. A fortnight later the hedgerows on the lane turned white with May blossom and the shady verges exploded into a riot of bluebells, Lady's Smock, violets, red campion, cow parsley, and a hundred other wild flowers I couldn't identify. By this time the hills were echoing cacophonously with the joys of the season as lambs and their mothers bleated relentless inanities to one another.

The moment I latched onto the idea of a garden, it seemed right. It licensed me to spend as much time as I wanted thinking about the place, and it would force us into making a plan. This in turn would give us purpose and structure and provide a deadline. Maybe it would even help me understand why the place meant so much to me. Two further comments acted like rallying cries. One, from a visiting friend as he got out of the car: 'God, there's nothing that doesn't need doing.' The other, from Jonny, who when I mentioned the plan, hooted with derision: 'A garden? What ... at your place? You're joking.' Followed a few moments later by: 'You *are* joking, aren't you?' At a stroke, a half-baked idea graduated into a clear personal challenge.

I'd heard of the National Gardens Scheme's 'yellow book' and was vaguely aware of the yellow 'Garden Open Today' signs that sprouted across the countryside from around the time the clocks went forwards. I'd even thought that, one day, visiting such gardens was something I might like to do. Now, with my own garden in mind, it seemed as good a place as any to begin my research into what might be achievable. Might we be able to get into the National Gardens Scheme? I bought a copy of the book: a fat yellow paperback entitled *Gardens of England and Wales Open for Charity*. Its 500 pages were crammed with brisk little one-paragraph entries beneath addresses of scarcely believable quaintness: 'Pikes Cottage, Hemyock', 'The Old Glebe, Eggesford', 'Mottisfont Abbey, Romsey'.* It was a remarkable collection. Here they all were: the cream of Britain's secret gardens. Thousands of them (3,542 to be exact) with directions and opening dates: precise instructions on how to see, at the best possible moment, the pride and passion

---

* Vita Sackville-West devoted one of her Sunday newspaper columns to the addresses in the National Gardens Scheme 'list': 'What enticements are therein offered! Who could resist the desire to penetrate without delay into precincts with such romantic names as Hutton John, Heronden Eastry, Nether Lypiatt, Bevington Lordship, St John Jerusalem, Castle Drogo, The House in the Wood, or Flower Lilies? All poetry is there, suggestive and evocative. One could go and sit in those gardens on a summer evening, and imagine what one's own garden (and one's life) might be.' *Observer*, 15 June 1947.

of some of the world's most dedicated gardeners. Scanning the descriptions at first glance revealed many to be disconcertingly grand ('60-acre deer park', 'Tudor knot garden', 'pleached lime avenue', 'Victorian fernery'), though there was also evidence of more modest attainments ('pot patio'). There was no sign of Derek Jarman's garden in the index, though endless other famous names were there: Sissinghurst, Hidcote, Stourhead, Newby Hall, Nymans, Bodnant. Was this the kind of thing we had a hope of getting into? And how on earth had such a scheme come about?

A little research revealed that the National Gardens Scheme was an institution that could have evolved nowhere but Britain. The inspiration arrived in 1926 at a committee meeting of the Queen's Nursing Institute. In those pre-NHS days, the QNI was a charity that raised money to pay for district nurses and to provide for the retirement of existing ones. Ideas for fundraising were being batted to and fro before the steely gaze of the committee chairman, the Duke of Portland, when one of the committee members, a Miss Elsie Wagg, piped up. What a shame it was, she said, that Britain had so many marvellous gardens, yet most were seen by nobody except their owners and a few friends. Why not ask those owners to open for the appeal one day next year?

It was genius. If the idea could be implemented, here was a way to tap into one of Britain's great hidden resources. But it was a big 'if', for the idea was presumptuous, impertinent, socially revolutionary even. Post-war Britain was still class bound. Garden-visiting was common enough, but only among a tiny minority. The thought of asking owners of large private houses to fling wide their wrought-iron gates to, well, anyone was outrageous. It smacked of Marxism, Leninism, Trotskyism or any of the other -isms which had been filling the papers recently. However, and this was the real genius, because the idea was to raise money for charity, and because it was approved by a duke, it looked mean-spirited to refuse. So suddenly, whether you were interested in gardens or just wanted a snoop behind the park wall, an irresistible opportunity presented itself. The Scheme licensed nosiness. It also sanctioned repressed British amateur gardeners to show off their efforts.

But what a feat of organisation. The idea lived or died by the contacts and persuasive powers of those setting up the Scheme. So, to be on the safe side, the first chairman of the new 'National Gardens Scheme' was a duchess (of Richmond and Gordon), who recruited a committee of well-connected county ladies, all with suitably fat little black books. And so was born the County Organiser: an imperious, horticultural version of the Pony Club's District Commissioner.

As I read on about the history of the Scheme, a picture began to emerge of a type. A handful of retired senior servicemen notwith-standing, most were women with names like Daphne or Phyllida or Veronica, who soon became the *grandes dames* of the gardening world. The County Organiser tended to be someone who'd grown up within, and now kept, a large walled garden, the kind whose obituary—and County Organisers, it became clear, were the kind of people who got obituaries—said things like 'could be impatient', 'fearsomely smocked and gaitered', or 'had a knack for engineering spectacular fallings-out, a process she thoroughly enjoyed'. She needed no reassurance about her place in the world, and had little time to spend reassuring those who did. As virtues, energy, efficiency and effectiveness took precedence over charm and humour; as a result, County Organisers were entirely immune to the latter. But in an imperial, *ancien régime* way, she Got Things Done. She was, in fact, my mother.

In 2002, to celebrate its seventy-fifth birthday, the NGS published a short history of the Scheme. There, on page 28, clustered around the Queen Mother on a staircase at St James's Palace, fifty-four of these Lady Bracknells stare out from beneath their hats, with gimlet eyes and don't-mess-with-me smiles—fifty-four iterations of the woman I knew best.

Under the organisation of these forces of nature, the Scheme triumphed from the start. In the summer of 1927 a printed list was

included free with *Country Life*, detailing 349 gardens that would open in June 'between the hours of 11 a.m. and 7 p.m.' for 'a shilling a head'. The 'Women's National Committee' responsible had done their work well. The list included the King's gardens at Sandringham, the Duke of Marlborough's at Blenheim Palace, those of such contemporary gardening giants as Norah Lindsay, and William Robinson's Gravetye Manor, not to mention 'the best of modern gardening' such as Edwin Lutyens and Gertrude Jekyll's garden at Hestercombe. Such was the success of that first June opening that the Scheme was continued into September, by which time 609 gardens had opened, visited by more than 164,000 people. The hitherto undreamt-of sum of £8,191 was raised for district nursing. Indeed, the Scheme was such a triumph that King George V wrote to the Gardens Subcommittee of the Queen's Nursing Institute requesting the event should become a permanent way of raising money.

By the outbreak of the Second World War, hardly a great garden hadn't been recruited. Chatsworth, Hatfield, Major Lawrence Johnston's Hidcote, Vita Sackville-West's Sissinghurst—they were all there. So, too, were the former Prime Minister, David Lloyd George's garden Brony-de, and Winston Churchill's Chartwell, and even the Welsh garden where Beatrix Potter wrote *The Tale of the Flopsy Bunnies*. In 1949 the guide acquired its distinctive yellow livery, and the NGS found its mascot. In no time, the slightly cumbrous *Gardens of England and Wales Open for Charity* had become affectionately known as 'the yellow book'.

Then, in the mid-eighties, Britain went gardening crazy, and a strange

thing happened. Where the County Organisers had traditionally had to plead, persuade or order grudging friends, relations, earls, spiky industrialists and absent-minded bishops to do their duty, suddenly they found themselves inundated with applications. From worthy institution, the National Gardens Scheme overnight became an elite club, to which a new class of Capability Browns, Smiths and Joneses all wanted admission. At last there was a formal goal towards which the ambitious amateur gardener could aspire. And as the only official horticultural yardstick available, the Yellow Book naturally became the gold standard. Applications tripled and the County Organisers found themselves in the eminently more in-character role of laying down the law. Numbers of gardens in the Scheme more than doubled between 1980 and 1990 (from 1,400 to 3,000*) and, for the first time, formal selection—and rejection—criteria had to be laid down. Getting into the Yellow Book became a whole lot harder, whether you lived in the Home Counties or on top of a Welsh mountain.

———◆◆◆———

To be considered for the National Gardens Scheme, a garden must:

1. Offer '45 minutes of interest'.
2. Be a good example of its type (cottage, alpine, herb, etc.)—if it is a type.
3. Have something of special interest (the view, a water feature, a national collection of plants, etc.).

This information was heartening. Forty-five minutes wasn't so long. The type of garden? Well, there was plenty of time to figure that out. As for having something of special interest, Tair-Ffynnon's setting and

* In 1991, the Yellow Book sold 100,000 copies, hitting the bestseller lists. By 1992 it was so familiar it featured on *The Archers*.

views must be as good as anywhere's. Yes, on the whole there was room for optimism. All I had to do was learn how to garden.

There was, of course, one other small matter. Would anything grow so high up? But here again, I was inclined to optimism. We already had evidence that potatoes, mangelwurzels and hay had been grown on Tair-Ffynnon's rocky policies, as that's what many of its previous inhabitants had lived on. If they could survive, no doubt other things could too. Derek Jarman had coaxed life out of shingle, by the sea, with all that that implied in terms of wind and salt.* Stuff must grow on mountains, too; it was just a matter of finding out what. In fact, in the circumstances, my course of action was obvious: ask Uncle William.

———◆———

Uncle William was the great gardener of the family, and my mother's half-brother. He and my Aunt Jeanette lived in a secluded nook of the Dorset Downs not far from Sherborne. Ranged around a seventeenth-century chalk and flint cottage (its thatched roof pulled well down over its eyebrows, at home in any book of idyllic English country cottages) was a garden that even I couldn't fail to notice was a plantsman's delight. The last time I was there, one August, summer was in its dusty and desiccated last gasp. Yet in Uncle William's garden greenery, foliage and flowers were positively clawing their way out of the ground. Apart from a lawn behind the house, there was hardly a square inch of space that wasn't bursting with trees, shrubs, climbers, pergolas and pots. In his extensive fruit and vegetable garden, the runner beans, raspberry canes and gooseberry bushes were so bowed down with the weight of provender they gave the impression that, however fast anything was picked, there was not the slightest chance of keeping pace with the output. The place had what I would learn was a hallmark of a plantsman

---

* How he did this mystified me until I read the secret in his garden book: shovelfuls of horse manure beneath the pebbles.

at work: narrow paths rendered almost impassable due to the rainforest density of vegetation spilling from either side. Should you dare level a criticism at Uncle William's garden, it was that you couldn't see the garden for the plants.

If green fingers existed, Uncle William's were of the most livid, fluorescent, Martian hue, and chlorophyll coursed through his veins. It was known far and wide that he had only to be handed a plant for it to perk up. Gardening rows between my parents concerning any matter of practical plant husbandry—where a particular plant was best placed, why it wasn't doing well, what the best treatment should be—invariably ended with a defiant, pursed-lipped: 'Well. We'll ask William.'

As a child, I'd found Uncle William slightly intimidating.* He was a naval captain and had a deep, husky voice that exuded peremptory command. I always imagined the huskiness had come from roaring orders across the wind and spray-swept flight deck of HMS *Ark Royal*, of which he'd been second-in-command in the 1970s, not that I'd ever heard him raise his voice or even seen him in his naval role (though he was wearing his uniform, holding an umbrella over them, in my parents' wedding photographs). It was a voice that implied that, once a task was stated, it might be regarded as done. I couldn't imagine any member of the plant kingdom defying it. He was a pillar of the local establishment and churchwarden in his local parish. I was sure he must open his garden to the public, and, on a hunch, looked him up in the Yellow Book. Sure enough, there was his garden: 'Planted over many yrs to provide pleasure from month to month the whole yr through.'

---

* The statement is qualified only because, in the scary stakes, Uncle William had stiff competition. The title-holder, by a clear head, was Uncle Hampden, a barrister and later a judge, married to my mother's sister Ann. He had a black patch over one eye from a war wound sustained at Monte Cassino. At breakfast he'd pull this patch up onto his forehead, releasing it with a loud snapping sound, before giving his empty socket a lengthy and luxurious rub, then adjusting his expression (though not his eye-patch) and fixing us, his nephews, beadily with his one good eye, daring us to speak. Thus, absolute silence was maintained as he contemplated *The Times* over a vast cup of coffee.

If anyone knew what would grow on a windswept hill-side 1,300 feet up, it was Uncle William. I hadn't spoken to him for years and was summoning the courage to make the call when, out of the blue, he called us. He gathered we'd bought an unlikely property in the hills and had ideas about making a garden. (Clearly, word had spread of our offbeat acquisition, though I did wonder how my father had described Tair-Ffynnon to trigger quite such prompt interest.) As it happened, he said, he and Aunty Jeanette were visiting a garden near Usk in a few weeks time as part of the local gardens society (I later asked him about his role in this: 'Chairman, for my sins'), and he suggested coming on to see us.

Which was how, one Saturday a few weeks later, Uncle William came to be pottering about Tair-Ffynnon's rocky and bracken-invaded acres. He seemed amused by the whole enterprise, as he poked cheerfully about with a stick. 'Well, your soil's alright,' he said, jabbing at the thick clump of nettles growing round the wood pile. 'Nettles only grow in rich soil.' The hundreds of molehills he thought were a good sign, too. 'Excellent potting soil if you collect it up. If you put bottles in the vegetable garden the sound of the wind in the glass discourages them.' We took him up to the gully where the spring ran. More jabs with the stick. 'You can increase the sound of the running water by adding stones,' he said. I'd briefed him about my Yellow Book plan as we progressed around the place, hovering behind him hopefully, biro and notebook at the ready for any suggestions about what we should plant. However, little apart from these general comments had so far emerged. Looking up and down the gully now, his gaze alighted on the stands of foxgloves. 'Foxgloves,' he said. 'There you are. You can grow fox-gloves.'

'But foxgloves ... foxgloves grow everywhere.'

Uncle William shrugged his shoulders. 'You can only grow what will grow. You need to look around you and see what's growing naturally.' He looked around again, taking in the clumps of gorse, the encroaching bracken. 'For instance,' he said, 'you could have a very fine *bracken* gar-den.' He dissolved into chuckles. 'The first bracken garden in Britain.'

I wasn't convinced Uncle William was taking me as a gardener, or the project, seriously. After lunch, however, he opened the back of his car and revealed a boot crammed with treasures. He'd brought with him dozens of trees: crab-apples and holm oaks, birches and sessile oaks and limes. Best of all, there was a yew, and yews, we knew, grew on the hillside, because many cottages had one (often calling themselves, imaginatively, 'Yew Tree Cottage' or 'Ty'r-ywen': 'the house by the yew'). 'The yew,' began Uncle William. 'D'you remember the yew at Rookwoods? Perhaps you were too young?'

'I remember it.'

'Well, this is its grandchild. When Granny left, I took a cutting and planted it in the garden. This is from a cutting from my tree.'

The idea of having a genuine piece of Rookwoods, of the garden in my head, growing in my own real garden … well, I need hardly say, the thought gave me goose bumps.

A week or two later, Uncle William emailed me. His advice boiled down to:

1. Get the place fenced. You can't do anything until that's done.
2. Look at what grows naturally around you.
3. Visit other Yellow Book gardens at a similar height and aspect.
4. Go to the Botanic Gardens of Wales, Edinburgh and the Lake District.
5. Consult your mother's books. She was a botanist, after all. Her shelves must be full of useful information.

As for getting into the Yellow Book, he said he could only speak from experience in Dorset, but he suspected they were 'far too stuffy' to take on such an unusual place. Which I presumed was his polite way of saying, 'Forget it.'

4

A short detour about
wood-chopping

The *Home Handyman*'s advice on smoking chimneys ... did
have one unusual suggestion to make: 'Perhaps you have
troublesome wind currents in your location. Find out if your
neighbours have trouble, and if so, how they tackle the problem.' What a good idea! We went at once to see what information we could gain. Our neighbours were sympathetic.
Yes—they too had troublesome parlour flues. How did they
get over the problem? Easy. They never used the parlour.

ELIZABETH WEST, *Hovel in the Hills*, 1977

Had you gone down to the woods—technically, the arboretum—of
Hawarden Castle, six miles west of Chester, in Flintshire, North Wales,
on any number of afternoons during the second half of the nineteenth
century, you might have encountered a diverting sight: Her Majesty,

Queen Victoria's sometime Chancellor of the Exchequer, latterly Prime Minister of England, complete with fine set of greying mutton-chop whiskers, in shabby tweeds, 'without a coat—without a waistcoat—with braces thrown back from off the shoulders and hanging down behind', setting to work with an axe. William Ewart Gladstone, aka 'The Grand Old Man', aka Liberal statesman, four-times Prime Minister, and *bête noire* of Benjamin Disraeli, the same man whom Churchill called his role model and whom Queen Victoria accused of always addressing her as if she were a public meeting, had an eccentric hobby. He was simply potty about wood-chopping, in particular, chopping down trees.

'No exercise is taken in the morning, save the daily walk to morning service,' recorded Gladstone's son, William, in the *Hawarden Visitors' Handbook*. 'But between 3 and 4 in the afternoon he sallies forth, axe on shoulder ... The scene of action reached, there is no pottering; the work begins at once, and is carried on with unflagging energy. Blow follows blow.' He seems to have possessed more enthusiasm than aptitude for his hobby. One Christmas he almost blinded himself when a splinter flew into his eye. On another occasion he almost killed his son Harry, when a tree Gladstone was cutting fell with the boy in it.

His tree-felling was achieved only by four or five hours of unremitting exertion, and much is made in descriptions of the terrific energies he expended, the way the perspiration poured from his face and through the back of his shirt; something that, according to his supporters (and, they claimed, the *vox populi*), emphasised his vital, heroic nature. His opponents did not agree. 'The forest laments,' remarked Lord Randolph Churchill, Conservative politician and later Chancellor of the Exchequer, 'in order that Mr Gladstone may perspire.' Wood-cutting even turned political when Disraeli spotted an opportunity to undermine his old foe. 'To see Lovett, my head-woodman, fell a tree is a work of art,' he declared smoothly in 1860. 'No bustle, no exertion, apparently not the slightest exercise of strength. He tickles it with the axe; and then it falls exactly where he desires it.'

Gladstone took up his tree-chopping in 1852, aged forty-two, and

continued with inextinguishable ardour until he was eighty-five, after which, he noted meticulously in his diary, he contented himself with mere 'axe-work' rather than 'tree-felling'.

———◆———

I mention Gladstone merely because, although he's possibly the most celebrated British example, in my experience most men find at least the idea of chopping wood appealing. In America the axe is an emblem of Abraham Lincoln, George Washington and Henry David Thoreau. It's the great symbol of the settler, the outback, of rural survival, self-reliance and the frontier spirit. Seven Presidents of the United States were born in log cabins.* Possibly this explains the axe's curious romance. All I knew was that if my idealised rural existence had to be summed up in a

* Andrew Jackson (7), William Henry Harrison (9), Millard Fillmore (13), James Buchanan (15), Abraham Lincoln (16), Ulysses S. Grant (18), James Abram Garfield (20).

single image, that image would be me either snoozing by the fire, or splitting logs on a frosty morning. Either way, the two elements were indispensable: a fire and logs to go on it.

Now, obviously lots of people like open fires. It's tempting to say everyone, were not my reason for bringing up the subject that the two most influential figures in my life emphatically didn't. My childhood was fireless. In the Woodward household, fires were one of the few subjects about which my parents were in complete agreement. They put their case peremptorily. Open fires were a chore. They had to be made, fed, poked and raked out. They were dirty. Their smoke ruined books. They were inefficient: everyone knew the heat went straight up the chimney, sucking draughts in its wake. They were dangerous, in a timber-framed, timber-clad house. None of these was the real reason for their antipathy, of course, which was that fires were yesterday's way.

To understand their viewpoint, it's necessary to remember the era. This was the 1960s and '70s: the nuclear age, the space race, motorways, comprehensive redevelopment, Concorde, and Harold Wilson's 'white heat of technology'. My parents were academic scientists: Da a research chemist,* Ma a botanical geneticist. Science, to my parents, was the way forwards. My mother was feeding us limitless quantities of instant food. My father was experimenting with disposable paper underwear. In our house there would be no ugly radiators or visible heat sources (at least not to start with). The future was electric: clean, silent, odourless and available at off-peak rates. Arguments (during one of my brother's and my periodic campaigns) that fires were cosy were ignored. The cottage chimney was bricked up.

My father was ahead of his time. Our new extension, complete with electric underfloor heating, was in place just in time for the 1973 oil crisis. The price of electricity shot up faster than heat up a chimney.

---

* He spent his days constructing weirdly beautiful models out of knitting needles and polystyrene balls, and writing papers with titles like 'Molecular Structure of Di-μ-chloro-bis-{[1-(dicarbonyl-π-cyclopentadienylferro)-2-phenylethylene]copper(1)}'.

The next six years (when, aged 10–16, my powers of recall were sharpest and my temperament most vindictive) saw strike after strike, power cut after power cut, culminating in the Three Day Week and the Winter of Discontent. Now, the all-electric house, without electricity, has a chilly comfortlessness that's all its own. With heating under the floor, there are no radiators to hug. I remember long, cold, dark evenings spent hunched round a Valor paraffin heater, as we tried to conserve our torch batteries. I left home fixated with radiators, Agas and roaring pot-bellied stoves; but most of all with dear, friendly, filthy, high-maintenance, chronically inefficient, open fires.

As it transpired, my mother, as she got older, softened in this area, getting me to draw the curtains close on miserable days, wrapping herself in blankets and hugging the electric fire. 'Granny-bugging', she called it. And even my father had the temerity recently to declare that he likes open fires—'in other people's houses'.*

———•◆•———

So, a fire and logs to go on it. With Tair-Ffynnon the archetypal lonely mountain cottage, a near-perfect enactment of almost every literary

---

* The patron saint of 'granny-bugging' is the nineteenth-century smack-head and (according to the *Sunday Times*) 'most unpleasant writer in literary history', Thomas de Quincey. His prose hymn to the joys of winter in *Confessions of an English Opium-eater* (1821) reads, for me, like a personal creed: 'I put up a petition annually for as much snow, hail, frost, or storm, of one kind or other, as the skies can possibly afford us. Surely everybody is aware of the divine pleasures which attend a winter fireside, candles at four o'clock, warm hearth-rugs, tea, a fair tea-maker, shutters closed, curtains flowing in ample draperies on the floor'—not forgetting the laudanum, of course—'whilst the wind and rain are raging audibly without.' It took years for this particular penny to drop—that a lust for wild weather goes hand-in-hand with a love of open fires because they're both part of the same thing: the pursuit of cosiness. The offbeat French philosopher Gaston Bachelard put his finger on it: 'We feel warm *because* it is cold out-of-doors. A reminder of winter strengthens the happiness of inhabiting.'

evocation of the granny-bugging fantasy, it clearly centred around an open fire, but for one small hitch. It didn't have one. It was patently meant to have one. There was a big stone chimney breast rising out of the sitting room. But the traditional cottage grate and bread oven were long gone, replaced by a tinny metal water heater connected by pipes to the hot water tank.

One of the first tasks with which the 'tidy' builders we'd engaged were charged was to remove this excrescence and 'open up' the fireplace. With it gone, I waited with mounting impatience for my big moment: an open fire of my own. In preparation, we'd bought an old iron fire-back in a salvage yard. This, with due solemnity, was placed in the hearth. I laid a fire, spreading the kindling into a neat pyramid, and struck a match. Almost immediately the room filled with smoke. It curled thickly out under the beam so it was clear none at all was going up the chimney. We endured it as long as we could until, eyes streaming, gasping for air, we had to stagger outside. Once the fire was doused and the smoke cleared, we peered up the chimney. We could see nothing. It was plainly blocked.

The following afternoon Frank the Sweep appeared with brushes and vacuum cleaners. The chimney was swept. No, he said, it wasn't blocked, but it was a bit tarry, which could have made a difference. Anyway, it was all clear now. As his van departed, we tried again. Precisely the same happened as before. I rang round for advice. It was freely available and readily dispensed: almost certainly the wood was damp and the chimney cold. It just needed warming through: all we had to do was light a really good blaze, keep it going for at least an hour and the problem would be solved.

As it had been raining we didn't have much in the way of dry wood, so we broke up some of the furniture that had been left behind by the previous owners. Pressing damp tea towels to our noses and mouths, we took turns to stoke the flames until they roared up the chimney so far sparks flew from the chimney pot. With such intensity of flame, it was true there was less smoke. But when we tried to light the fire the following time, it was just the same. More advice was solicited. 'Screen the chimney breast,' our experts said confidently. That was the standard procedure. So screen it we did. But however low we brought the screen (and we lowered it almost to the hearth itself), tendrils of smoke snaked determinedly under it into the room. 'The opening should be more or less square,' we were told, 'with neither width nor height less than seventy-five per cent of the depth.' I measured the fireplace and found this was already the case. 'Raise the hearth: fires need air, for goodness sake.' So we splurged £300 on a fine wrought iron grate and fire dogs to go with the fireback. And with like result. 'Raise it further,' we were briskly advised, as the smoke billowed forth no less prodigiously. So higher and higher we perched the iron basket, until it looked eccentric, then comic, then ludicrous and, finally, proving our advisers right, the fire no longer smoked. But that was only because it was out of sight up the chimney.

As the weeks passed our advisers' confidence never slackened. 'Try a hinged metal "damper" to block out cold air and rain.' It made no difference. 'It'll smoke when the wind's from the east,' said someone else. 'A lot of fires smoke when the wind's from the east.' And they were right, it did smoke when the wind was from the east. But as it came round, we were able to determine that the fire also smoked when the wind was from the west, and the south and the north. It even smoked when there was no wind at all. And on it went.*

We transferred our attentions from hearth to chimney. The chimney had been more messed about than the fireplace. The original, sturdy stone stack, when the house was enlarged, had been given mean, spindly

---

* I consulted Vrest Orton's *The Forgotten Art of Building a Good Fireplace: How to Alter Unsatisfactory Fireplaces & to Build New Ones in the 18th Century Fashion: The Story of Count Rumford & His Fireplace Designs that Have Remained Unchanged since 1795*—a slimmer volume than its title implies. Trying to follow the Count's precise specifications for 'throat' measurements and 'smoke shelves' in pursuit of the elusive 'continuous draught' (magical phrase) yielded only more builders' invoices and streaming eyes.

brick extensions. But rebuilding the whole chimney was too expensive. Besides, fresh advice informed us that this was not the fundamental problem, which was almost certainly one of downdraught, caused by the position of the house relative to the rise of the hill and the prevailing wind. Just as we were about to despair, one day in the builders' merchants a leaflet caught my eye. It advertised chimney cowls. And there, amongst the chimney cappers and birdguards, the lobster-back cowls and 'H' cowls, the flue outlets and 'aspirotors', was the very item for which we'd been searching:

> In constant production for thirty years, the **Aerodyne Cowl** has abundantly proven its worth in curing downdraught, showing clearly that the laws of aerodynamics don't change with the times. As wind from any direction passes through the cowl the unique venturi-shaped surfaces cause a drop in air pressure which draws smoke and fumes up the chimney for dispersal. The **Aerodyne Cowl** is offered with our money-back **guarantee**. If it fails to stop downdraught simply return it with receipt to your supplier for a full refund.

Why had no-one suggested this? An 'Aerodyne Cowl' was duly ordered. It took three weeks to arrive, two more to be fitted, but at last we were ready once more. All I can say is it was lucky about that money-back guarantee. If anything, the fire smoked more than before.

So we gave in. We ordered a wood-burning stove. By this stage I had my doubts that even this would work, but the man in the stove shop guaranteed it. And it did. The fire roared and crackled: it just did so behind glass. And thus, at last, we had an authentic need for logs. Which is how, by the convoluted way of these things, I came by my first tractor.

Amongst the chattels that came with Tair-Ffynnon (which included two mossy Opel Kadetts, a collapsed Marina van, numerous bathtubs and an assortment of broken and rusting bedsteads, trailers, ploughs, cultivators, rollers and diesel tanks) was an iron saw-bench. A farm saw-bench is a heavy cast-iron table with, protruding through a slit in the top, a big circular blade with scarily large teeth. They date from the time when farmers cut their own planks, gateposts and firewood. Many old farms have one somewhere, superannuated, rusting away in a corner. The moment I saw ours, I wanted that saw-bench back in action. It spoke of self-sufficiency and self-reliance, of replenished wood stores and cold winter months. It was, to an almost baleful degree, a renegade of the pre-health and safety era. Like most of the older ones, ours was worked by a pulley belt, which connected the bench to a parked tractor. Modern tractors ditched pulley wheels decades ago, but a couple of the older makes, Fordsons and Fergies, still had them. All I needed to get the saw-bench into action was one of those.

The more I thought about it, the more obvious it became that an old tractor was just what Tair-Ffynnon was missing. Now the requirement for firewood spelt it out. Jonny's remark came back to me: 'Looks as if you'd better get yourself a tractor.'

'Why?' said Vez.

It was one of those typically female questions that, on the spot, it's surprisingly difficult to answer. Arguments that a tractor was self-evidently a Good Thing to have, that it would lend tone to the place, in our straitened financial circumstances, lacked weight. 'For towing and mowing and pulling stuff. For cutting logs … everything.' My answer was necessarily vague, as I wasn't absolutely sure myself of all the myriad uses to which an old tractor might be put.

'You can buy a lot of logs for the price of a tractor,' said Vez. 'How much does a tractor cost?'

'Well, you could probably get an old Fergie or a Fordson for about £1,000, but I should think …'

'A grand! A *grand*! Are you out of your mind? When we haven't even got a dry place to store anything. And Maya needs shoes.'

There's no arguing such a case. Even I could appreciate that an inclination to see an old saw-bench back in harness, coupled with the knowledge that we could cut our own logs, sounded a little thin when ready-cut firewood was available for £40 a load.

All this I had only half worked through in my mind when I arrived on a Saturday in mid-July at the annual East Wales and Borders Vintage Auction, held, conveniently, in a field at the bottom of our hill. Over the last few days the field had been cut for silage and a tented village had sprung up so that now, although it was windless and grey, the white canvas and bunting presented a cheerful scene. Vintage auctions being the sole recreation my brother and I shared, he and my nephew Thomas had come over for the day, taking the opportunity to see us all, as had my father from Somerset. Jonny had arrived early for his usual forensic examination of the lots and announced that, amongst the collections of old railway sleepers, feed bins, mangles, chaff-cutters and nameless implements and agricultural bits and bobs, there was 'a very nice Fergie'. And sure enough, there amongst the junkyard tractors, Lot 571, was a peach of a machine.

The finer (and indeed the broader) points of tractor mechanics meant nothing to me, but I could see this was something special. For a start, unlike the other tractors on sale, it was complete. It had four wheels, two matching mudguards, and so on. No-one had attempted to spruce it up; it had a couple of dents, a buckled number plate, but still a fair amount of original grey paint. Headlamps either side of its radiator grille gave it a friendly, if slightly melancholic air. Here was one of those gems, it was clear, one might never forgive oneself for missing. Befitting its exalted status, it was one of the final lots, but the auctioneer and his throng were already working their way steadily down the rows towards it.

53

Jonny, who knew about old Fergie prices, said not to go a penny over £1,200. By the time the brown-coated auctioneer approached, he had established himself as a waggish figure whose skilful manipulations of his bidders was drawing a larger-than-average crowd. The auctioneer hoiked his foot onto the front wheel and, as his sidekick clambered into the seat, made a whirling motion with his hand. 'Start 'er up, Jack.' The sidekick pressed a button and the Fergie clattered cheerfully into life with a cloud of black smoke and diesel fumes, settling down to a homely chugging rattle.

There was no shortage of interest. The bidding flicked rapidly upwards. Soon it narrowed down to me and a small, sharp-eyed, fox-faced man with a peaked cap pulled well down over his eyes. By the rubber overalls under his shapeless tweed coat, I was pleased to note he was a hill farmer rather than a restoration enthusiast, so presumably wouldn't have absurd amounts of money to spend. £1,160 ... £1,180 ... £1,200 ... I could feel my pulse quickening. My adversary looked shrewd, informed, sure of himself. If he wanted the Fergie, it was plainly a good buy so it would be doubly foolish to miss out. £1,220 ... £1,240 ... My opponent's face was a mask. He communicated his bids by tiny, almost imperceptible nods, hardly more than twitches. £1,360 ... £1,380 ... £1,400 ... Would the man never give up? How much did these hill farmers have tucked away? The auctioneer sensed my wavering. 'Go on, Sir, you've come all this way'—(where did he get that idea?)—'Not going to lose her for a couple of quid, are you?'

'£1,500,' I said crisply.

He turned to my adversary. 'He's way over his limit, Sir. I think you've got him.'

Another expressionless twitch. The auctioneer turned back to me. 'Come on, Sir. You know it's got your name on it.' The crowd was loving it. Well, suffice to say, I got her. In the adrenaline rush it seems I also bought Lots 572, 573 and 574, the all-important pulley wheel, assorted bars and links that Jonny had announced went with the Fergie, and a complicated-looking hay mower with scissor blades that looked like a big hedge trimmer. As the crowd moved on, and the Fergie was again deserted, I sat on its front wheel in a daze of mixed emotions: happy fulfilment (I owned a tractor!), guilt (the purchase was indefensible), trepidation (what was I going to tell Vez? How did the thing work?). My father looked nonplussed. 'How much was it?' he said. 'What ever will you do with it?'

Jonny climbed onto the Fergie and pressed the starter. Nothing happened. 'Notoriously bad starters, Fergies,' he said. He fiddled with various switches and levers and tried again. Again, nothing. 'That's odd,' he said. He ordered me into the driving seat, while he tinkered in the engine. I was instructed to press a button in with my right ankle, while pressing the gear lever forwards. 'Are you sure this is what you do? It doesn't sound very likely.' I was told I knew nothing and just to do as I was asked. It made no difference.

'It started a minute ago. There must be something you're not doing.'

But there wasn't. Or there didn't seem to be. The crowd had moved well away by this time. Did I catch a frisson, a lightning backwards glance towards us, from my foxy friend in the low peaked cap?

An hour passed. People started arriving in pick-ups with trailers to collect and load their lots. We buttonholed any likely looking person who wandered past. They leant under the raised bonnet. They pored over the engine. They prodded and poked. They said Fergies were notoriously bad starters. But everyone agreed, it all looked fine. The field began to empty. My father went home. As I drove back to Tair-Ffynnon to look for tools for Jonny to start dismantling the engine, the full idiocy of what I'd done sank in. It had never occurred to me that the tractor might not work. In the excitement of the auction I hadn't given a thought to any practicalities. I knew not the first thing about tractors. I was amechanical. What was I to do next time she wouldn't start? Call the AA?

A couple more hours passed while Jonny dismantled and reassembled the engine. It made no difference. At length, he puffed out his cheeks. 'Well, I don't know what's wrong. Everything works fine. It should start.' By this time, the field was almost empty and a steady drizzle was falling. We were saved by an old boy wandering by. He told us to check a tiny lever hidden out of sight on one side of the engine. Somehow it had mysteriously moved from 'ON' to 'OFF'. 'I think someone's played a joke on you,' he said.

It was months before we finally got the saw-bench rigged. After a rudimentary course of tractor-driving instruction, Jonny departed, leaving me to make jerky, undignified forays up and down the track, trying to master the clutch. This tended, however gently it was engaged, to snatch, catapulting the machine forwards in ungainly kangaroo bounds. Vez, presented with my sly fait accompli, was magnificent, even agreeing the tractor looked just so, and made us appear less like urbanites (an accommodation assisted, unquestionably, by an envelope from my father which arrived a few days after the auction containing a cheque for the price of the Fergie and a fairytale about finding more money in an account than he'd expected).

From a company Jonny told me about ('A & C Belting'), I ordered a rubberized canvas belt and the next time he visited, we heaved the eye-poppingly heavy bench into position, pegging it into the dirt floor of the barn with eighteen-inch iron pegs.* Then Jonny oiled and greased the blade shaft and pulley wheel spindles. With much to-ing and fro-ing, we positioned the tractor. We chocked the wheels and connected up the pulley belt between the tractor and the saw-bench. We engaged the tractor's pulley wheel, setting the belt turning. Then I pulled the iron lever on the saw, which slid the belt across to drive the blade. The saw cranked into life.

It was simply terrifying. I'd never been so close to a machine that

---

* These are the kind of things you find lying around when you go to vintage auctions.

was so blatantly lethal. The belt flapped and slapped between the pulley wheels, hungry to snag any loose clothing or inquisitive passing child. The blade whirred and squeaked like a giant bacon slicer, though the sound was quaintly soothing and almost musical: the rattling rhythm of the Fergie's engine, the regular *ting-ting* of the staples in the belt as they passed over the iron pulley wheels. I found some small branches and pushed them towards the blade to warm it up (something the man from A & C Belting had advised). The saw scarcely noticed. After a few of these I pushed a thick old stump forwards with a stick. The blade screamed as it bit into the wood, and the tractor engine chugged harder, reverting to its gentle clatter as the cutting finished, the blade ringing as the severed timber thudded onto the ground. The smell of sawn wood filled the air. It was sensational.

Wood was strewn all over the place at Tair-Ffynnon: shambolic heaps of logs and stumps, hedging offcuts, old fence posts, sections of telegraph poles and sleepers, as if a giant had been playing Pick-Up Sticks before being called away mid-game. To at last be clearing it was satisfying work. Some timber cut more easily than others. Yew and old oak were so hard their sawdust was as fine as flour. Sappy larch and fir released a delicious piny smell, but the resin gummed the blade, making the belt slip. As my confidence increased I discarded my stick, pushing the logs forwards by hand. Occasionally, with the scrap wood, the saw would hit a nail or a staple, screeching and sending out showers of sparks. Soon the iron table top shone and the feet of the bench were lost in deepening heaps of sawdust that dusted every surface like snow.

True, I couldn't quite banish the image of a gross-out, splatter-movie death. A momentary lapse of concentration, a trip from catching my foot on something buried beneath the sawdust, and—the wood chipper scene from *Fargo* or Johnny Cash's brother in *Walking the Line*. My hand, or arm (or head) in the log pile. But the tangle of timber was transmogrifying into a neat pile of logs for splitting. And all that fear worked up a prodigious appetite.

Maybe stockpiling wood is in our genes as hunter-gatherers. Stacked wood bespeaks security, cosiness, preparedness for winter. Perhaps it's because it's exercise with a purpose, or a way of clearing one's head. 'I chop wood,' Gladstone told the journalist William T. Stead, 'because I find that it is the only occupation in the world that drives all thought from my mind.'*

Maybe it's all the associations that come with an axe: the forest clearance, the ancient oaks of England on which a navy and an empire were built. Or the perfection of its form. If an hour's wood-chopping is soothing work, it must be because quite so much hopping around, swearing, trying to extricate the wedged head has taken place over the 1.2 million years of steady R&D devoted to this, the prototypical tool. Though in fact it's not a tool, it's a simple machine, using leverage to

---

* In *The Woodlanders*, Thomas Hardy, writing at much the same time, asserts precisely the opposite: 'Being an occupation which the secondary intelligence of the hands and arms could carry on without requiring the sovereign attention of the head, the minds of its professors wandered considerably from the objects before them; hence the tales, chronicles, and ramifications of family history which were recounted here were of a very exhaustive kind, and sometimes so interminable as to defy description.'

ramp up the force at the cutting edge, and dual-inclined planes to enhance the splitting action. That head is drop-forged from medium carbon steel (the flaring cheeks averaging twenty-nine degrees): hard enough to hold an edge, yet not so brittle it shatters. The shaft (of ash or hickory so it won't splinter or split from the strain) is kinked for easy swinging by anyone of average height. And it's a philosopher's axe—not a rake or broom—over which we puzzle: is it still our grandfather's if our father replaced the head and we the shaft? The Director of the British Museum recently called the axe 'the most successful piece of human technology in history'.

Not bad for twelve quid from Homebase.

5

Winter on the hill

A glance around at the landscape should have warned us
what we were in for. Where rowan and hawthorn trees
bend at permanent right angles, man wasn't meant to plant
Jerusalem artichokes and rhubarb.

ELIZABETH WEST, *Hovel in the Hills*, 1977

'Was Granny's garden in the Yellow Book?'

'It was.' My father could compress much meaning into two words.

'At Rookwoods?'

'At Rookwoods. And again when she moved to Bath. She was very
much the magnanimous charity worker, remember' (that was pretty
loaded, too). I'd been sporadically quizzing him about the National
Gardens Scheme since hatching my plan, but it had only recently
occurred to me that Rookwoods itself might have been in the Yellow
Book.

'And ...?'

'Well, it was the kind of menace you might imagine. We all had to dance attendance and ended up doing most of the work. On one occasion she announced she was going on holiday the week the garden was opening, leaving us to take care of it. You can guess how well that went down with your mother.'

'So you helped, too?'

'We all had to help.'

'Didn't it occur to you to mention this?'

'Mention what?'

'The fact that Granny was in the Yellow Book? I've been asking you about the Yellow Book for weeks.'

'No. You never asked that.'

It was July and our move to the sheep-run pastures of Tair-Ffynnon was complete. We'd driven over to the Mendips for one of our periodic Sunday lunches with my father. He greeted us with his usual mock exasperation. 'Late as ever.'

'You'd be disappointed if we weren't.'

He gave me a bottle of champagne to open. He always gave us champagne when we came now: a reminder how special these occasions were, and how seldom we saw each other since my brother and I had young families. Today, however, I had a private purpose in coming. If I were going to make a garden I needed to learn all I could about gardening—fast. It was so vast a subject it was hard to know where to begin, and my father seemed a good start. My mother may have been the botanist, but the garden of our family home was very much his. So I did something I'd never done before: I requested a garden tour.

I regretted it almost immediately. Full of pre-Sunday-roast bon-homie, we'd hardly carried our glasses to the low raised bed outside the kitchen—'This, as you know, is the *Eucryphia* ... it has the most wonderful big flowers in August'—before the first pang of deep boredom set in. It wasn't what he was saying so much as what it brought back. Suddenly I was at Stourhead, aged seven, standing on aching legs by some tree or other, while my parents banged on and on about it. And it wasn't just Stourhead. It was Hestercombe, Barnsley House, Prior Park, Westonbirt Arboretum ... all names whose mere mention made me thankful never to have to be a child again.*

With specialised interests, opposite characters and very different backgrounds, my parents ostensibly had nothing in common. The garden was the closest they came. 'This, as you know ...' my father's voice brought me back to the present. '... is the *Philadelphus*. It has the most glorious scent ...' Then there were the Latin names. I could almost hear my mother shouting from the kitchen window: 'Behind the *Eucryphia* ... No, you noodle, the *Eucryphia,* not the *Euphorbia* ...' I didn't discover plants even had English names until my mid-twenties. As academics of the pre-spin school, my parents never seemed to feel the need to make their subjects interesting or accessible, to supply context or simplify.

My father had now moved on to explaining his principles for choosing plants, his preference for foliage over flowers, but it was hard to separate the information from the associations. 'This is *Rhus cotinus.* Another shrub you grow only for its leaves ...'

'What are these, again?'

'*Stachys lanata.*'

'Do they have an English name?'

'I think some people call them Lamb's Ears.'

It struck me that going round a garden with its owner is not unlike looking at someone else's holiday snaps at their pace. ('That's Jackie,

---

* Stourhead was infinitely the worst, a position secured after my grandmother took it upon herself to supplement our spring (rhododendrons) and autumn (leaves) visits with a summer evening Open Air Theatre performance. These were staged round the bridge across the lake and as night fell on the waterside setting, the hot stage lights came on and the midges and mosquitoes went to work, illuminated in vast clouds as they feasted, unable to believe their luck, on their captive prey. Following one August performance of *Charley's Aunt*, we were all so bitten even my parents decided enough was enough.

the person I was telling you about. She was *so* funny.') Yet, having specifically requested the tour, I could hardly ask to speed things up.

We walked back up the lawn, past the kitchen, and up the steep path towards the open fields behind the house. The garden wasn't large, perhaps a quarter of an acre, but it was much divided around the house because of the way the site had been bitten out of the hill-side.

'Did Ma help much with the garden?'

'Did she actually *do* anything, d'you mean? Heavens no. She was far too busy with her horses. Full of advice, of course. Sometimes she used to "pop things in", as she called her cuttings. She was extremely tiresome in that regard.'

As we returned to the front door, we encountered something I could confidently identify. 'Purple sage,' I said.

'Mmm ... *herbs*.' The word was invested with a scorn it's hard to convey in print.

'Why, don't you like herbs?' I knew perfectly well what his views were on herbs, and the reasons he'd give for them, but I couldn't stop myself.

'They're a nuisance.'

'A nuisance? How can herbs be a nuisance?'

'You have food that tastes of nothing but herbs, rather than what it's supposed to taste of.' For my father, cooking was a chemical experiment: instructions were followed, tasting was unnecessary and final temperature (piping hot) was the key indicator of the success of the meal.

We had to go back into the house to reach the patio. The house was my father's Great Modernist Experiment, the product of his love of architecture in general and Mies van der Rohe's 1929 Barcelona Pavilion in particular. In time for my arrival in 1963, they needed to add onto my mother's cottage, which had only one bedroom and a wide landing where Jonny slept. My father devised a contemporary solution. Modules precision-machined off-site by Vic Hallam, the Nottinghamshire company made famous by its pre-fabricated classrooms, were bolted to a pre-formed, cantilevered concrete deck. Twenty-eight polished Ilminster stone steps led up from the poky cottage's front door to an airy, light-filled, flat-roofed glass box, containing sitting room and bedrooms. These were furnished accordingly: razor-edged steel-and-glass coffee table, brick-hard, angle-iron and foam-rubber Hille sofas, Ercol bentwood table and chairs. Comfort took a holiday. And so Modernism made its brazen progress from Bauhaus Germany, via New York, to our ancient Mendip lane. Nothing like it had been seen before in rural Somerset.

The patio arrived in Phase Two of the Great Modernist Experiment, an extension forced upon us by my mother's riding accident almost a decade later. It was my father's most successful garden space, enclosed on three sides by the house, and on the fourth by the rising ground of the hill. It was, as he'd intended it, an astonishing suntrap. In raised dry-stone beds he'd planted acers, a green one with broad leaves and a couple with more dissected leaves in red and bright green. I ran my hand along one of the smooth, shapely branches. After thirty years the trees were sculptural, contributing a calming, vaguely Japanese air to the space that set off the severity of the square brutalist concrete pond and the glass and cedar of the house.

During the Modernist years, my father had maintained the pond, with its floor of raked pea shingle, in a state of stark clinical perfection, washing it clean of algae several times a summer so the water never clouded. But in later years he'd given up, planted lilies in the corners, stuck a round stone bowl in place of the water jets and even, the final capitulation, added goldfish. It was softer now, but less dramatic or coherent.

I wanted another drink and for the trip to conclude. We took the path round to the back of the house, north-facing and enclosed by a conifer plantation. Towering into the sky, straight as a missile launcher, was the tree with my favourite name.

'There you are: *Metasequoia glyptostroboides.*' My father pronounced it perfectly, slowly, with just the right amount of ironic inflexion to wring out its full, polysyllabic absurdity. 'It's a remarkable tree,' he said. 'One of the few in the country when we planted it. Your mother got hold of it through some botanical thing she was doing. Looks ludicrous now, of course, it's got so big.'

It wasn't the only giant. Blocking the view in or out from the lane was a stand of three vast leylandii.

'What possessed you to plant those?'

'It's all very well for you to be sniffy about them now, but at the time they were the wonder tree. We'd never come across anything like them. Fast-growing. Dense. Evergreen.' He sighed. 'But they do grow like triffids. I'll have to take them out.'

Was any of this remotely useful or relevant for Tair-Ffynnon, I wondered? We went in for lunch. Midday sunshine streamed through the south-facing floor-to-ceiling glass, the same glass that on winter nights used to seem so cold and black and endless (and still makes me yell at wide-eyed couples on Channel 4's *Grand Designs* as they order their steel and glass boxes: 'Don't do it! You'll feel cold and vulnerable and watched! You'll spend a fortune on curtains and ruin the look!').

Four candles on wall sconces in the dining room, comically drooped and corkscrewed, testified to the opposite extreme. But today, with the doors open, the house was perfect: warm and light and airy.

———◆———

After lunch, while Vez, pregnant with our second child, lay snoozing on the sofa, and my father played songs on the piano for Maya, I ransacked my mother's bookshelves, as Uncle William had advised. Here were floras and herbals, catalogues and regional guides. Many of the names were familiar: Hillier's *Manual of Trees and Shrubs* and H. J. Bean's doorstop volumes of *Plants and Shrubs Hardy in the British Isles* (a title which for some reason always conjured images of plants swathed in brightly coloured cagoules and scarves battling up a hill), though I'd never opened them before. And I now saw, as I pulled a few out, what a wise course this had been. It would be hard to devise books more calculated to repel a potential plant lover. All appeared to share the same striking characteristic: not a picture to be seen. I was puzzled because these volumes, I knew, were mere holiday-reading, lightweight warm-up acts, alongside the *vade mecum* of my mother's day-to-day existence: the much-thumbed *Flora of the British Isles*, which I now pulled out. Its cheerful yellow jacket, with a picture of a flower, was at iniquitous odds with the 1,591 pages of closely written print within. This was the immortal 'Clapham, Tutin and Warburg', named after the three distinguished professors of botany who were its editors. Each entry matched absolute incomprehensibility with mildly pornographic language. A sample might run:

Basal sinus wide, coarsely dentate; cauline lvs. Pedicels erect, with small sessile glands. Densely tormentose with pickled, blue-veined spectricals. Sparsely ciliate on the petiole. Stipules and peduncles filiform indehiscent. Sepals lanceolate-aristate, hairy. Petals obovate cuneiform. Carpels pubescent. Naturalised in North America. Endemic.

Was this, I wondered, why places seemed so much more interesting than plants? Alongside Clapham, Tutin and Warburg, the architectural jabberwocky of my father's Pevsner's county-by-county *Buildings of England* series (another collection for which a few more pictures might not have gone amiss) read with Orwellian clarity.*

Further meditations were interrupted by the soothing, familiar rattle of my father bringing the tea tray. Tea was an inviolable 4.15 tradition in the Woodward household (equal mix Lapsang and Earl Grey, minute, much-stapled tea cups, and, when she was alive, one of my mother's cakes). As Vez stirred and sat up, and Maya hurled herself at my legs, I wrenched my thoughts from stipules and peduncles.

———·•·———

That summer was the record-breaking one. Back at Tair-Ffynnon, it seemed as if clouds had become extinct. Exchanging our hard-won London pad for a derelict hilltop smallholding seemed the cleverest move we'd ever made. We bought a big army frame tent (big enough to accommodate a Land Rover) to act as a spare room for friends to stay in. It came in two vast canvas bags, so heavy the delivery driver and I could only just move them. The military instructions specified at least five to erect it ('pitching party—five men') so we did it one day when friends came for lunch. We weighted the wide 'mud cloths' with con-

---

* My mother's doctoral research had been completed at Leicester University (partly, it emerged, to permit regular hunting with the Quorn and the Pytchley) under none other than 'dear old Tom Tutin' as she called him, the Tutin of Clapham, Tutin and Warburg. I've since heard it said that the great trio's *Flora* was part of a deliberate conspiracy within academic botany—one to which my mother evidently subscribed—to keep botany complicated. As one of the great ancient subjects of Oxford, in the late nineteenth and early twentieth centuries, botany was in danger of being overtaken and eclipsed by the other, more 'difficult' natural sciences: biology, physics and chemistry. By using obfuscating language, the theory went, and arid descriptions instead of pictures, plus masses of Latin, it might have a chance.

crete joists and breezeblocks and whacked in two dozen enormous iron pegs with a sledgehammer. Then, inside, we decked it out, until, frankly, it was the cosiest room about the place.

We'd got a new black Labrador puppy (christened Beetle after her propensity for eating dung) and twice a day I'd walk up to the trig point with her. The place bustled with activity. During the day there were walkers and riders, bemused school orienteering parties, pony trekkers, runners, mountain bikers, radio modellers, occasional motocross riders (on plateless scrambling bikes and always careful not to remove their helmets). Gliders would fly down the ridge, almost brushing the bracken, so close you could hear the air rushing over their wings. There were falconers, racehorses exercising from the local yard, whinberry pickers with faces and fingers stained purple-black. Walkers would stop to ask for water, or, exhausted, if we could drive them to their B&B. And when we heard muffled shouts and bright canopies billowed up on the far side of dry-stone walls, we'd know the wind was from the east. Then dangling figures suddenly appearing out of the sky would drive Beetle into paroxysms of territorial barking, a remit she soon extended to anyone wearing a backpack, rendering our walks a good deal less relaxing for all concerned.

But as evening came, calm would descend; the hill would empty, until the moment when it was deserted apart from the swallows. After all the bustle, the quiet seemed twice as intense. Day after day dawned cloudless and warm, some so clear and still that, in the way that silence amplifies space, the sky seemed twice the size. Far above us, vapour trails dispersed like gradations on some vast protractor. Stonechats arrived, their characteristic call like two stones smacking together. At ground level, the forests of thistles left by the sheep went to seed, sometimes filling the air with so much thistledown it seemed to be snowing. A redstart nested in the baler. As the hill got drier and drier, the ponies brought their foals to drink at the bathtub in the yard.

October brought the first serious hill fog. We were used to intermittent fogs lasting the morning, shifting with the wind which interrupted their opaque evenness, perhaps affording a glimpse of the shining white disc of the sun, or offering fleeting vignettes of things made strange by the randomness of their selection—a wind-blown thorn tree singled out from the hill across the valley, a distant farm, the top of Skirrid or Sugar Loaf. Occasionally a confused-looking pigeon or crow might make us feel momentarily less alone. Usually these fogs burnt off during the morning, but this one was different. It arrived one Sunday when our friends Nick and Kate were staying. Kate, who was pregnant, went out for a ten-minute stroll, only for dense cloud to sweep across the hill. When after an hour she hadn't returned and twenty minutes of bawling her name into the murk met with no response, we began to worry. What made it worse was Kate was a by-word for self-reliant competence. Another hour later, neighbours just the field below us called to say she'd found them, having lost the path and stumbled over tussocky moor, scrambling over five foot walls and barbed wire fences in her desperation to find civilisation. We sensed, as Nick and Kate's red tail lights faded into the gloom, that they left few regrets behind them in the fog, now denser than ever.

Next morning it was still there, deadening everything. Usually, depending on the wind direction, the sound of tractors, farmers calling dogs, chainsaws or even the railway were audible from the valley below. But not now. We could hear nothing. By Tuesday the oppressive atmosphere had begun to affect us; we were getting on each other's nerves and taking headache remedies. Escaping to walk Beetle, usually the best remedy for every irritation, brought no relief; indeed, it seemed to compound the problem, confirming the impossibility of escape, while the heavy air made me breathless and left my clothes damp. We would compete for the chance to go down the hill, once we'd discovered the fog stopped at the hill gate and life seemed to be carrying on as normal down there.

After four and a half days, I opened the bedroom curtains and stood blinking. The fog had gone. No, that wasn't strictly correct: it had moved. It was below us. Now we, Skirrid and Sugar Loaf occupied a lofty world above the clouds. Tendrils of water vapour lapped at the yard gate, sometimes reaching up as far as the front door, like waves on an incoming tide. Occasionally, the mist would rise up and engulf us completely, then sink back down again, the water vapour sliding off the roof of the house and rolling round the yard, as the first pink shafts of the rising sun broke over the roiling sea of cloud. We pulled on our clothes and walked to where the hang-gliders launched, then climbed the hill in the chilly stillness, to see how far this ocean extended. Over the entire world, it seemed.

Then, at the end of November, came the wind. It was not cold, but it was fierce. It arrived from the south-west and its strength, at least to start with, was amusing. It blew so hard we found ourselves frogmarched across the yard. It clawed at our mouths and eyelids, messed with our balance and made it hard to breathe. Walking up the hill became a comedy stagger, coats flattened like Lycra on the windy side, snapping and flapping crazily like loose sails on the other. Dustbins had to be weighted. Anything light and unfixed was swept away, collecting against west-facing walls. Parking her car crosswind, Vez found herself a prisoner, the door pinned shut. Unthinkingly, I parked the Land Rover with its back to the wind, opened the door and found it wrenched clean away. It clattered and bounced for thirty yards.

After a few days the novelty of this began to wear off. Loose corners of tin sheeting on the barns flapped and banged, the cut edges screeching like fingernails down a blackboard. Fast as I could screw them back down, the wind tore them loose again. The gale howled in the chimney. It tugged and strained at the house, searching for the weak points. The windows fitted so badly, or were so holed by rot, there were draughts everywhere. Open a door and the curtains would be sucked against the windows. We could feel the pressure changes in our ears as we moved from room to room. Lying in bed, I'd listen as the wind funnelled between the outbuildings and the house, and on round the tin barns, setting up a haunting, organ-pipe moan. Every now and again the note would change, as it veered or gusted. As it strengthened, its note rose from a scream to a shriek. I found it soothing and it lulled me to sleep, but it kept Vez awake. After a week, despite earplugs, she looked so grey and shattered I feared we might have to abandon Tair-Ffynnon altogether.

———————◆·◆·◆———————

We knew we should be taking the tent down. We'd known it since October; not even our hardiest friends would volunteer to sleep under canvas now. We'd taken out the rugs and lights. But, as the terse military instructions declared ('striking party—five men'), the tent was just too heavy for us alone and we never seemed to have enough pairs of hands. On Boxing night, we were woken by what sounded like a strong man vigorously and repeatedly slamming a door downstairs. The internal doors were all secured by Suffolk latches, but the sitting room door didn't catch. I went downstairs to wedge it closed, to discover that even the doors whose latches caught were rattling. Usually inert parts of the house had come alive: newspapers rustled, dust filled the air, draughts howled around my ankles, window panes creaked and groaned. I shoved a chair against the door and returned to bed. An hour later we were woken again, to the sound of glass smashing. The heavy velvet bedroom curtains were billowing, and there was the unsettling patter of rain on paperwork. The bedroom window had been sucked out.

In the morning, the wind had dropped. As I drew open the bathroom curtains and peered out, something looked different. I couldn't for a moment tell what it was. There was a patch of brown grass outside the barn. What had made that? Then I realised. The tent had gone. There was nothing left at all, apart from the row of breezeblocks and concrete lintels used to weight it. No frame, no ropes, no eighteen-inch iron pegs, no ground sheet, no mattress. It was a tidy job, as if the recommended striking party had come in the night. We eventually found it about a mile away, wrapped round the top of a tree. It seemed we'd had our last guests until the spring.

6

The Not Garden

This, then, leads up to what I believe to be the great secret of
success in garden-making … we should abandon the struggle
to make nature beautiful round the house and should rather
move the house to where the nature is beautiful.

SIR GEORGE SITWELL, *On the Making of Gardens*, 1909

As we parked on a grassy common alongside a vast leylandii hedge, I
couldn't suppress a pang of disappointment. I'd been waiting months
for this moment. We'd just driven for two hours, deep into mid-Wales,
specifically to see the garden behind this hedge. In the last few miles
the first hints had appeared that we were entering a landscape that was
weird and interesting. We were following a Scenic Route through an
undulating, much-folded massif of the Cambrian Mountains. There'd
been a sign to a sailing club, pointing to a road that led steeply *uphill*.
And now, before I even got out of the car, let alone stepped through the

garden gate, I knew with resounding certainty that the garden was not going to deliver, that anyone who had a leylandii hedge in such a place couldn't possibly have a garden I liked. It wasn't so much the leylandii per se,* as what this high and impenetrable barrier implied. Which was awkward, given that its owner was very kindly putting herself out entirely on our account.

We were on a fact-finding mission. It was proving a good deal trickier than I'd expected to work out how our garden should be. Apart from spending an inordinate amount of time standing about staring at patches of mud from various angles, trying to imagine this scenario or that— the collapsing ex-army Nissen hut in the yard replaced with a stone barn, a dry-stone wall in place of a tangled wire fence, the house magically made pretty, even, in more futile moments, a tree moved twenty yards to the left—my efforts hadn't amounted to much. We knew Tair-Ffynnon was to be a mountain garden, but what did that mean? If I tried looking up 'mountain gardens' or 'mountain flowers' I just found a lot of stuff about rockeries and alpines, which didn't feel right. Reading Derek Jarman's diaries and garden book revealed that his garden had come about by accident and had grown gradually and haphazardly from there. But we needed more of a plan than this. The most hopeful avenue for inspiration seemed to be Uncle William's idea of going through the Yellow Book, finding other gardens at a similar height, and seeing what their owners had done. It quickly became apparent, however, that there weren't many. For good reasons, people tended not to make gardens on top of mountains. Perhaps as a result,

---

* Though, let's be clear about this, I do believe that anyone who plants leylandii should be put in prison. This malign, greedy, evergreen emblem of instant gratification and territorial hostility now asserts its homogenising presence across every part of Britain, once one of the world's most diverse landscapes. Upland, downland, dale, wold, fenland, forest, coastline, moorland—nowhere is safe. It's become a close call as to whether barbed wire, the moulded concrete brick or *Cupressocyparis leylandii* takes the laurels as the key force in Britain's rural desecration.

everyone with a garden more than 700 feet above sea level mentioned the fact, prompting the thought that we might be higher than the highest garden in the Yellow Book. If so, that would effectively mean— delightful notion—we might be able to make Tair-Ffynnon into the highest garden in the National Gardens Scheme.*

As only areas with high ground were competition—the Pennines, Lake District, Yorkshire and Derbyshire Dales, Dartmoor, Bodmin Moor, Exmoor and Wales—I set about working through the relevant counties. Cumbria had not a single garden in the running. I thought this must be a mistake until it occurred to me that, of course, most places in hill country were not seeking altitude but the exact reverse. It was only the poorest dwellings that were forced up onto the high, marginal ground. This boded well. In Derbyshire, the appealing-sounding 'Cloud Cottage, Simmondley' boasted of being at a scarcely numinous 750 feet, while 'Spring Tops Cottage, East Sterndale' was pleased to be 'over 1,000 feet above sea level'. Neither Devon nor Somerset had a single contender, neutralising Exmoor. In Cornwall, a garden between Bodmin and Launceston, claimed, 'at nearly 1,000 feet', to be 'probably the highest garden in Cornwall'.

It was all most promising stuff. In rising spirits, I reached the Wales section. Moorland Cottage, on the side of the Preseli Mountains,

---

* We'd already detected a quiet, understated competitiveness from locals who lived up in the hills. If we casually let slip that we lived high up, a gentle sparring match would ensue.

'How high are you?'

'About 1,500 feet,' I'd say. I deliberately hadn't checked, not wanting to know if we were lower than this.

'Oh.' A wounded silence would follow, which a shared bond of elevation was seldom enough to recover.

Subsequent examination of the contours on the Ordnance Survey 1:25,000 map revealed that we sat on the 360 metre contour, putting us at an unambiguous 1,182 feet. A friend with a GPS modestly improved this to 1,214 feet, with the top of the highest field a hundred feet further up.

sounded bleak but was a mere 720 feet. Denbighshire and Colwyn had just a single garden at 800 feet. Flintshire and Wrexham, nothing. Glamorgan, nothing. Gwent, our own area (combining four counties), nothing. Gwynedd, one garden with 'panoramic views ... 1,000 feet up in Snowdonia'.

And so, with just five pages of the book to go, I reached Powys. A 'stunning view of Black Mountains' from 900 feet and a 'spectacular view of Black Mountains' from 850 feet were speedily dismissed. But then, on page 510 of 512, like a punch to the solar plexus, I read:

NEW! CWMLLECHWEDD FAWR, Llanbister ... 2-acre garden at 1,500ft.

I couldn't believe it. And 'New!' too, so had we been applying a year earlier, it wouldn't have been listed. And the height slipped in so casually, as if it was hardly worth mentioning. I hurled the book into the waste paper basket. When I retrieved it a few moments later, however, things got worse. Three entries later, a garden was described as 'set on a windswept hillside and at just under 1,400 feet, reputedly the highest garden in Montgomeryshire'. Three entries further on, a '1,350ft windy location' promised 'stunning views'.

Disappointment aside, one thing was clear: it was plainly possible to garden at these heights. With this thought annoyance turned to curiosity. What could they be like, these places? What had their owners done with their wild and windswept settings? In my head I conjured images of low stone cottages huddled into bleak, heather moorland; quarrymen's houses beneath slate cliffs or walker's bothies with cheerfully painted tin roofs weighted against gales in bleak, treeless settings, dwarfed by mountains. Unfortunately, I wasn't going to get an early answer. While the National Gardens Scheme opening season began in most areas in early spring, these gardens (presumably owing to their altitude) didn't open until mid-July.

With the gardens themselves out of bounds, elevation became a fixation. I visited the three highest villages in Britain: Garn-yr-erw, near Blaenavon (1,315 feet), a few miles south of us; Flash in the Peak District (1,489 feet) and Wanlockhead in Scotland (1,393 feet), each demolishing Tair-Ffynnon's pretensions to altitude.* When I read in Evelyn Waugh's *Diaries* that, on 12 August 1926, he'd visited a house in Aberdeenshire 'said to be the highest in Britain', I wrote to the owners asking their elevation and received a courteous response to the effect that yes, the house did sit on the 1,500 foot contour, but that, although the owner's father-in-law always used to say it was the highest occupied house in the UK, this probably meant 'mansion house' as there were numerous cottages on the estate higher up. By then I'd joined the Mountain Bothies Association and discovered that many of their mountain shelters sat at over 2,000 feet.

Eventually, impatience got the better of me. As the second and third highest gardens were within a few miles of each other, I rang the owners and asked if we could make a private visit well before their official open days. Which was how we came to be contemplating the leylandii hedge on a lifeless day, grey and pregnant with rain, in early May.

As we walked round the hedge to meet the owner, a substantial stone house came into view. In front was a large lawn and wide herb-aceous borders. The place was overflowing with rudely healthy herbage. Unquestionably, the lady now showing us round was a most talented plantswoman. I nodded behind her, trying to sound like a gardener, while Maya played hide-and-seek happily around the pond and walk-ways. I could see that the garden was a triumph of energy, determination and organic manure. There was no doubting the owner's skill in coaxing such prolific growth from such unyielding terrain. But, and this was

---

* Alston and Buxton, both at around a thousand feet, slug it out for 'highest English market town'. The highest pub is the Tan Hill Inn, 1,732 feet up in the Pennines above Swaledale in the Yorkshire Dales, leaving the Kirkstone Pass Inn between Ambleside and Troutbeck, on the highest road pass in the Lake District, a distant speck below at around 1,400 feet.

my problem, there was no sign of that terrain. It had been carefully and deliberately shut out. I couldn't see the point of it. Why, I wondered, so proudly state the garden's elevation, yet not make it a feature? Then I realised, of course, it was a feature, in as much as the garden was a remarkable advertisement for the owner's skills in succeeding despite it. It was, really, no different to the Middle Eastern water gardens which defied the desert. But it felt wrong.

By the time we set off for the second garden, I knew it would be the same, and it was. For once I was grateful for the rain and Maya's crying. It meant we could make an early escape.

Disappointing as I found the gardens, the trip wasn't wasted. It helped clarify what I wanted. My father had always said there were two types of gardener: 'There's the kind like your mother, potty about plants, who couldn't really care less about design. Then there are the people like me, for whom gardening's just architecture. So far as we're concerned, you don't need to know much about plants, so long as they'll grow where you put them.' It looked as if he was right. Plants or place. But why couldn't it be both? For me the perfect garden should be able to exist only where it is and nowhere else. The trick was to find what naturally grew there, then, however limited the palette it offered, to create within those limitations. That, surely, was what creativity was about. I consoled myself with the thought that perhaps the highest garden in the Yellow Book, up at its dizzying 1,500 feet and open in July, would prove more satisfactory in its relationship to its landscape.

It did, as it happened, when the impatiently awaited date finally dawned, but for a different reason to the one I expected. We arrived shortly after lunch, parked and joined the queue for tickets by the entrance to a walled garden. On the table there was a photocopied sheet providing a brief introduction to the garden. While we waited, I scanned the sheet. 'Welcome to Cwmllechwedd Fawr,' it began. 'Situated at

1,100 feet above sea level ...' I stopped and read it again. Then a third time. 'Excuse me,' I said to the woman from whom we bought our tickets. 'I could've sworn your entry in the Yellow Book said something about you being at 1,500 feet?'

'Did it? Yes ... well ... ha ha, I don't think we are. No, I don't think we can claim to be that ... no.' She leant forwards, lowering her voice conspiratorially. 'I think they probably encouraged us to say that, you know, beef it up a bit, make it sound a bit more interesting.' She gave a musical laugh and turned to take someone else's money. 'Have you got your ticket? Teas up on the left. Yes, and that's a sheet about the garden. Just a bit of history ...'

Not a blush. Not a missed beat. That was how the pros did it. If they were out of the running, who was to say the other two gardens we'd visited were the height they said they were? Why, it opened up all kinds of possibilities.

'Stop looking so pleased with yourself,' said Vez.

<hr />

Still without a plan for Tair-Ffynnon, and with Vez fully occupied with our latest arrival, a boy, Storm, I wondered what to do. I decided to cut down the row of conifers and leggy sycamores that blocked the view and the light in front of the house. The effect was dramatic. It revealed a ten-mile view down the Gavenny valley, and the discovery that we looked directly onto Skirrid. This was our local mountain and the most characteristic local landmark. It was freestanding, an outlier of the rest of the Black Mountains on the eastern side, with a cracked, asymmetrical profile half resembling an extinct volcano, owing to a vast landslip that broke its top. (This event, supposedly coinciding with the birth of our Lord, was depicted with high melodrama on the sign of 'The Skirrid Inn'.)

Yet strangely, instead of being delighted with our new view, I felt mildly unsatisfied. Partly this was because Skirrid was only 1,594 feet,

in a mountain range already stretching the envelope of that categor-
isation. If we were to have a mountain view, I'd have greatly preferred
it to be onto the classic 'table top' escarpment of the higher, prettier and
altogether more 'mountainous' Sugar Loaf to the west. Still, whether I
liked it or not, Skirrid was now the garden's main feature. I had yet to
grasp that the trick of garden-making, as of life, is not to moan about
what you haven't got, but to make the most of what you have. It was
only later, when a mountain-minded neighbour (with whom, we'd
discover, the Black Mountains were teeming) pointed out Skirrid's
intrinsic qualities, that I learnt to look at it differently. Following some
remark I'd made about the poxiness of the Black Mountains, she
reminded me that the Brecon Beacon chain was, in fact, the muddy
remains of the vast Caledonian Mountain range, alongside which the
Himalayas were lowly parvenus. She finished by saying that anyone
with eyes to see would also spot the blindingly obvious mirror image
resemblance between the 'Holy Mountain' of Skirrid and the sacred
peak of Nanda Devi in the Kumaon Himalayas, the highest peak in
India and patron Goddess of Kumaon and Garhwal. Finally, she pressed
onto me a book entitled *The Nanda Devi Affair*.

The book chronicled its author Bill Aitken's decade-long obses-
sion with that peak. Reading it, I began to realise how callow and
unsophisticated my mountain appreciation was. Aitken brooked no

truck about size being any indication of a mountain's quality.* Skirrid, now I came to examine it properly, had many of the qualities of the greatest peaks in the world. The mere fact that it was the one peak that most visitors managed to confidently identify by the end of a weekend, well, what better indicator of character was there than that? It had any amount of myth and legend attached to it. Most important of all, however, was its relationship with the clouds. During temperature inversions, it floated, towering, forbidding and seemingly as vast as the Matterhorn, over a white sea of low-lying mist. Sometimes it trailed a pale plume on its downwind side like the jet stream 'flag' off Everest. Other days, when the hills seemed to steam like an Amazonian rain forest, rags of cloud appeared to catch on the conifer plantations on its lower slopes, like sheep's wool on gorse. At other times again the cloud spilt off the summit, like lava from an erupting volcano, or just leant on it, as if the sky were taking a break.**

To appreciate Skirrid properly, I began to see, was a matter of adjusting my scale and state of mind. Now, as I began to look, I noticed the layered rocky ledges to the north, like terraces, revealed by a hard

---

* 'Mere verticality is no measure of a mountain's beauty any more than a tall woman should be accounted desirable before a shorter but more attractive companion. This might be a criterion for distinguishing the true mountain lover from the mechanical; the one drawn by the lure of aesthetic satisfaction, the other driven by the mass demand for statistics with their sheep-like acclaim for physical priority.' Bill Aitken, *The Nanda Devi Affair*, 1994.

** Wordsworth noted this effect in response to the general British chippiness about the height of our mountains that followed the Romantic 'discovery' of the Alps in the nineteenth century. In his *Guide to the Lakes* (1810), he comments: 'A short residence among the British Mountains will furnish abundant proof that after a certain point of elevation, viz. that which allows of compact and fleecy clouds settling upon, or sweeping over, the summits, the sense of sublimity depends more upon form and relation of objects to each other than upon their actual magnitude; and that an elevation of 3,000 feet is sufficient to call forth in a most impressive degree the creative, and magnifying, and softening powers of the atmosphere.'

frost or snow, and how the extent of the landslip of two millennia ago was marked as clearly by the tree line as if it had happened yesterday. There was no question about it: it was, by any standards, a fine mountain. And 'mountains', as Ruskin told us, 'are the beginning and end of natural scenery'.

After that things began to click. One afternoon in mid-August, we were sitting around the bathtub where the spring came into the yard when inspiration struck. The spring had subsided to its high summer trickle, a barely audible dribble from the iron pipe into the surface of the filled tub. Watching the overflow seep away down the stony track to the gate into the Hang Glider field, it suddenly seemed obvious: that's what the place was about. Water. The spring was the reason the small-holding was here, in this particular fold of this particular hill. That was why the place was called Tair-Ffynnon, which, I now belatedly recalled, meant 'Four Springs'. No water, no Tair-Ffynnon. So we should do more with the water: maybe divert it so it ran across the yard. Having grasped this fundamental, it was suddenly easier to see what else the place was about. And those features, too, turned out to be under our noses. Principal among them, snaking away down across the common for almost a mile, was a dry-stone field wall, five foot eight inches high, with big uneven coping stones and a tombstone stile a third of the way along. Such a thing would probably cost hundreds of thousands to build, and we had it already: ours, so to speak, for the taking. All we had to do was rebuild our own collapsed or missing wire fences as dry-stone walls in the same way and Tair-Ffynnon would be knitted back into the landscape of the hill. That handsome wall would become part of our garden. From here it was but a single step to see that the dominant aesthetic of the place was—or should be—stone. Stone walls, stone slates, stone troughs, stone flags. Stone was what the hill was made of. However poor Tair-Ffynnon's inhabitants had been over the years, stone was the one thing of which they had a limitless supply.

Plant life, too, suddenly seemed simple. If coppiced (sawn off at ground level so that they sprouted new growth), and with the gaps replanted, the hedges in the more sheltered areas could be coaxed back into a useful barrier, and in due course cut and laid. There was scope too for all the pleasing idioms that went with walls and hedges: gates and gateways, stiles and water troughs. There'd be a vegetable garden, of course, and maybe a small orchard. Just one more feature seemed worth considering; one that we'd noticed every farm and smallholding in the Black Mountains shared. When a farm implement had run its course, it seemed, farmers didn't trade it in, or sell it for scrap. They abandoned it in the corner of a field.* There was charm to some of these bits of junk, a sort of wistful melancholy, especially with bracken or foxgloves growing through them. Admittedly, the scene wasn't always enhanced by a collapsed caravan, or stack of rotting pallets, but by an old hay rake or a tractor, it was. Perhaps the odd carefully chosen example, with a bit of (but not too much) art direction ...?

---

* I later learnt there was method in this policy. With lots of hard, pointy bits these junked implements made ideal rubbing posts for sheep, thereby saving the dry-stone walls which would otherwise have been used and pulled down in the process. 'That's not to say,' the farmer who told me this was anxious to clarify, 'they're not usually there just because the farmer couldn't think where else to put them.'

There was just one thing missing. Even with the spring tinkling merrily across the yard, even with the most exquisitely rebuilt dry-stone walls, even with the mountain views properly appreciated according to my developing mountain sensibilities, one critical element was still absent: flowers. Here I already had a plan. Wild flower meadows were just becoming fashionable and I'd been reading up about them. It turned out that all you needed to do to get a plethora of ludicrously poetic-sounding flowers* was to make hay. And as most of the rusty machines lying around Tair-Ffynnon—mowers, rakes, tedders, balers, flat-bed trailers— were all about hay-making, what could be more obviously right as the floral element of the garden?

Throughout this process I'd been periodically pestering Uncle William with calls and emails. Where would be the best place for the vegetable garden? ('I should think an allotment down in the valley.') What did he think about my art-directed junkyard idea? ('Someone near here, quite famous, used to do that. He made a garden with bits of metal and rusty sculptures like you're talking about. Unfortunately no-one came to look at it, so he was asked to take them away.') What about a wild flower meadow garden, like the celebrated one in his village?

---

* Such as sneezewort, ladies bedstraw, common knapweed, yellow rattle, fragrant agrimony, pignut, meadowsweet, mouse-ear hawkweed, autumn hawkbit, creeping tormentil, fleabane, pepper saxifrage, stitchwort, goat's beard, common vetch, great burdock, gipsywort, purple loosestrife, garlic mustard, hedge woundwort, bird's foot trefoil, slender speedwell, kidney vetch, eyebright, dropwort, fairy flax, rockrose, milkwort, vervain, sweet vernal, sheep's fescue, Yorkshire fog … well, you get the idea.

What did he think of our chances of getting into the Yellow Book with something like that? ('It's amazing what you can get away with.')

Sod it. We had structure. We had features. We had sculpture. We had flowers. Or, at least, we *would* have these things. What more did we need? It was appropriate. It was confident. It had taken us a while to get there, but, finally, we knew where we were going.

My father called. 'I've been thinking about your garden,' he said. 'Do you want to know what I'd do if—heaven forbid—I lived where you do?'

'Yes, very much.'

'Nothing at all. It's such a lovely setting; it would be quite wrong to have a garden there.'

'What's prompted you to say this now? I've reached the same conclusion after months of research and thought.'

'It occurred to me when I was shaving. But really, it's quite obvious.'

'What, not to have a garden?'

'Yes. A Not Garden.' My father had evidently misheard me. 'A Not Garden. Yes, very good.'

So, a Not Garden it would be.

7

The perfect country room

A wood-panelled railway carriage is hard to beat as a perfect
country bedroom: there you can dream that you are rattling
through the night on some great adventure, and the dimin-
utive box that is your bedroom has something in common
with the traditional cupboard bed.

EMMA-LOUISE O'REILLY, *The Perfect Country Room*, 1996

'I *want* to give you permission.' The Head of Development Control at
the National Park was choosing his words carefully. 'Does it move?'
Over the phone, with only his voice to go on, I couldn't be certain if it
would be better for it to move or not. We weren't necessarily trying (as
my mother would have put it) to 'pull a fast one'; the planning situation
was hazy when it came to old railway carriages. It seemed wisest to
hedge.

'It's on wheels. So it *could* move, I suppose.'

'Hmmm … you know, I'm not sure you even need permission.' It wasn't quite the unequivocal 'yes' I'd been aiming for. But then it definitely wasn't a 'no'. The implication seemed to be: if we could get the carriage up to Tair-Ffynnon without drawing attention to ourselves then we could have it.

———◦—◦◦—◦———

In the flush of euphoria after getting the place, I'd bought us a modest celebratory present in the form of a book entitled *The Perfect Country Room*. This delightful volume featured a succession of enchanted rural dwellings, from Swiss mountain farms to New England clapboard houses opening onto sun-dappled orchards. For months, *The Perfect Country Room* was our most coveted possession, hunted out for coffee breaks and trips to the loo. Two of the most-thumbed pages featured old wooden railway carriages: one adapted into an airy bedroom, another as an office. Early on we'd agreed that we had somehow to contrive a sturdy, weatherproof room where I could work, that could maybe double as a spare bedroom, ideally away from the house. We'd noticed that many of the local farms had old wooden railway wagons in their yards, usually in use as stock shelters or storehouses. So many places had them we assumed a job lot had been sold off cheap by British Rail in the wake of the Beeching cuts in the 1960s. The more we thought about it, the more we agreed that an old railway carriage seemed dreamily in keeping with the recycling spirit that pervaded the place.

But where to get one? Old wooden railway carriages weren't available at the local builders' merchants or garden centre, or even at the train station. I assiduously called heritage railways (all 170 of them), but the answer was always the same: some version of, ''Fraid you're ten years too late, mate.' No-one had a carriage for sale. No-one knew of anyone with one for sale. I'd almost given up hope when someone at the Heritage Railway Association offered to place an ad for me in their quarterly newsletter, *Sidelines*, the parish magazine of the railway preservation fraternity. I dictated my plea, put the phone down and, when I heard nothing, moved on to the equally time-consuming task of tracking down shepherd's huts and gypsy caravans.

Eight months later, the phone rang. 'Bruce MacDougall here, Keighley and Worth Valley Railway. Are yer still looking fer a railway carriage?' For a moment I couldn't think what he was talking about. The sorry fact was I'd more or less given up looking for anything. All my research into gypsy caravans and shepherd's huts had taught me was how exactly right a railway carriage would have been. Gypsy caravans were gaudy, gimmicky and overpriced. Shepherd's huts, suddenly chic, were either antique and overpriced, or new and overpriced. As for railway carriages, they simply weren't available. 'We 'ave an old brake van due to be scrapped next moonth. Do yer think yer may be interested?' *Interested?* We'd stooped to considering shipping containers. A brake van, Bruce explained, was like an old guard's van. It went at the back of a steam train, but this one was surplus to requirements. A thought occurred. The railway wagons we'd seen around the Black Mountains sat flat on the ground. 'It's just the top bit you're talking about, isn't it, Bruce? She's not still on her wheels?'

'She's complete, yes.'

A railway carriage still on her wheels. That was quite something.

'Where are you again, Bruce?'

'Keighley.'

'Keighley. Ah yes, Keighley …' Where the heck was Keighley?

'Yer know, Brontë country: Charlotte, Emily, *Wuthering Heights* and all that.' I arranged to meet him the following week. Then I went to look up where Keighley was.

It was in West Yorkshire. I collected Bruce at Haworth station in the picturesque Worth valley. He directed me along a winding, stone-walled road that followed the river to Oakworth station (where, Bruce told me, *The Railway Children* had been filmed). He unlocked the gates and led me onto the platform. And there, wedged between a smartly restored guard's van and a goods wagon … there she was.

'She looks a bit sad, but there's a lot sound about her.' I certainly couldn't argue with the first statement. About twenty feet long, she was little more than a rotted wooden box resting on a rusty iron chassis. What paint remained was faded to a murky pink-brown. Chipboard was nailed over the worst timbers, which meant most of them. The roof sagged, and patches of roofing felt were clumsily tacked over the ends. 'Brake still works. She's perfectly restorable.' Mighty foot-long chain links hung from her couplings and she had the oily smell of heavy industry. 'Doors are on oother side,' said Bruce, dropping down onto the track and ducking under the couplings. I followed. The carriage's underside was, if anything, in worse condition: a mass of rusty levers and flaking ironwork. It seemed best not to look too closely. 'Been messed about a good bit, of course. She had open verandas either end originally, but at soom point British Rail boarded them up. Far more room, presumably. Be easy enough to put them back, though.' Verandas. Vez would like those. 'Now then,' he searched about on a vast ring of keys, then opened the padlocked door. 'See? Yer can still see the joints perfectly clearly. Joost be a matter of putting the doors back.'

'How old is she, Bruce?'

'Now yer askin'. We think 1920s. About 1921 or 2 ah'd guess, but we'll have a look later.'

Inside, hinged bench seats ran down each wall. The space was stacked with bollards and plastic crates. The smell wasn't oil, I realised. It was coal. Near the middle, on a heavy pedestal, was an iron wheel, like a giant stopcock. 'That's the brake wheel,' said Bruce. 'The guard would apply the brakes when he heard the driver whistle.' From inside it was clear that patches of the roof timbers were completely rotted away. A pool of glistening oily water had collected on the coal-dusted floorboards beneath a neat six-inch hole in the roof. 'That's for the stove pipe,' said Bruce. 'The stove's probably around here soomwhere. Otherwise we can probably find yer one. Well, there she is.'

I imagined her up at Tair-Ffynnon, the verandas opened up, the doors restored to their proper place, books lining her walls, a fire crackling in the stove, smoke puffing from a crooked stove pipe. It was irresistible. But would we ever get her up the hill, with all its sharp and narrow kinks? I banished such negative thinking. Of course it was possible. Anything was possible. This was a once-in-a-lifetime opportunity. 'How much d'you want for her, Bruce?'

'She's yours, if yer want her.'

'She's wonderful. If you mean it, I'd love to have her.'

'Well, that's good,' said Bruce. 'We'd far rather she found a home than went fer scrap.'

'How do I move her?' A happy thought occurred: 'By rail?'

'Ah'm afraid, Tony, the railways don't exist joost fer yer convenience. But plenty of hauliers can take her by road.'

A couple of days later, Bruce rang me. 'Turns out we made a mistake about 'er weight. Yer know ah said two or three tons? Well, we brought her down to the Ingrow yard, weighed her, an' turns out she's not three tons, she's twenty.'

Two tons, twenty tons, the figures meant nothing to me. Yes, it sounded heavy. But so what? A conversation with the first of Bruce's recommended carriers, Don, at Power Run, confirmed my confidence.

I outlined, and if anything overemphasised, the difficulties of reaching Tair-Ffynnon: the narrowness of the lane, the sharpness of the bends, the steepness of the gradient, the overhanging trees. 'Put it this way,' said Don. 'We ain't been beat yet.' To be sure, he said, he'd better inspect the approaches.

At seven o'clock next morning, I duly awoke to find a white car parked outside the house. 'Don?' He wound down his window. 'What time did you get up?'

''Bout four.'

'Jesus.'

'Like to make an early start.'

'So, can you do it?'

'No way,' he said. 'We wouldn't even get under the low bridge. Forget the first bend.'

'Really, no way?'

'Aye, really. An ah'll tell yer summat else. If we can't do it, yer won't find anyone else who can.'

He was right. I spoke to several other carriers and they all said the same. If Power Run couldn't do it, they wouldn't be able to either as they all used much the same-sized lorries. The problem wasn't getting the brake van from Yorkshire to Wales; it was what to do once it got here. The hitch, it seemed, was that twenty tons was really very heavy. It was heavier than a big bulldozer. Heavier than three double-decker buses. It would require a low loader of considerable size and scale, no problem if you were shifting, say, a turbine between an engineering works and a power station; but up narrow sunken lanes, hairpin bends, steep gradients and a rough track, unthinkable.

I refused to abandon hope. I measured the bridge heights and gate widths, and then visited the local agricultural contractors, Mervyn and Martin. A father and son team, I already knew them by their machines. If a field contained a tractor that was big, new and working fast, chances were it was one of theirs. Their yard outside the village, empty by day, at night became an Aladdin's cave of macho yellow Caterpillar crawlers, diggers, JCBs, giant green John Deere tractors and oversize ploughs and harrows. However their heaviest trailer, for carrying big earthmovers, would only carry sixteen tons. 'We could make a carriage up there for you,' suggested Martin. It struck me for the first time how odd my mission must sound from someone else's perspective. Besides, was the difference really so great?

'Trouble is, I want this one,' I said.

'Fair play to you.'

After that, unsure where to turn, I'd asked anyone and everyone who might conceivably be able to help. I stopped farmers pulling heavy-looking loads on short trailers. I called specialist hauliers I spotted on the motorway. I found myself in an alien world, discussing 'axle weights' and 'gross payloads', comparing the rival merits of 'six-wheelers' and 'eight-wheelers'. Each time it was the same story. The trailer or truck was only licensed to carry up to sixteen tons. If it was a question of going just a ton or two over, they'd risk it. But twenty tons, it was just too heavy. I even called the Army, on the off chance I could persuade them to use a helicopter as a training exercise. But a Chinook, their biggest helicopter, could only lift ten tons. I wasted so many months on a cowboy near Hereford, who promised the earth, but then failed to show up on the day Bruce had marshalled his men, that I suspect Bruce regretted he'd ever dialled my number.

The problem was compounded by the unresolved planning situation. I had worded a careful email to the Head of Development Control espousing the aesthetic merits and appropriateness of old railway carriages, attaching a photograph of the brake van. In response, he'd made encouraging noises and I'd hoped this call would swing it. 'As I say, I *want* to say yes to this,' he said. Perhaps I thanked him a little too effusively. His tone became sterner. 'Obviously, if there are complaints, we'll have to investigate.'

Everyone asked the same question. Why exactly was this old carriage so important? I gave a different answer each time. I said I just liked it, its friendly barrel-vaulted roof and cute doors, its cosy stove and romantic verandas. Or I said I simply wanted a den, because all men want dens. Or maybe that it was a reaction to growing up in a Modernist house. Invariably they pursed their lips, nodded politely, and wandered away, looking like Obelix when he taps his temple and says: 'These Romans are crazy.' The truth was, I hadn't the faintest idea. I just wanted it. Maybe it was sheer pig-headedness. But whatever it was, one thing was certain. That bloody brake van was coming up the mountain.

Finally, Bruce called time. Unless the brake van was removed from his yard within days, it would be scrapped. The trouble was, even if I got it to Wales using one of Bruce's recommended hauliers, even if I could find somewhere to keep it until I figured out how to get it up the hill, this still raised the problem of how, if the thing was so damn heavy, we'd ever get it off the lorry at this end. Which, I suppose, is what made me think of calling a crane company. Probably they didn't do little jobs like this. Still, I'd made so many pointless calls by now, one more could do no harm. There was a crane company in Hereford called Jay and Davies. I recited flatly: 'I need to get a twenty-ton railway wagon up a mountain. There are narrow, windy lanes with high hedges and overhanging trees. It's incredibly steep. Endless people have told me they can do it, only to later admit they can't.'

'I can do it.'

'There's a low bridge, less than fourteen feet. I can't find a trailer to carry the weight,' I said.

'I can.'

'Be difficult, I should think, to get a crane up here at all.'

'I can do it. Don't worry, I can do it.'

I'd heard such a lot of boasts and broken promises that I couldn't share his optimism, but I agreed, with low expectations, for him to call round that afternoon.

The figure that unfolded itself from the cab of the new, black pick-up labelled 'Jay and Davies Cranes' was not unlike a crane himself. There seemed to be more and more of him, until about seven feet had assembled itself in front of me. He had intense, deep-set eyes, wore a black leather jacket, and otherwise looked (and, as it turned out, sounded) like Will Self. He gave me a winning grin. 'Me and my big mouth,' he said, extending a huge hand. 'Russell Davies.'

The problem, he explained, was that to unload twenty tons required a sixty-ton crane. '*Sixty* tons ...' (I was more familiar with weights now) '... up *here?*'

Getting a brake van up the hill, he said, would need specialist industrial equipment, a trolley small enough to fit up the lanes. It was a highly unusual requirement.

'I see. So you can't do it.' I wasn't surprised. What was one more wasted meeting? At least I'd tried everything. But it was a shame. There'd been something about Russell that was different to the others. His promises had sounded less like empty boasts and more like determined declarations of intent.

'No, you don't understand. Of course I can do it.'

I felt as if a great weight—a twenty-ton weight—had lifted from my shoulders.

———◦•◦———

'Well Antney, where d'you want me to dig?' Mervyn and Martin had just arrived at Tair-Ffynnon with a big new JCB and a tractor and trailer that dwarfed the house. The brake van, having got to Wales had for the past year sat in Russell's yard, until he, like Bruce before him, had declared that unless the thing was moved forthwith, it was going for scrap. Which was why we were urgently digging foundations in preparation for its arrival. It was my first experience of having professionally operated earthmoving equipment at my beck and call, and the responsibility felt bracing but onerous. Feeling important, I indicated the general area where the van would sit on the east side of the yard and went in to make coffee for everyone.

By the time I emerged, I was alarmed to see that a swimming pool-sized hole had already appeared. As Martin dug, Mervyn hauled the spoil away to build up the site of the vegetable patch (which after infinite deliberation we'd decided to keep exactly where it was before). They worked with a steady, confident precision. Watching the scoops of Martin's bucket, I'd be disconcerted to find Mervyn had quietly reversed his empty trailer to a few inches behind me without my even noticing. 'What d'you think then, Antney? We winning?'

Over the next couple of days, as Martin and Mervyn prepared a base of drained gravel for the carriage to sit on, then scooped decades of accumulated muck out of the tin barns (whose floors we were about to concrete), we got to know them a little. They combined astonishing efficiency with a mischievous turn of phrase (swift retorts prompting a 'fair play to you') and the appealing gift of knowing when to say the right thing. Witnessing my hopeless over-ordering of gravel, Mervyn merely observed: 'Useful having a bit of spare gravel up here, Antney. Useful thing to have. Other folks might not think about it, when they order a bit of gravel, but it don't exactly jump up here, does it?'

When they'd finished, despite all the heavy machinery, everything was left as if it had been swept with a dustpan and brush. Russell had requested a spare tractor to drive in front of the one pulling the carriage up the lane, in case extra horsepower were needed, so we'd booked Mervyn's big green John Deere. Now, rather than leaving in the blue tractor he'd been using all day, he parked it up by the barn before climbing into the JCB with Martin. 'We'll leave that one there, Antney, just in case,' said Mervyn. 'You never know. And nothing'll get past once that thing's in the lane. Thank you,' he said to Vez as she handed him a final cup of coffee. 'You're a super girl, I congratulate you.' She flushed pink to her dimples. It was with a tinge of disappointment that we saw their work done.

In fact, I saw Martin sooner than expected. In my bid to find some railway track—the carriage had to be 'moveable', after all—I'd managed to locate (after another eternal goose chase) an enthusiast near Hereford called Mike. Initially Mike was friendly, informative and helpful, but his repeated additions to the agreed price and attempts to alter what we'd arranged quickly started to grate. After insisting he bring the track over himself, he'd started prevaricating about the delivery date until the afternoon before the carriage was due. A steady light rain had fallen during the day and, as it was getting dark, I received a call announcing he was in trouble on the hill. Somehow, towing a trailer bearing the thirty-foot section of track up the lane, he'd come off the tarmac. In his subsequent to-ing and fro-ing in his lorry, he'd spread greasy mud everywhere until he was hopelessly stuck.

Martin came to the rescue, towing him up to Tair-Ffynnon, but received no thanks for his pains. When Mike's lorry then ran out of diesel at the crucial moment and a jerry can of my own diesel proved insufficient to restart it, the only option was to siphon further fuel out of Martin's tractor, a task promising the pleasure of a mouthful of diesel for someone. As Mike remained silent, I volunteered—again, no thanks or apology—but still his accursed machine wouldn't start. ('Even I'm beat,' Mike declared.) Another hour passed before, finally, he left, taking with him, we discovered next morning, most of the dry-stone wall by the mountain gate.

Still, we were, belatedly, ready for the Big Day.

———◆———

It was now the third week of November. Several days of gentle rain had erased the iron-hard dust bowl left by one of the driest autumns on record. The day Russell had selected was, at least, a Wednesday, far enough from the weekend for the hill to be deserted. For once, I hoped fervently for hill fog. In cloud, there was no reason why the whole operation shouldn't pass unnoticed. Wednesday dawned, however, clear and cold, and by 8.30 we were bathed in bright sunshine.

The schedule of events ran as follows:

8.30 a.m.:	Crane arrives at bottom of hill.
Mid-morning:	Crane reaches Tair-Ffynnon, hoists track into place, gets into position for lifting brake van. Brake van arrives at bottom of hill on special rig arranged by Russell. Mervyn drives ahead in big tractor just in case.
Early to mid-afternoon:	Brake van arrives at Tair-Ffynnon. Crane hoists it onto track.
Teatime:	Everybody goes home.

I felt a sense of pleasant excitement. Jonny had arrived, bringing my nephew Thomas, who'd taken the day off school. We were all looking forward to seeing a sixty-ton crane in action (and how it would get up the lane). Not to mention the sense of progress, the first visible, tangible step, that today marked in Tair-Ffynnon's transition from dereliction to hilltop Nirvana. It was good to be a mere spectator, having handed my worries over—and Russell certainly looked worried. Businesslike red overalls had replaced his leather jacket, a continuous frown hovered across his brow and he fidgeted about, preoccupied, constantly looking at his watch. 'I think it's going to be OK,' he said. 'We tried her in the yard this morning and the tractor pulled her sweet as a nut. It was as if she wasn't there.' I felt just the tiniest tinge of disappointment.

The first part of the operation, the hoisting into place of the track, went almost perfectly according to plan. The crane arrived at the bottom of the hill shortly before nine, like a huge blue and yellow toy with six wheels, flashing lights, two drivers and, confusingly, two steering wheels. It fitted the lane exactly, centimetring its way up the hill, sometimes so slowly it appeared not to be moving at all. But by mid-morning, apart from a tense moment when the road beneath started to give way, and some skidding where Mike had greased the road for us, it made it safely to Tair-Ffynnon.

The driver, visibly relieved, set about extending rams and raising the booms, accompanied by a lot of high-tech beeping noises, while I loitered, pestering him with questions. In no time, the stretch of track had been lifted into position.

At noon, news arrived that the brake van had reached the bottom of the hill, so we scuttled into our various cars and headed down to join it. On the way we met Les the Post. 'You having a delivery today? If you are, I don't think he'll make it. I nearly got stuck with four-wheel drive, there's so much mud on the road.' Cursing Mike, we pressed on down. The first thing we encountered was a vast green tractor with yellow wheels, a steroid-enhanced version of Mervyn's, which was also waiting. It required eight steps to climb up to the cab and appeared to have come directly from the showroom: the tyres still had a waxy sheen; the paintwork and glass gleamed glossily in the sunshine. 'Biggest tractor in the county,' said Russell. 'Three hundred horse power. Borrowed it from Alexander and Duncan, the John Deere dealership in Hereford. Calling in a favour.' Behind the tractor, meticulously packed and strapped onto a short yellow low loader with eight wheels running across its full width, a 'dolly' Russell called it, was the dear old brake van.

It was a year since I'd seen her, and I'd forgotten how tatty she was, an impression emphasised by all the fancy machinery around her. She looked a wreck, with her rusty chassis, rotted timbers and sagging roof. Russell had brought a second crane, too, a smaller one, in case help were needed getting round sharp bends.

And so the cavalcade started up the hill. First us, in the Land Rover, then Mervyn, huge chains swinging off the back of his tractor in case they were needed. Then, with a roar, Steve, pulling the brake van, followed by the smaller crane and then Russell in his pick-up. For the first quarter-mile straight, Russell's optimism seemed justified. The brake van was hauled at a brisk six miles per hour up the deeply sunken lane. At the first right-angled bend, the big tractor neatly rounded the corner ... and the dolly trailer wedged like a cork in a bottle. The four shiny yellow tractor wheels span uselessly, digging little crescent-shaped impressions into the tarmac. For forty-five minutes it looked as if this was as far as we were going to get. Every move seemed only to jam the trailer tighter. But I had underestimated Russell's determination in his role as Master of Ceremonies. After interminable pushing and shoving, the big tractor got just far enough round the corner for Mervyn's tractor to be coupled up. Then, working together, they yanked the dolly through. The first hurdle was negotiated.

Free once more, a second burst of progress carried the caravan half a mile to the next obstacle, another sharp corner, where the trailer stuck fast again. More minutely tedious manoeuvrings, a garden wall demolished, the verges churned to pulp, another tug from Mervyn, and we were onto the next straight. And so it went on, a curious afternoon of snakes and ladders.

We soon faced the first major obstacle: a switchback bend with a gradient of one in four, the steepest on the journey. From here it was straight almost all the way to the mountain gate. Both the tractors were coupled together now, their linking chains taut as steel bars. They rounded the corner and pulled onto the straight; the trailer followed, but as the gradient hit its steepest pitch, the dead weight of the load asserted itself. The crane, with its wide wheelbase, had churned the verges. Now, as the tractors hit the mud, their wheels started to spin, spreading the greasy film across the road like a floor mop. Russell's countenance, which had been growing steadily more harassed, brightened visibly at Mervyn's news that he had parked a spare tractor up at Tair-Ffynnon. There was a delay while Mervyn went to collect it and we all wondered what we'd have done without his foresight.

By now the box-fresh tractor was beginning to look a little shop-soiled. The treads of the tyres were wearing badly from skidding on the tarmac. Several broken hawthorn branches were caught in the cab mirrors and any number of scratches had appeared. The immaculate green paintwork was liberally flecked with mud. 'What've you done to my nice new tractor?' said Steve as I walked past.

'You should see *his* tractor,' said Jonny helpfully. Frankly, I was more concerned with the state of the disappearing road, which was, after all, a public highway.

With Mervyn back, installed in the lead tractor, Russell behind him in Mervyn's other tractor, and Steve in the big John Deere, synchronising the drivers' actions (so that everyone released their brakes and moved off simultaneously) became a problem. At the first attempt, everyone jerked forwards independently, pulling against each other. A chain snapped. A new chain was produced. The second time, the transition was smoother. With professional skill, Mervyn, then Russell, released their brakes and moved gently forwards, taking up the slack, until the moment when Steve could do the same. For an awful moment everyone, the whole cortège, lurched backwards. Then those twelve tractor wheels, their differentials locked, ground forwards. The lane shook to the sound of seven hundred straining horses. The dead weight was taken, held, then slowly, with an eerie creaking, the low loader began to move upwards round the bend. Its wheels turned so slowly I watched as they picked up pieces of grit and grass: five yards … ten yards … twenty yards … fifty yards. After a hundred and fifty yards, however, Mervyn in the lead tractor hit the spot where Mike had slid off the road the night before. As his wheels touched the mud, they began to spin.

With a third of the traction gone, the twenty-ton weight was too much. The wheels of the two John Deeres also lost grip. Slowly, ineluctably, despite its twelve forward-turning wheels, the entire cavalcade began to slide backwards down the lane. 'Get out the way!' yelled someone. 'Look out!' shouted another voice. Red brake lights flashed brightly in the darkening afternoon gloom. With the eerie groans of metal carrying more strain than it's supposed to, the low loader dragged the three tractors slowly backwards, and sank into the soft verge.

During the break that followed, a new thoughtfulness entered the proceedings. Caps were removed. Heads were scratched. An awful lot more machinery than had been scheduled (or budgeted for) was now assembled in the lane and it was, plainly, nowhere near enough. More importantly, even if more tractors were available, there was no way to get them to the front of the convoy because the lane was the only route up the hill. It was now around three and would soon be dark. At this point the crane driver called Russell from Tair-Ffynnon to say there was a problem. I joined Russell—who was beginning to look a little wild-eyed—in his pick-up and we sped through the mountain gate and up the track. Was this his worst ever job, I asked cheerfully. ('Not yet … but getting there.') The sight that confronted us on entering the yard was baffling. We'd left the crane drivers, hours earlier, contentedly man-oeuvring their machine. Their task was simply to get the crane into a stable position straddling a corner of the prepared site, ready to hoist the brake van off the low loader and swing it into position. Now, as we came through the gate, not only was the crane almost tipped onto its side, nowhere near its supposed position, but there was no longer a yard. The surface of stone and broken concrete had disappeared, replaced by a ploughed landscape of turned earth and three-foot deep ruts.

As I gaped at the devastation, Russell listened to the explanations of his distraught head crane driver. As he'd extended his stabilisers, he said, they'd simply broken through the patchy concrete. Trying to move the sixty-ton machine to more solid foundations, the surface had broken up around him, and with six wheels simultaneously churning and steering, it hadn't taken long for the machine to dig itself in ever deeper. He'd become so stuck by the time Mervyn arrived to fetch the third tractor that he, Mervyn, had had to pull him out. He was now grounded again. Nor was that all. The strain of all this on the crane's engine had begun to tell: the cylinder head gasket had blown, so he was now operating at greatly reduced power. 'Damn,' said Russell thoughtfully. 'I knew that pot was going.'

Mervyn was called to rescue the crane again, and by the time everyone reassembled in the lane, spirits were definitely dipping. It was now after four. The red winter sun was disappearing behind Sugar Loaf and the temperature was plunging. I was having to wriggle my fingers and toes to stop them going numb. A question mark hung over what to try next. We couldn't go back. And we hadn't even got to the hardest part yet: the rocky bottleneck along the track. Mervyn explained the problem. 'Well, see, Antney, it's not the shortage of power. If it were just a matter of power, the big John Deere could do it on its own. Problem is, there's no weight on the wheels. Tractors grip best with a good heavy load on 'em, see, to press the wheels down. A low loader doesn't work like that. It's got a dolly on the front, so all the load's on the dolly, not the tractor. An' tractors aren't so good at that. To make 'em grip they need the weight. 'Specially when it's slippery like this.'

Another attempt only resulted in another thirty feet lost. In the end, it was Mervyn who solved the problem. 'We'll call my boy Martin,' he said to Russell. 'He'll be back just now. He can bring the JCB. If he lifts the back of that bumper, gets some of the weight on his wheels, we'll be away.'

And, by golly, he was right. When Martin arrived, half an hour later (I tried not to think how much this would be costing), he duly hooked the JCB's front bucket under the buffers of the brake van. The JCB's big tyres flattened with the weight. Then he simply pushed the whole caboodle up the road. The convoy steamed up that steep quarter mile in twenty seconds. As Sugar Loaf disappeared in a pink glow, around five, there were muffled cheers as the low loader passed through the hill gate and onto the hill. We'd reached the difficult bit.

After the gate, the track climbed steeply and curved left to enter a narrow gully about a hundred yards long, kinking as it did so. There was no give here, as the high bank to the right was of solid rock, atop which sat an ancient fort. The curve and the darkness compounded the difficulties: for, despite dazzling lights on all the tractors, the front two drivers now couldn't see the two behind them. Another driver was found for the second tractor and Russell clambered up onto the ancient mound to co-ordinate the next series of heaves, his lanky form silhouetted against the glare below, a ghostly conductor with his diesel-powered orchestra.

Two or three bursts brought the procession to the kink, where, as expected, the low loader wedged fast. I wandered down to talk to Martin. The yellow metal of the JCB was already coated with a hard rime of frost. I apologised for hijacking his second evening in a row. 'Don't worry Antney. You know ... we quite enjoy this sort of thing.

But I'll tell you something. You won't get that thing through there.' He nodded towards the kink ahead. 'No way.'

Moments later, his prophecy appeared to be proved correct. The first properly co-ordinated shove, on the count of three, Martin pushing just as the three tractors pulled, moved the low loader about an inch. The second and third attempts moved it half that. The brake van, it seemed, had found its final resting place. Undaunted, Russell urged them on, 'one ... two ... three ...'. Four great engines drowned out the word 'Go!' as he hurled his arm groundwards as if starting a race. Again and again he did it. With almost a thousand-horse power so brutally applied, something had to give, and on about the fifteenth attempt, it did. There was a shriek of metal, a shower of sparks, and with a grinding screech, the low loader, brake van and all, bounced upwards and over the rock. We were through to the final straight.

With that the mood changed. A spirit of near euphoria entered the proceedings. A problem had been solved by a team effort, in which everyone had played their part. The Sisyphean task had become a fine shared adventure. There was a pause while thermos flasks were produced and cups of tea were poured. All that now remained was to pull the brake van up the rocky track. The two front tractors were uncoupled; from here Steve should be able to manage on his own. Perhaps the atmosphere went to his head, perhaps he just wanted to get home, but for whatever reason Steve then did something mad. He took it upon himself to leave the track and take a short cut across the common. We watched in disbelief as the low loader sank axle-deep into the soft ground, then heeled over on one side and nearly tipped over. He tried to reverse. The low loader jack-knifed.

By now I'd ceased to care what the problems were or how they were being solved. I was tired, starving, frozen and bored. How Russell, Mervyn, Martin and the others were able to concentrate, let alone come up with new strategies was beyond me. But in another hour they had somehow unhitched the low loader, pulled it round, re-attached it, and we were back on the track. One hurdle remained: the last bend in the track, where it switched from following the slope of the hill to running along the contour, squeezing between a bank on one side and a dry-stone wall on the other. I was lost in thought, dreaming of toasted crumpets and melted butter, hands deep in my pockets, when Russell appeared at my shoulder. A decision was required. The low loader couldn't get round the sharp corner. Did I wish them to dig up the hill with the JCB or knock down our neighbours' dry-stone wall? 'Neither,' I said. 'Both options are out of the question.' The wall was a work of art (and I was acutely aware how much they cost to rebuild). But digging up the hill was infinitely worse: this was common land, adjacent to a Site of Special Scientific Interest, sacred turf belonging to the National Park, the very body whose feathers it was so crucial not to ruffle.

I was spared too much agony, as it happened. Moments later Russell reappeared at my elbow to announce they'd knocked down the wall but there still wasn't enough room, so they were digging up the hill. The JCB roared in the darkness as Martin started scooping great bites out of the ancient, springy turf. The freezing air filled with the smell of freshly dug earth, while I wondered how I was going to explain this the next day. After that, it was merely a matter of digging up a concrete run-off pipe by Tair-Ffynnon's gate, tearing down two sections of fence that enclosed the yard, and we were there. The crane was in position, stabilised on banks of railway sleepers. Nylon slings were looped under the brake van, and suddenly it was dangling in the air as, with two fingers, Russell guided it over the track and, to a ripple of applause, it was lowered gently down. The job was done. It was one in the morning: seventeen hours after leaving Hereford, Brake Van 112 had completed her final journey.

If my intention had been to bring the carriage up the hill, well, if not incognito, then at least without drawing unnecessary attention to the fact, then the view from our bedroom window the following morning was a sort of grim practical joke. Tair-Ffynnon sat in a blasted landscape. Our grassy, stony yard no longer existed; all traces of vegetation were gone. From the churned earth of this no-man's land, where wheel ruts were three feet deep, a brown trail of devastation led away down the hill. The general effect, once we'd emerged from a hasty initial survey, was of a Paul Nash war painting of the Western Front, as if a small railway station on a hill had been used for target practice by an inexpert artillery battery, leaving just a solitary item of rolling stock, an old brake van, intact but badly damaged.

An inspection of the track and lane told a tale no less scary. Everywhere were tell-tale signs of the battle that had been fought through the night: mounds of broken concrete, tangled remains of wire fences, deep tractor ruts, heaps of earth and broken branches from the overhanging trees. Two dry-stone walls had been damaged or demolished. No tarmac was visible for at least a quarter of a mile below the hill gate due to the mud on the lane, nor was the roadway itself distinguishable from the verges. By mid-morning, word had got around and sightseers were out with their dogs. It got worse. It transpired that it had taken until three in the morning for the crane to reach the bottom of the hill (the road so slippery from mud and frost that the driver had to winch himself down inch by inch). Pausing, no doubt for a well-earned breather at the bottom by the farm, leaving their engines running, they'd disturbed the farmer's stock. So now the farmer was pissed off. Most of our neighbours on the way up the lane had had something, a wall, a hedge, a tree or verge, damaged. Word, via my brother, had even reached my father. 'I hear no bird sings,' he said.

I called Clive, our area warden for the National Park, sensing it was better to break the happy news to him before someone else did. 'I'll get it all cleaned up,' I promised his answerphone weakly. 'I'll repair the common where it's been dug up, rebuild the walls, clean the road, roll the verges. Just give me a couple of days.' By the time he arrived, fortunately, I'd hired a roller and Martin was already at work with his

JCB, doing what plastic surgery he could to the hill before rebuilding our yard so we could get in and out. 'Phone's been red-hot at the park office,' Clive said, inspecting the damage. We held our breath, wondering what he'd say. I knew that damage up on the hill was far worse than in the valley. Ruts and wheel tracks hung around like footprints on the moon. But all he said was—and not for the first time we congratulated ourselves on having such an outstanding warden—'Well, it's just a bit of mud. Things grow back pretty quickly once the growing season's here. Pity you chose to do it at the beginning of winter.'

I did all the things I'd promised Clive's answerphone. I rolled the verges. We rebuilt the walls so they were better than before. Martin swept the road. We delivered bottles of sloe gin to neighbours up and down the hill. It was just unfortunate timing that we'd booked ready-mix lorries for the following day to deliver concrete for the barn floor, so most of these reparations were promptly undone.

In due course, a letter arrived from the National Park entitled 'Unauthorised Siting of Railway Carriage', ordering us to apply for planning permission within fourteen days. I called my friendly Head

107

of Development Control to reassure him there was no need for concern as it was only me, with the brake van he liked so much, to discover that he'd left a year earlier and there was no record of our 'agreements'. In the end we did get permission, and restored the brake van. We stripped it down, opened up the veranda on the south end, returned one of the doors to its rightful position, insulated the walls and ceiling and installed electricity. We put in shelves, a small fold-down writing table, a bed and an old top-loading cast iron stove which crackles and roars as I write. Vez hung Welsh blankets over the doors and windows. Then we painted it a deep maroon to match one of the colours it had been painted before. So, all in all, things didn't turn out too badly. I'm still often greeted with the words: 'Oh, you're the bloke with the railway carriage,' though it's not always clear this is a compliment.

Just for a few days at the time, however, we deemed it wiser not to answer the phone. It seemed everyone in the Black Mountains had some reason to be annoyed with us. Everyone, that is, except Mervyn and Martin, in whose estimation I appeared to have soared for instigating such an adventure.

8

The County Organiser

A beaky nose, an eagle eye, and a lot of grey hair, and the
general effect is pretty formidable.

               P. G. WODEHOUSE introducing Bertie Wooster's
               Aunt Agatha, *The Inimitable Jeeves*, 1923

The moment could be put off no longer. Another winter had somehow come and gone in a blur of mud, nappies and general non-
achievement, and it was April again. The time for theorising and
procrastination was over. It was time to grasp the nettle, to get things
moving, to—as my mother would have said—'get on with it'. It was
time to call the County Organiser.

I'd known the name of our County Organiser from the start, having
looked it up when I bought the Yellow Book. She was a Mrs Joanna
Kerr and lived in an old rectory in the Usk valley. Numerous times
since then, in case I'd missed some subliminal clue, I'd returned to the

relevant page to reread her name, address and contact details. I'd also asked around continually in case anyone had come across her and any useful information was to be gained that way. And it was. One of the builders knew of her. Intensive cross-examination had elicited the following observation: 'Tell you one thing, boss, you'll 'ave a job impressing her. I remember the place. Sun has to wipe its feet before it's allowed in.'

This image had lodged itself in my head, surfacing whenever I thought of her in the context of Tair-Ffynnon's ramshackle policies. It hardly boded well. Then, perusing the magazine *The Garden* (which came with my new Royal Horticultural Society membership), her name leapt from an article about people who chose to open their gardens to the public. And there she was.

She certainly looked steely enough. A potted biography informed me she was not only Gwent's County Organiser, but Regional Chairman, and on the Management Committee of the National Gardens Scheme. All serving to underline my initial presumption that here was a horticultural heavyweight.

As I prepared to pick up the phone to her, I felt curiously nervous. I knew I wasn't the first person to be struck by such feelings. A friend had told me the story of how a distinguished magazine editor, during the inspection of her garden by the County Organiser with a view to admission to the Scheme, had suffered the misfortune of a bee flying up her skirt. Rather than risking the distracting hiatus and concomitant indignities of hoisting her skirt up to pursue the miscreant insect, she simply pinched it silently between thumb and forefinger, sustaining a prolonged and agonising sting. The point being, it might only be gardening, but there was more at stake than perhaps I cared to admit.

I dialled her number. A cheerful voice answered. I explained my mission to create a garden, that we were high up in the hills with some nice views, but not, yet, much by way of planting. 'Oh, that may be alright. Have you got some walls and things like that?' Not a trace of the grande dame. Disarming friendliness, in fact.

'Well ... we *will* have.'

'Hmm, I'd better come and have a look. How about tomorrow?' Her tone switched to one of businesslike efficiency. Tomorrow. It seemed a bit precipitate, after such a long gestation.

'Er ... yes, why not?'

'Shall we say ten o'clock ...?' She didn't need to add 'sharp'.

'Watch the weather, it can change quickly in the hills,' warns the National Park's sign at the hill gate, and it stated no more than fact. On any given day the weather at Tair-Ffynnon might show an almost Icelandic range of conditions, from bright sunshine to glutinous fog. I was learning to distinguish slight differences, however, such as between the apparently similar rolling mist that affected just us, and the settled gloom which reached down to the valley floor. And yet for nearly a month now the weather had been uncharacteristically consistent. It had rained incessantly that April, and gradually, as always happened when one set of conditions predominated, we'd forgotten that any other weather existed. The spring now rushed down the hill, sloshing and gurgling out of the old bathtub in the yard, its default meandering tinkle forgotten. Dry weather was forgotten. Sunshine was forgotten. Frost was forgotten. Everything but rain was forgotten.*

Up early the morning after my phone call to plan a suitably compelling itinerary for Mrs Kerr, I opened the curtains to find that someone had apparently glued tracing paper over the windows during the night. Rubbing the glass, in case it was ice or condensation, made no difference. Fog had descended. On the only day of the last five years when it really was crucial to be able to see the view, we couldn't see a damn thing. Visibility was fifteen yards and drizzle filled the air. There were three hours to go. Should I cancel Mrs Kerr? With no improvement by nine I called to break the news.

'Hmm. It's perfectly alright here.' (Was it me, or was there a hint of accusation, the faintest insinuation that I was being dishonest?) 'Let me look outside.' A pause. I imagined French doors opening onto a terrace enclosed by a precisely clipped yew hedge, a well-coiffed head appearing through them (not a bad guess, as it transpired), the sky receiving curt appraisal, then the phone was picked up again. 'No, it's perfectly clear here.'

'We're high up,' I explained. 'Thirteen or fourteen hundred feet, so sometimes visibility is much worse. It often clears by mid-morning ...'

'I'm afraid it's now or never, unless you want to put it off for a fortnight. I'm in London for a meeting this afternoon. I have regional meetings all Thursday, and Friday I go away. Do you want me to come or not?'

---

* Later, when the builders were working, and the descent of dense cloud and lashing rain set them packing up, I was able to impress them by saying the sun would be shining again within half an hour and be proved right almost to the minute. When a similar-looking situation occurred the following day, and they were to be found sheltering in the barn ('We're not going as it'll be over in half an hour'), having seen the weather forecast that morning, I was able to send them home in the sure knowledge that conditions wouldn't improve all day, thereby cementing my reputation as a gifted weather diviner.

In some ways, why not? Let her see it at its worst. It might even, if the fog was swirling across with occasional glimpses of peaks, make the place more dramatic. I decided to risk it. 'Very well. I'll leave it an extra half an hour. I'll see you at 10.30.'

The fog began to clear around ten, and by 10.28, when a blue car appeared on the track, tentatively picking its way up towards us, even the drizzle paused respectfully. I'd been careful to warn Mrs Kerr about the state of the track when giving directions. After weeks of rain, it was in its worst ever state: a boulder-strewn river bed of criss-crossing channels, with loose stones the size of breezeblocks (many were breeze-blocks), kerb-sized steps, and places where the wheel tracks were deep enough to ground a car. However, a few minutes later, a pristinely clean, almost new Volkswagen Golf turned into the yard and parked. Somehow the newness of the car emphasised the near-dereliction of our surroundings. Mrs Kerr stepped nimbly out, tidily dressed in blue quilted jacket and trousers, with a pair of pearl studs in her ears. She exuded order and control. She gave the place a sweeping glance, taking in the mud (the yard had not even begun to recover from the brake van's arrival), the tangled and broken fences, the house with its rotting windows. However, if the scene offended her, she didn't let it show. She looked younger than her photograph suggested. We shook hands and I offered her a cup of tea or coffee.

'Why don't we look round first.' It wasn't a question.

From the boot of her car she hoisted a pair of spotless blue welling-tons. She carefully removed a court shoe, revealing an immaculately stockinged foot, which she slid into the first boot, then repeated this operation for the second. She placed the shoes together in the car, square to the angle of the boot space. For some reason, the action reminded me of someone drawing on rubber gloves before an unpleasant task. Certainly, with her boots on, she looked, if anything, cleaner than before. I said something about it being lucky the fog had lifted. She said yes it was.

At this point Maya, standing beside me, said: 'Daddy, is this the dragon? She doesn't look like a dragon.' I shot her my dirtiest possible look.

'Shush, poppet,' I said. Vez picked her up.

'Come on, chops, let's go and get you some toast,' said Vez, pulling her hastily towards the house. Maya was not so easily fobbed off. She started wriggling out of Vez's grasp. 'Why did Daddy say she was a dragon if ...'

'Enough!' said Vez. The front door shut firmly.

Why didn't we start the tour at the point where the hang-gliders launched, I suggested brightly, as that offered fine views? 'Whatever you say,' said Mrs Kerr. And off we went.

'How did *that* get here?' she nodded towards the brake van as we passed. I gave what I hoped was a lightly comic, self-deprecating account of the brake van's arrival, finishing—to remind her that I was in no way straying from the matter in hand—that it was to be my 'garden room'.

'Mmm.'

Her gaze alighted on the collapsing corrugated iron Nissen hut. 'That's going,' I said quickly. 'Replaced by a stone cart shed. We've already got planning permission.'

'Oh, I rather liked that.'

As we walked along the track, she said: 'I'm afraid I must tell you immediately that you have a serious problem with access—' This was bad news. In a bid for inside information, I'd taken the precaution of calling a few County Organisers, in safe, far-off counties like Surrey and Northumberland, on the pretext of researching a newspaper article. This had revealed a crucial tip: if a garden was deemed, for some reason, not up to standard, then the routine procedure for rejection was to blame access or parking problems. It neatly avoided subjective discussions and hurt feelings and closed matters without having to enter potentially controversial areas. '—these steep, narrow lanes are difficult at the best of times, and if two cars meet and one has to back, it soon becomes chaos. You only need one person who isn't very good at backing. As for the parking and the track, I'm afraid—'

114

'Wait! Please wait!' This had to be nipped in the bud. 'We've got it all worked out. One-way systems. Lots of alternative parking. Obviously the track's got to be re-done. Just look round first, then we'll explain.'

'Hmm.'

To get to the place where the hang-gliders launched, we had to pass the rusting skeletons of old bits of farm machinery which lined the final approaches to Tair-Ffynnon. I explained my plan for harnessing the romantic qualities of abandoned junk, using them as evocative sculptures. For modesty's sake, to avoid any presumption that this was all my own intuitive brilliance, and to emphasise its appropriateness, I explained how the inspiration had been local farmyards themselves.

'So people can come all the way here to see exactly what they see all around them at home?' she said.

'Er ... well ...' It had not occurred to me that visitors would mainly be local.

We reached the grassy patch on the edge of the escarpment where the hang-gliders and paragliders took off. By any standards the view was a fine one. To the east, the hill fell away hundreds of feet to the Monnow valley, from which Monmouthshire takes its name, and the patchwork fields of England. To the south-east was the long ridge of the Graig and Monmouth beyond, with May Hill and the Cotswolds in the distance. To the south were the mountains of Skirrid and Blorenge, the Severn Estuary glinting, the Mendips, the Quantocks and Exmoor. To the south-west was the wide Gavenny valley running seven miles down to Abergavenny. To the west was a mountain panorama with Sugar Loaf in its midst.

'Uh-huh. Right.'

Was she deliberately stonewalling? Was a poker face part of her job? We walked back to the yard. I explained that the mound of spoil in front of the house was to be a terraced vegetable garden, and how we planned to re-route the spring so it tinkled attractively through the yard.

'Right.'

Then we headed out of the opposite side of the yard, across the rough patch of ground we'd designated for the orchard. 'This will be the orchard.'

'Not very sheltered for an orchard.'

I'd recently attended a one-day orchard course. 'We hoped that so long as we grafted onto vigorous M25 root stock, then bush-pruned them, they should be alright.' (Take that.)

'Hmm.'

'We'll have some chickens pecking about,' said Vez, rejoining us, Maya eyeing Mrs Kerr suspiciously. 'Chickens always cheer a place up, don't you think?'

'I'm not really a chicken kind of person.'

By now we'd reached the two furthest fields. They should have been a healthy green by this late in April, and possibly (I'd hoped) a sea of spring flowers. But with no gates and more holes  than hedge, they looked exactly like the rest of the place: a pale mat of shorn turf, mud and sheep droppings, the only notable sign of life the thistles pushing through. 'These will be wild flower meadows,' I said, with a sweep of my hand. 'The hedges will be coppiced and the gaps replanted.'

'They should look splendid in fifteen years.'

I couldn't help thinking things could be going better. I'd been rather assuming she'd be eating out of our hands by now. Having shot our bolt, scenery-wise, and with the romantic abandoned machines idea junked, there wasn't much left. We were at the Far Field now.* 'This would be the parking field.' Pointing to the gaps in the hedges where there should have been gates, I told her about my plans to make gates myself, in the traditional Monmouthshire pattern, from cleft oak. 'Gates are so important. For framing views and all that.'

'Hmm.'

116

'And this hedge ...' We were walking back towards the house and we'd reached the gateless opening into the orchard field. The scrappy boundary scarcely merited the word hedge, simultaneously moth-eaten and absurdly overgrown. 'This hedge will be cut-and-laid,' I said. 'I love the look of a cut-and-laid hedge, don't you?'

'Who'll you get to do that?'

'I'll do it myself.'

'Will you now?'

We were approaching the house again, from the west. Its lumpen boxiness, its cement-grey complexion, especially in that grey light, made it an unavoidable blemish on the pretty hillside.

'Why ever don't you do the house first?'

It was a fair question—to which I didn't have an answer. 'Yes, I suppose we should, really.' The fact was, we still hadn't the faintest idea what to do about the house.

In silence, we trooped up the hill to the patch of disturbed ground I'd started calling 'The Quarry' (more because I was hoping we might find stone in it than because of any material evidence to that effect), up above the anthills near the top of the Top Field. Surrounded by clumps of gorse, it was a wasteland of nettles, but also a natural vantage point. From here the immediate locality was spread beneath us like one of those papier-mâché landscapes people build for toy train sets, with tunnels and bridges and rivers. Indeed, the Abergavenny–Hereford line ran directly through the middle of it. Covered with gorse and bracken, it felt a notch or two bleaker than the level the house sat at. 'We thought

---

* We'd finally named our fields. Having discovered that local fields had ancient and poetic names—Big Lool-A-Bout-O, The Swards, Caer-mawr, Little Quoika—I'd been hoping to institute something similar. After months of deliberation, however, dull expediency had stepped in. The field nearest the house had become the Near Field and the others, by the same unimpeachable logic, the Middle Field, the Far Field, and for the one rising up the hill behind the house, the Top Field. The field to the east of the yard, where our predecessor had encouraged the hang-gliders to park, became the Hang-Glider Field.

we might build something in stone here. An Andy Goldsworthy-style sculpture or a stone cairn. Something mountainous, anyway.'

'Hmm.'

We crossed the field to the soggy bowl of gorse and dead bracken where the spring emerged. 'This'll be a pond. We'll dig out the boggy area round the spring a bit. Try to establish heather and whinberries in place of the bracken.'

'Hmm.'

I was running out of steam. As we picked our way down the hill, over the soaking tussocks and anthills towards the house, tendrils of mist swept across our path. They reflected my mood. As we neared the house, it seemed as well to get the bad news straight up. From speaking to the other County Organisers, I knew potential entrants had to be approved in September for inclusion in the following year's Yellow Book, which came out in February. Still, Mrs Kerr didn't know I knew that. 'It's a lot to ask, I know,' I said. 'And obviously I don't know when you have to make your decision for next year's Yellow Book. But knowing the forty-five-minute-rule, if we worked incredibly hard between now and, say, September, and if we could demonstrate then *exactly* what else we'd get done over next winter ... I don't suppose there's any conceivable chance that ... er ... I mean to say ... that you might ... er ... might *consider* including us in the ...' Suddenly, in the fog, the whole notion seemed so absurd, I could hardly bring myself to finish my sentence: '... in the Yellow Book for next year ...' I trailed off.

'We could put in disclaimers,' chimed Vez.

'We can put in no disclaimers,' said Mrs Kerr.

'Caveats, then.'

'Caveats? What, caveats about access? About reversing? And parking? Caveats about no flowers—in fact, about no garden?' The mist chose this moment to close in completely. 'And caveats about the weather?' For the first time, she smiled.

'So ... it's out of the question?'

'Well,' she said, pausing and looking around her, as if to give the place a final appraisal. The mist thinned momentarily. '*Well ...*'

Another pause. Another appraising look. 'The Scheme *has* been considering a move to include more unusual gardens. Natural gardens ... wild gardens ... gardens which promote wildlife and so on.'

Another look around. I caught Vez's eye.

'So I suppose if you could show me, by September, that you had made *real progress*. And there was some chance that people coming here might actually have something to *see ...*'

'Definitely we could.' Dear good kind sweet lady (as Alan Clark said of Margaret Thatcher).

'And access and parking remain a major problem.'

'I'm sure there's a way round it.'

'Obviously I can't promise or guarantee anything.'

We had five months.

9

The important matter
of gates

The five-bar gate is made to just the right height for a
comfortable lean, and round where I live there are plenty of
gates to choose from. I could happily lean on a gate all the
livelong day, chatting to passers-by about the wind and the
rain. I do a lot of gate-leaning while I am supposed to be
gardening; instead of hoeing, I lean on the gate, stare at the
vegetable beds and ponder.

TOM HODGKINSON 'The Best Things in Life Are Free',
Guardian, 6 January 2007

'Nice green field like this,' said Mark, casting an appraising eye over
the newly-fenced Far Field where he'd been helping me replant a
hedgerow. 'You'll have fun keeping the sheep out of here.' I attached
no particular significance to his remark. Surely once a field was properly
fenced, the sheep would be excluded (or contained). It seemed a

straightforward equation. The larger significance of our afternoon together—of which Mark was not aware—was that I was spending it with a *real, live farmer.*

Having lived in proximity to farmers throughout my childhood without ever knowing any, they occupied, in my mind, a hallowed position in the rural firmament. They didn't just live in the country like the rest of us; they used it to make a living: they were *of* the country. They knew about animals and machines. Their dogs were working dogs. Farmers married farmers' daughters and were all related to each other. Other rural activities ranked in significance and authenticity entirely according to their proximity to farming. Apart from Mervyn, who had been a farmer before he became a contractor, Mark was my first close contact with a world which, for all its ubiquity, still seemed closed and remote, with its own institutions, rituals, buildings, machines, livestock, smells and sounds, even hours. There was no logic to my position. I knew perfectly well that farmers couldn't be that different, that I was certainly more similar to them than, say, to the apes, and that as a group they were at least as responsible for the destruction of the countryside as any urban dweller. Yet, nevertheless, they retained a mystery and elusive allure that beguiled me.

Mark farmed the fertile land at the bottom of the hill and we drove through his farmyard on the way to Tair-Ffynnon. I'd known him by sight since we first arrived, but had only recently met him on a local hedge-laying course where he'd been instructing. Since then his unexpected approachability and dry sense of humour meant I found myself pestering him constantly for advice about an ever-widening range of matters, from mole-trapping to installing water troughs. He was plainly a paragon of his species. His farm and fields always looked tidy and workmanlike. His animals looked healthy and contented. His wife Liz, the daughter of a long-established local farming family, was an elegant presence in the lanes as she exercised her hunters. His standing rose even further when I discovered he not only looked after his own flock of sheep and herd of beef cattle, but also acted as dairyman for other farmers. He was Chairman of the Llanthony Show and a governor of the local school to which, in spring, he brought baby lambs, and where, in autumn, he acted as auctioneer after the Harvest Festival. In fact, a more burnished pillar of the local agricultural community it would have been hard to find.

Following the County Organiser's visit, the most pressing matter was to secure our boundaries: no small task since not a single field offered a remotely stock-proof barrier.* The sheep simply did as they pleased, a lesson we'd learnt when friends brought us a couple of oaks, a rowan and an apple as moving-in presents. Unthinkingly sticking them in the ground with just a stake and a rabbit guard, I'd returned to inspect their progress a week later to discover they'd apparently been fed into a shredder. A quarter of their previous size, they'd been stripped, gnawed and de-barked. All died. This was, though I didn't realise it, the opening salvo of a long and bitter wrestle for control of our land. Shortly afterwards, the sheep got into the tiny walled enclosure by the front door, where, for safekeeping, we'd placed the trees Uncle William had brought. Locusts couldn't have done a more comprehensive job. Of the still pot-bound stumps, but an inch of stalk remained. Most were torn from their pots, the discarded root balls flung aside in an apparently deliberate attempt to antagonise.

I'd called Martin. I hated the idea of wire, especially barbed wire (its introduction in 1867 marking the precise moment when the British countryside's inexorable decline began). However, in the short term

---

* The fence being, as the gardening theorist Simon Pugh has pointed out, the basic, minimum condition of the garden. The word 'garden' supposedly originates from the same Old English root as *geard* or 'fence'. Paradise, from the Greek word *paradeisos* (derived, in turn, from the Persian *pairi daêza*), means 'enclosed place'. Walpole's claim that William Kent, first of the eighteenth-century landscape gardeners, 'leaped the fence and saw all nature as a garden' still confirms the fence as the integral feature of the garden. Except in the case of Derek Jarman, of course, who noted that 'the charm of Dungeness is that it has no fences—to build one would go against the grain'. But then Jarman didn't have sheep to contend with.

there didn't seem much alternative. And so, after a day and a half, a series of mighty barricades of gleaming high-tensile galvanised steel had been erected around the Far Field, which now resembled a border crossing from Cold War Europe. Double fences allowed the replanting of hedgerows in between: tiring, repetitive work, which is why, once Martin had finished with the wire, I'd gladly accepted Mark's offer of help. Together, we'd planted double, staggered rows of mixed 'gapping' whips—hawthorn, blackthorn, hazel, dog rose, holly and field maple— interspersed with the odd standard trees of oak, ash, birch, rowan, sycamore and wild damson. As we worked, I grilled Mark about the sheep. The ones on the hill, he said, were Welsh Mountain ewes, at least two years old. They were bigger than his Suffolk Crosses, with white faces and longer tails. 'Why don't you have Welsh Mountains in your flock?'

'We-e-ell ...' Mark had a way of pausing between words for emphasis. 'Suffolk Crosses aren't so ... bloody-minded ... as the Welsh Mountain. Your Welsh Mountain's a real bruiser. A born survivor. Tough as they come. And if they get in anywhere, they destroy everything.' Once upon a time, I thought. But not any more.

After we'd finished and Mark had left, I walked our newly secured western perimeter. No Roman guard patrolling Hadrian's Wall can have felt greater satisfaction. Periodically, I'd try a post. Not a hint of give; they might have been bedded in concrete. As for the wire, each strand was taut as a steel bar, the barbs so sharp I cut my finger. There was no doubt that, with fixed points of entry and exit, the feel of the space had changed. It was an enclosure now, a compound, no longer just part of the open hill. Savouring our new control, I almost pitied the knot of sheep outside, staring hungrily in.

It was now the last week of April, spring was springing and the prospect of seeing, for the first time, what one of our fields looked like when left to grow, ungrazed, was exciting. I had high hopes it would be carpeted with wild flowers, a *Heidi*-like alpine scene. And by the end of the month the field had duly erupted into a frothy blaze of yellow buttercups and dandelions. Because of the curve of the hill, we couldn't actually see the Far Field from the house. The one place where we could check its progress without a special visit was coming up the track, where it crossed the common lower down, about half a mile away. And it was here a few days later, humming with the joys of spring, that I was surprised to spot a white blob in that very field. I was so taken aback I stopped and reversed the car to check my eyes weren't playing tricks. No doubt about it. There was an unmistakeably sheep-sized blob, right in the middle of the field. Wondering what it could be—a stone? A piece of clothing? Unmelted snow (in May)?—I parked and hastened over to it. There, ambling contentedly amongst the buttercups, was a sheep. It didn't even trouble to look up as I climbed the gate. Eventually it raised its bullet head and surveyed me indifferently. Some fool had plainly opened the gate into the lane and not closed it and, cursing ramblers in general and my family in particular, I strode down to shut it. Only to find it shut and tied, exactly as I'd left it. What was going on? Furiously I paced the perimeter. We must have overlooked some point where a persistent animal could get in. But the fence was as strong and sound as ever. The only other possible explanation was that I'd somehow missed a sheep when we cleared the field, but it seemed unlikely. I opened the gate, chivvied out the recalcitrant ruminant and tied it even tighter than before.

Two days passed. I found myself approaching the vantage point on the track with a certain apprehension. I knew there was no way the sheep could now get in, but even so … Happily, however, the intrusion seemed to have been a one-off and I was just beginning to relax when, on the third day after the incident, Maya piped up from the back of the car: 'Why are there sheep in the field you said we made a fence around to keep the sheep out?'

'There aren't poppet. You're imagining …' But—and it was like a knife-stab—she was right. Not one white blob, this time, but two. I strode to the field to check, and there they were. One looked up and gave me a bored look. Once again I paced the barricades, forensically examining every inch for kinks, glitches, tell-tale tufts of wool on the wire. Nothing. The boundary was as intact and formidable as before. The gate was tied with the same double knot. I looked around. Was someone playing a practical joke? If so, who could it be? Bill the Shepherd, our neighbouring hill farmer, in his seventies? A rambler? It seemed unlikely. The children? They could neither undo nor tie knots. Really, it was stranger than crop circles. Once more, I herded them out and retied the gate.

As I pondered the mystery, it occurred to me that there was one place where, just conceivably, the sheep could have jumped a post-and-rail fence, scrambled up onto a tumble-down wall, navigated some wire and thorn bushes and, from this vantage point, jumped the wire. I spent an irritable, joyless afternoon scheduled for something else erecting a spiky barricade of old pallets, scrap timber and tangles of barbed wire. The result closely resembled the messy blockades we'd inherited, about which I'd been most derogatory and which the fancy new wire replaced. Still, I sank into a bath that evening in the certain knowledge that, finally, the matter was closed.

Next day there were four sheep in the field. After chasing them out, the following day (when the bill arrived for the fencing) there were seven. After this, a sort of madness possessed me. I took to staking out the field from the track below or the hill above with binoculars. However long I waited, nothing happened. I never saw a sheep enter. But if I left and returned, there were always more. It was like magic. Getting them out, too, as their numbers increased, was becoming less straight-forward. Perhaps unsurprisingly, they were unwilling to relinquish the 'nice green field', as Mark had predicted. It now required a co-ordinated effort from all of us, Beetle the dog, Maya and Storm (now just walking) armed with long bamboo canes, Vez and myself, also with sticks. After closing or opening the relevant gate, we'd begin a steady sweep. The sheep would be compliance itself, docilely allowing themselves to be herded ever nearer the appropriate exit. This continued until the final moment when, just as we were closing in and the task seemed as good as accomplished, they'd veer past the opening, separate like mercury and, now in twos or threes, plunge between us, ignoring our frantic yells, halting when they were a hair's breadth out of range to resume grazing as if nothing had happened. It was a study in insolence.

As more of our ground got fenced, this routine became increasingly frequent. It wasn't (given the sheep's Houdini abilities) quite as pointless as it sounds because sometimes, once evicted, they'd stay out. It all depended on the time of year and what alternative food sources they had. Late winter found them at their most determined and devious. On these occasions, once we'd been outmanoeuvred three or four times, we'd have to wait for reinforcements in the form of Bill the Shepherd, with his dogs, or visiting friends. Occasionally I'd lose it, running at the nearest smirking animal—they always seemed to be smirking, and many seemed to have a lazy eye, compounding the effect—howling war cries and brandishing my stick. Once, incensed beyond endurance, I threw a stone. This unfortunately missed the sheep and hit one of the chickens, which exploded in a cloud of feathers and startled clucking. The sheep looked on, chewing, smugger than ever.

And so our acquaintanceship with the Welsh Mountain ewe deepened. For some time, Storm believed the correct procedure on seeing a sheep was to run at it screaming and flapping his arms wildly. Perpetually ravenous, they ate most things: hay, straw, silage, horse and cattle feed, chicken feed, bird seed, cat food, grass cuttings.* Particular favourites were anything clearly forbidden and protected, particularly newly planted saplings. They toyed with kitchen waste, potato and orange peel, compost, hedge, gorse and tree prunings. They ate ivy—supposedly poisonous. As for yew—according to William Robinson's *The English Flower Garden*, 'deadly for stock in all states, and if a record could be made of its destructiveness it would amaze'—they consumed it with impunity and in as much quantity as available. The only vegetable

---

* The reason Britain's mountains and moorlands are treeless has nothing to do with weather or altitude, and everything to do with sheep.

matter they left untouched were the few things it might have been genuinely helpful if they did eat: nettles, thistles, bracken and docks.

The cute, gambolling fluffballs that appeared in the spring and briefly made the hills echo to an oratorio of *maa-aaaa-aaaa-aaa*-ing, metamorphosed in eighteen months into burly, lumpen, daggy-coated opportunists, patrolling the hill in twos or threes. They were incurably nosy, peering into the kitchen window, craning and ducking to improve their view.

They bullied the cat, putting their heads down to move it on for no reason. And they were master dissemblers, affecting utter indifference, even wandering absently in the opposite direction as we scattered chicken feed with a wary eye. A blind feint. The instant our backs were turned they'd reappear, en masse, butting the hens away.

As individuals, they displayed a slyness seldom attributed to sheep, which accumulated into a remarkable herd wisdom. They learnt to lift the latch on the garden gate, to knock the twist top off the chicken feeder and were reputed to be able to cross cattle grids by rolling. 'People say sheep are stupid,' Robert, a neighbouring farmer I'd meet in the lanes, told me. 'Nothing stupid about sheep. They learn. People don't know that. Sheep learn.' What they couldn't get by guile, they often achieved by brute force. We roped the garden gate, so they battered it down. Wire fences they dealt with by forcing their heads beneath the lowest strand then wrenching it up. Yet they could also display considerable agility, reaching up on their hind legs onto the bird table, climbing over stacked furniture in a barn, or strolling along the jagged top of a new stone wall. Any object inadvertently left out—a wooden bench, say, or a climbing frame—would be rubbed against until broken. In frosts, their spherical droppings, which were everywhere, turned into lethal ball bearings, sending us flying.

And yet, grudgingly, we had to admit we quite like them. They kept the turf springy and the grass short without the mechanised evenness of a mower. As for how they were getting into the Far Field, it remained a mystery—until one afternoon a walker knocked on the door, visibly excited. Did we own the field just along the track? Yes, I said, we did. Then he thought there was something we ought to know. He'd just seen the strangest thing. It was so extraordinary he had to tell someone. He'd watched sheep hopping the fence like pole vaulters. They took a run up from the high ground of the field above, he said, then did a vast, comedy, grasshopper leap as if propelled from beneath by a giant spring. 'I suppose it's no surprise,' he said. 'Nice green field like that.'

———◆———

Fields aren't enclosures, of course, until the gateways have gates. And, apart from the two in the Far Field, we had none. The departing owners had (following, I later learnt, long agricultural tradition) taken the gates with them, at least the half-decent ones. We had fourteen gaps to fill. If the 'features' of our garden were to consist of no more than the idioms of the countryside—gates, walls, hedges, stiles, paths, cairns, views— then they had to be shining examples of their kind. So those fourteen gaps represented an important opportunity. I had an idea that every part of Britain had its own regional style of gate, so it clearly made sense, if we required gates, to have local ones. I was also fairly sure that gates were traditionally made from oak or elm or ash or larch, or split chestnut, or some other noble and ancient-sounding British wood, that they should be pegged together with wooden pegs, rather than nailed or bolted, and that such gates, without supplementary treatment, should last a lifetime.

When I started checking them out, however, the gates available signally failed to match these criteria. There was no shortage of companies offering ready-made gates, but they all looked the same. Timber gates were offered in a standardised, diamond-braced pattern of various widths, mainly in 'tanalised' or treated softwood that gave them a sinister green tinge. All were held together with clearly visible galvanised bolts. Enquiries about regional patterns, British hardwoods and wooden pegs drew indifferent responses of the 'Nah, no call for it, mate' school. The top-of-the-range gates, offered in imported hardwoods (with strange names like idigbo, keruing or iroko), looked too dark, too orange or too shiny and tended to have inappropriately flamboyant raised 'heels' (the side with the hinges). They were immediately recognisable from the places for which they were clearly intended: suburban driveways. Metal field gates meanwhile (available from agricultural suppliers) were grimly utilitarian affairs with no pretence to style of any kind, in lightweight galvanised steel tubing.

Then, at the annual Royal Welsh Show, I picked up a little book entitled *Gates and Stiles*. Here, in one slim volume, was all the information I'd wanted—even a surfeit perhaps. It was crammed with photographs of lychgates and tapsel gates, wrought-iron gates and cleft chestnut gates, and hewn stone posts in every regional style. 'You will probably find, once you have read this book,' boasted the author, 'that as you drive along the country lanes in future, you will see the gates you pass with entirely new eyes.' And, goddamit, he was right. I became a connoisseur of gates and gateways, though I still wasn't quite sure what their fascination was.* In the book was a series of maps showing, county by county, exactly which pattern of gate belonged to each region. Some had five bars, some six, and the permutations of bracing seemed endless, from the crudely rudimentary to the frankly finicky. The design for a Monmouthshire gate, however, was one of the simplest. Unfussy and elegant, its braces and struts gave a pleasing vertical emphasis while also, conveniently, forming the shape of an 'M'. I couldn't recall actually having seen one, but this was clearly the gate for Tair-Ffynnon.

———— ◆ ————

'Hello, is that Mr Morgan?'

'No, no, this is his son.'

'Oh is it? Is Mr Morgan there?'

'He's standing right beside me.'

'Oh … could I speak to him, please?'

'You'd like to speak to him, would you? OK … *Father!*'

'Hello? Mr Morgan?'

''Allo there!'

'D'you remember, we've spoken a couple of times about some stone gateposts you've got?'

'Yes, yes. I remember.'

'I was wondering if I could come and have a look at them.'

'Well, yes of course. The trouble is we're in chaos at the moment. Chaos. The yard's all over the place. We're moving, you see. I don't think I've ever worked so hard. I was working all the Bank Holiday.'

* Doubtless something to do with the myriad appealing things they evoke: weekend rambles, unspoilt countryside; pausing, leaning and musing. They're also natural 'viewfinders'. A field gate framed by a tree has the same 'aspect ratio' (the proportion of a rectangle's shorter dimension to its longer one) as 35mm film, an old-fashioned television and human vision (about 1:1.3). If the British countryside needed a logo, what more elegant symbol could there be?

'I'm sorry to hear that. But I was wondering ... those stone gate-posts ...'

'Yes, the gateposts. Well, let me see. What size do you want them?'

'As we discussed, about seven feet. That's about normal, isn't it?'

'All depends what you want them for, see.'

'Well, as posts for a metal field gate. Or maybe an oak one.'

'Oak? Totally different matter. Different thing altogether. Wooden gates are much heavier than metal ones, see. So they'd need to be bigger for that.'

'What sizes have you got?'

'You could have 12 x 14, or 14 x 32 ... I can cut them to size, see? You just need to do some measuring. You might like them just as they are!'

'Well, exactly. That's my point. I think I need to see them before I can decide.'

'In that case, you'd better come over and have a look.'

'When would be a good time?'

'Well, you see that's the problem. I'm never here. We're in chaos at the moment.'

'Well, when are you there? You must be there sometimes.'

'Tell you what. Let me know when you're coming this way. I'll have a look and see where I am. Then we'll go from there. Now I'm afraid I've got to go. I'm right in the middle here, see, everything's in chaos ...'

I put the phone down feeling, as I often did these days, slightly seasick. Trying to arrange anything in Border Country was almost impossible. Everyone was as friendly as could be. They seemed genuinely pleased to hear from you. They listened attentively, chatted away unhurriedly, were keen to help. But when it came to fixing anything—a price, say, or a date in a diary—they were pathologically non-committal. How was one supposed to get anything done in this part of the world?

I'd found Mr Morgan's salvage yard only after a protracted session of ringing around in search of stone gateposts. Other stone wall areas—Dartmoor, the Lakes, the Yorkshire Dales, the High Peak, Scotland, Ireland—had posts rough-hewn from lumps of local rock, with iron hinges set into them with lead flashing. It was clear this was the model to which all gateways aspired. Such a post would last for ever without rotting or breaking. They looked better the more moss and lichen they attracted. Appraising Black Mountains gateways with my new connoisseurship, I was pleased to spot the occasional stone post, though, it had to be admitted, there weren't many, and those there were were frequently so oddly shaped it seemed remarkable that anyone had thought to use them as gateposts. Plainly the flaky sedimentary beds of the local Old Red Sandstone didn't lend themselves to pillar-shaped blocks half as well as Dartmoor's granite or Yorkshire's Millstone Grit.

Finding a source for such menhirs quickly escalated into the kind of goose chase that was fast becoming the hallmark of every Tair-Ffynnon-linked project. The big quarries advertising in Yellow Pages or online met my enquiries with incomprehension. The specialised quarrymen that I needed, I gradually learnt, were so obscure I might as well have been searching for scythe-snaiths or corn-dolly weavers. They weren't registered anywhere and certainly didn't advertise.

The only way to find them was word-of-mouth, by asking around, calling local architects, dropping in on building sites, gradually narrowing down my search to villages, then pubs, then, hopefully, individuals. 'There was a bloke over Michaelchurch way a few years back … what was 'e called, now? … 'E might still be goin'.' Or I'd be given a number: 'Don't know if it still works.' (It never did.) Or be told 'Drop by the Bull's Head on a Monday evening. Or the Post Office—try Mrs Powell. If anyone knows, she will.' Gradually, I'd compiled a list of names and phone numbers, only to find that this was the easy part. Getting hold of anyone—invariably they worked in places well out of mobile reception—then finding them, was far trickier. Theirs weren't quarries as I imagined quarries to be. There were no big machines or lorries; just a few heaps of stone in a field around the seam they were working, usually by hand. It soon became clear why so few people built in stone, and why, when they did, they felt compelled to make such an overt feature of it: the prices were enormous. But regardless of cost, no-one had any stone suitable for gateposts. No call for them, I was told. 'There's a bloke you could try down Longtown way, if you can find him,' someone said. 'South African. Tony Something.'

Which was how, when Mr Morgan's gateposts failed to materialise, I tracked down Tony.

Tony was dressing flagstones with a disc-cutter when I first encountered him. Cheetah-thin and bronzed from his outdoor life, his high cheekbones supported a pair of mirrored wraparound sunglasses and everything about him except his gleaming silver earring was lightly coated with stone dust. His quarry was in a sloping field on the English side of the Monnow valley. Behind, rose the great, dark ridge which hinted at how the Black Mountains acquired their name. Tony's stone was identical to ours, pale purple-pink, and thin rather than blocky. He showed me how he used steel wedges to split off great slabs from the horizontal face, which he then split and cut further to make flags, roofing slates and tombstones. 'Yis, yis. Ah know the sortuf thing you mean, yis,' he said when I asked about gateposts. He was the first person who'd shown a flicker of recognition. 'Ah've none et the moment. But ah'll kip ma eyes open. Something'll turn up.' His accent sounded improbably exotic, but no longer surprised us. One of the features of Border Country, we were learning, was the number of inhabitants not from Border Country.

Since then, at periodic intervals, Tony had arrived with great pillars of stone, some of which, he said, weighed more than half a ton. It was riveting to watch him unload these from his light, flat-bed truck. Waving away offers of help, and using just a crow bar and fence posts as rollers, he'd manoeuvre them until they hung so far over the back it looked as if they must crash to the ground. At which point, like a see-saw, the cab and front wheels would rear dramatically into the air, dropping the back of the truck and gently depositing its cargo.

Once we'd accumulated eight of these monsters, Tony helped me erect them. The first problem arose when he asked which way we wanted the gate to open, and which side, accordingly, should be the hanging post and which the receiving post? Fortunately, having an instinct for this kind of thing, I was able to reply immediately: 'Left to right.' At this I got an odd look from Vez, who'd at that moment arrived with coffee. 'You mean right to left,' she said. It was hard to know what to say. Anyone could see it should be left to right. 'What do you think, Tony?' she said, with practised guile.

'Yis, right to left,' he said, ever the gentleman. And so it went on, gateway by gateway, over a wearisome day. By comparison, setting the posts in the ground was a doddle.

※

It seemed insane to be calling a Dorset number about a Monmouthshire gate, but I couldn't see any alternative. Most of our gates, we'd decided, would have to be metal ones. These we could get inexpensively copied by a local forge from a rusty old angle-iron gate on the hill, dating from the 1950s. ('Ah. New, old gates,' said Martin when he saw them.) And so ten gaps were quickly and easily filled. But for the gateways into the Middle and Far Fields, between hedgerows rather than walls, nothing but traditional oak would do.

Finding someone to make such things, however, proved a formidable task. No-one handmade gates any more; it was that simple. Any number of local joiners offered to make one, if I gave them the plans, on the principle that if it was made of wood, then they could make it (at a price). But somehow this missed the point. I wanted gates made by a gate-maker, someone who didn't need me to tell him how, because he already knew everything there was to know about gates, and all the strains and stresses they came under, so he could allow for whatever had to be allowed for. The only company I'd come up with that might conceivably meet this brief was based in Dorset and had advertised in

Gates and Stiles. 'Winterborne Zelston Fencing, The supply and erection of fencing, gates, agricultural and leisure based products', with its Royal Warrant and 'Proprietor: Major J. R. I. Bower', sounded disconcertingly patrician. I decided to call them anyway.

The phone was answered by a man with so many plums in his mouth I could barely understand him. The major, I presumed. My enquiry as to whether he could make a gate prompted a testy response.

'Yes, yes. Of course, we can make gates … mmm … mmm … How many d'you want?'

'Can you do them to regional patterns, you know, not a standard design?'

'Can do anything you want.'

'What are they treated with?'

'Nothing. Whole point of oak is it requires no treatment. Just gets harder and harder as it seasons. Can have a coat of linseed oil, if you want.'

'How long will they last?'

'Seventy years … mmm … maybe a hundred.' The sound with which the major interspersed his comments was halfway between a thoughtful pause and an impatient grunt. Either way, it sounded disapproving.

'Can you do them with pegs, you know, without using bolts?'

'Can do, yes … hmmm … mmm … very foolish thing to do, though. Green oak warps you know … mmm …. pegs might come out. That's the reason they're bolted. Couldn't guarantee the thing if you want it pegged. Why'd you want to do a thing like that?'

I explained that I wanted an absolutely traditional gate, as they would originally have been made.

'Hmmm.'

'Could you could do that?'

'Yes, yes. Just send the design over as you want it.'

After I'd put the phone down, however, I realised it felt all wrong. It had been too quick, too remote. How could I trust a gate made without me? It would be hardly different from buying one mass-produced from a garden centre. I redialled the major.

'Hello? Antony Woodward again. We just spoke about some gates.'

'Yes, yes. I remember.'

'There's a condition. Can I come and see the gates being made?'

'What?'

'I said: can I watch the gates being made?'

'What d'you want to do that for?' The request seemed to wrong-foot the major. 'Want to see the gates being made? Hmm ... mmmh. What? Mmmh ... Why?'

Why indeed? I didn't demand to see how most things I bought were made. Why a gate? Why did I want to slog all the way to Dorset to watch someone perform a bit of carpentry so straightforward I was probably capable of doing it myself? The answer, I supposed, was that this gate was not any old gate for any old field; it was for a tiny patch of countryside which had to be perfect. Normal rules did not apply. I had an image of an old estate workshop, perhaps in a wood, surrounded by piles of sawn timber and woodshavings, with racks of wooden-handled chisels and an old band-saw, where a couple of old timers in brown coats and flat caps with pencils behind their ears worked in an all-pervading smell of sawdust. I needed to see my gates' provenance for myself, maybe to confirm that—in a world where, in Ruskin's words, 'there's almost nothing that someone can't make a little cheaper and a little worse'—at least one simple item could still be made as it was meant to be. My gates, in their own small way, were a conduit to a better world. I wasn't absolutely certain, however, how this explanation would play with the major.

'I'm making a garden. The gates are part of it. I just want to know the story behind them.'

'I don't know.' He sighed. 'Mmm ... I think it's too difficult ... I really don't think ... Look, I'll think about it and get back to you.'

A week passed. I left the major a couple of messages, but there was no response. A cynical thought occurred. Had my modest order already been processed and passed tó a factory in the Ukraine? Did that explain the major's reluctance? Then he called back.

'Look, they're pretty odd people you know. Don't say much ... mmm ... 'cept a few grunts. You won't get much out of 'em.'

'I'll chance that. I just want to see a gate being made.'

He sighed. 'Very well ... mmm ... if you really want to spend a day coming down here.'

I met Major Bower the following week at his timber yard. Wearing a tweed cap pulled well down over his brow, he was almost as inscrutable in the flesh as over the phone. He showed me his great stacks of seasoning oak and sweet chestnut, and explained how most of the timber he used was 'cleft' or split by hand, rather than sawn. The result was gates and stiles and post-and-rail fences of the kind that characterised Surtees's England. Mid-morning, we dropped back to his cottage where, in the downstairs loo, a framed article from *Country Life* documented (alongside the major's two-goal polo handicap) his struggle to compete alongside the giants that sold the mass-produced softwood gates I found so wanting. I realised I'd underestimated the major. Here, beneath the plums and the mild testiness, was a romantic who could recite Oliver Rackham's *History of the Countryside* almost by heart. Getting into my car, he told me how he'd gradually assembled a coterie of craftsmen, dotted about the place, one of whom was making my gates.

After a pub lunch, we crossed the New Forest until he directed me into a row of ordinary-looking brick houses in a clearing. He led me into what looked like a garage but turned out to be a workshop. Everything—workbench, chisels, radio, kettle—was so thickly coated with sawdust only vague shapes were discernible. I was introduced to Robin, a young man in his twenties. He wasn't wearing the brown coat I'd imagined, nor did he have a pencil behind his ear, but the hairs of his forearms were sprinkled with sawdust. He'd already cut the various parts of the gate to size, and the three heaviest members, the 'top bar', 'heel' and 'shutting head' (latching post), were laid out on trestles. While we watched, Robin assembled the four horizontal 'bars' into the morticed slots in the heel and shutting head. When he'd smacked them fully home with a mallet, he drilled right through the joints, took a wooden peg from a ready-cut pile, dipped it into linseed oil, then hammered it through until it emerged the other side. The planks started to resemble a gate.

He laid on the rest of the timbers and started drilling busily, explaining, as he did so, that because no bolts were being used each joint had to be double-pegged, with each pair of pegs at opposing angles. Unseasoned green oak, he said, would warp and could pull in any direction as it seasoned and hardened. Chances were, some pegs would come out. But this way, whichever way the oak warped, hopefully some pegs would always hold firm. This, I thought, was why I'd come: to understand as well as to witness. When he'd hammered in all the pegs, he trimmed them off flush. Then he chamfered the square edges of each 'brace' and 'downright'. 'D'you want them painted with linseed oil?'

'What does that do?'

'Nothing really. Makes them smell good. They'll still weather to a silver-grey.'

'Why not?'

In three quarters of an hour both gates were assembled. Not a drop of glue, not a nail, bolt or screw had been used. As they leant up against the workshop wall, I ran my hand over the smooth, still dusty surfaces.

The two gates were delivered the following week. We had builders working at the time, and we all watched, transfixed, as the lorry in its immaculate white livery with ostrich feather crest and Royal Warrant entered the yard. I couldn't help wishing, as this regal vehicle skidded and struggled on the yard's vertiginous slope, to-ing and fro-ing between the rusting junk and nettles, that the gates had been delivered when no-one was about, ideally at night. It felt ludicrous to have gone so far for something so ubiquitous.

The gates seemed ridiculous too, as I helped the driver unload them; unbelievably heavy, with their extravagant cricket club whiff of linseed oil. But once we'd heaved them to their respective gateways, hooked them onto their hinges, and stepped back thirty yards, suddenly they changed. They fitted in perfectly. They were a bit wide, certainly. An eight-foot gate would have looked prettier than these ten-foot ones. Nevertheless, they did something magical. Where previously there'd been a space, now there was a place.

10

The orchard

Apples grow much better in sites that are no more
than 500ft above sea level.
MONTY DON, *The Complete Gardener*, 2003

'So, how do most people pick a site for an orchard?'

Our tutors for the day were a husband-and-wife team, Tony and Liz.
Tony, it turned out, did most of the talking, while Liz interrupted
periodically from the front row. There was no doubt that Tony inspired
confidence. A big man with a deep voice, he sounded as if he had earth
under his fingernails. And he seemed to have the measure of us, the
twenty or so novices assembled with our cups of coffee in the country
house drawing room, as thoroughly as he did his fruit trees. 'Ah'll tell
you how most people pick a site for an orchard,' he said. 'They say to
themselves: "Well, I've got a piece of land I can't do anything with. I
might as well put an orchard on it."'

Which, of course, was precisely what we'd done. The lower half of the small, steep field immediately west of the house was good-for-nothing ground. Bisected by a track crudely bulldozed along the contour into a rough step, it was so steep even the turf couldn't hang on, ruckling into those little crinkles called 'terracettes'. It was strewn with docks, thistles and tussocky grass, running down to an old tin shed at the bottom. In the Black Mountains, most farms and smallholdings had a few wind-stunted fruit trees, often with hens pecking about amongst them, and we were, after all, only yards from the border with Herefordshire, by-word for apple country. Besides, what self-respecting Eden didn't have at least one apple tree? Every other field had acquired a character of its own except for this one. So for quarter of an acre that we couldn't think what else to do with, it made perfect sense: plant an orchard.

But would an orchard grow at 1,200 feet? My knowledge of fruit trees was non-existent. In my tiny London garden, I'd inherited a highly productive peach tree only to preside over its steady decline and eventual demise from leaf curl, despite sousing the thing, as books instructed, in toxic preparations of copper. Apart from this, my only experience of fruit growing was the damson tree we'd had in Somerset in the middle of the steep front lawn. Charming as this looked, at least as I first knew it with its trunk and branches bearded with lichen, it fell victim to the unspoken horticultural battle between my parents. My father never liked it. The low branches caught his head as he passed with the mower, the lichen scratching his bare arms and shoulders if, as he often did, he mowed shirtless. In the autumn it dropped hundreds of damsons on the lawn, which didn't chime at all with the Great Modernist Experiment (requiring perfect order at all times), especially when the damsons began to rot and squelch under foot, attracting platoons of wasps. My mother claimed she loved the fruit, and wanted them for making damson jam, chutney and gin; but in practice, only the jam ever got made, and that rarely. Sharp tasting and consisting largely of chewy skins, it was certainly the nastiest jam I've ever eaten. No-one but she

and my father would go near it. The Kilner jars
sat for years at the back of the kitchen cupboard,
their lids rusting, until one year, to our
disbelief, my mother wrapped them up as
Christmas presents and gave them to our
relations. When a drain was dug across the

lawn during the building of the extension, doubtless chopping many of
its roots, the tree's end was assured. My father lopped off dead branches
at every opportunity until, finally, it caught some kind of fungus and,
bleakly triumphant, my father cut it down.

On the whole, however, I was inclined to be optimistic about Tair-
Ffynnon's fruit-growing potential. True, all the orchards I could think
of were in flattish, sheltered lowlands rather than on steep hillsides re-
claimed from bracken, but still, was our field so bad? It faced south, the
slope must surely assist the drainage everyone specified was so critical,
and there was a sheltering hedge, albeit moth-eaten, on the side from
which the prevailing wind blew. Also, what hedgerows we had were full
of bullaces, crab-apples and sloes, evidence that some fruit, at least, was
happy enough on the hill. William Robinson struck an encouraging
note in *The English Flower Garden* (in a chapter appealingly titled 'The
Orchard Beautiful') declaring that suitable ground was 'none the worse
if too hilly for the plough'. My mother's copy of *Fruit-Growing, Modern
Cultural Methods* (1939) by N. B. Bagenal of the East Malling Research
Station had little advice for the mountain fruit-grower, though I
reassured myself he was too preoccupied with maximising yields to
concern himself with anything so frivolous. It was only when I consulted the supposedly user-friendly *RHS Encyclopaedia of Gardening* that
my heart properly sank at the enormity of the research project ahead.
Forty densely-written pages advised on a bewildering array of tech-
nicalities, from pollination compatibility to root stocks and grafting.
Hoping a more practical approach might help, after that I'd ordered
some nursery catalogues. They were like spreadsheets, with table after
table of dates and codes and jargon. Was I seriously meant, from a

standing start, to be able to pick the most suitable varieties for Tair-Ffynnon from the 3,500 extant alternatives? And that was just the apples … never mind pears or plums. I marvelled that any amateur ever managed to fill a fruit bowl.

After months of catalogue-induced paralysis, I'd confided my woes to a small, forceful woman on a stand much-decorated with colourful pictures of apples at the Royal Welsh Show. Before I knew it, I was signed up to the 'Marcher Apple Network' and their quarterly news-letters were arriving. Their progress reports on the 'Welsh Marches Pomona', topical discussions of Codling Moth control and new trans-lations from the Latin *Priapea* about protecting orchards had the effect, if such a thing were possible, of confusing me further. However, amongst a list of forthcoming events I'd spotted an 'Introduction to Orchards' training day for a tenner, which was how I came to be listening to Tony and Liz in mid-Wales one spring Saturday.

The course was well pitched. Tony correctly surmised that words like 'grafting', 'pruning' and 'pollination' were scary ones, so the emphasis was firmly on reassurance and encouragement. Grafting didn't seem half so technical once the reason for it had been explained: that it was only by grafting a particular variety of tree again and again and again that *exactly* the same fruit, genetically, could be eaten today as the Vikings had once eaten, or the archers at Agincourt. (Tony had a knack for romantic examples like these.) As for pruning, if we didn't care how much fruit we got, he said, pruning was optional. And when it came to pollination, again we were told, no need for panic. All we had to do was plant at least two trees that blossomed at the same time and leave bees and the wind to do the rest.

The main question still remained, however: would apple trees grow at over a thousand feet? I didn't even have to ask. A thousand feet? Two thousand feet? Even three thousand feet? No problem at all, according to Tony. 'Apple trees are *very* hardy. Sap is like anti-freeze. They'll grow on top of Snowdon,' he declared. 'It's blossom that's vulnerable. You just have to accommodate the site conditions. In Russia, they grow apple trees in the Arctic Circle, by growing them horizontally, in a fan. Covered by snow they're completely out of the wind. On very windy sites, get trees on vigorous root stock, but cut them off at eighteen inches and grow them as bush trees. And pick late flowering varieties.' Simple.

I'd come away from the course inspired and better informed. Even so, there was still the question of exactly what varieties to choose. The thought of picking root stocks, of buying and planting trees, only to discover in three or four years that I'd cocked up somewhere, seemed too risky. And it was then that it struck me: much the most useful information I'd left the course with was, in fact, Tony and Liz's telephone number. They offered a comprehensive orchard survey service. I called them.

———— • • ————

A few weeks later, Tony and Liz visited. The orchard field duly got the thumbs-up, and a few days later a workmanlike 'Orchard Management Report' arrived in the post. With it—alone justifying their visit—came a nursery catalogue in which they'd ticked suitable varieties of apples, pears, plums and gages, thereby reducing my range of options from thousands to a manageable fifty or so.

Even with the field narrowed, however, choosing was far from easy. Did I prefer, for example, the authenticity of a Bardsey ('Wales's unique apple') or the familiarity of a Bramley 'original' from the original tree in Nottingham? The allegedly beautiful blossom of Ashmead's Kernel ('raised by Dr Ashmead of Gloucester about 1800') or King of the Pippins ('perfect for open tarts'), or the aniseed flavour of Ellison's Orange (not that I liked aniseed)? Or should one think practically? Go for a 'reliable cropper' like James Grieve, a 'late keeper' like the ancient

Court Pendu Plat or the red-striped Tom Putt ('prolific even in wet, windswept situations')? And how did one balance such claims against the Golden Noble, which I encountered a few minutes later, whose 'creamy texture when baked' made it perfect for Apple Snow, my favourite school pudding? And weren't a few silly names *de rigueur*? Sheep's Snout, say, Slack-my-Girdle or Bastard Rough Coat? Really, it was impossible. Faced with so many decisions, there seemed only one solution: cram in as many as possible.

Official planting distances allowed for three rows of six trees, but if we shoved them up a bit, there really seemed no reason why we couldn't have four rows of seven. With those ten extra choices to play with, it just became a matter of whittling down Tony and Liz's recommendations to a final shortlist.* Apples went on the highest rows, because they were hardiest. Pears below them. Gages and plums lowest. And so, at last, all the reading and agonising and day-dreaming about tapering fruit ladders and glazed *tartes aux Normandes*, boiled down to a single sheet of A4 (*see page 146*).

———◆———

Although the trees couldn't be planted until the winter, we decided to mark out their positions at once. Transferring an orchard from a paper plan to a field sounds straightforward enough, but we were soon in difficulties. Taking as our datum the bulldozed track at the top of the plot—which was roughly parallel with the track at the bottom—we carefully measured out seven lines of four trees. A contented hour was spent, Vez paying out and spooling in the measuring tape, I tapping in

---

* Naturally, once the trees were planted, I discovered the varieties I should have included: Landore ('widely planted in Powys farm orchards in the past ... mentioned by the diarist Francis Kilvert ... grows well, even at higher altitudes'), Royal Jubilee ('late flowering of this useful cooker enables it to produce regular crops in bleak sites and at higher altitudes'), etc.

APPLES	APPLES	PEARS	PLUMS & GAGES
Ashmead's Kernel	Tom Putt	Williams	Quince: Meeches Prolific
Scotch Dumpling	Newton Wonder	Pitmaston Duchess	Damson: Shropshire Prune
Bardsey	King of the Pippins	Onward	Victoria
Bramley Original	James Grieve	Jargonelle	Opal
Court Pendu Plat	Golden Noble	Conference	Excalibur
Ellison's Orange	Crab-apple John Downie	Quince Vranja half-standard	Crab-apple *Malus floribunda*
Red Falstaff	Red Falstaff	Conference	Gage Jefferson

UPHILL/NORTH

DOWNHILL/SOUTH

the stakes. Vez said it looked splendid, like a mathematical model of receding perspective.

When I walked up the slope to join her, however, it was clear none of the stakes were in line at all. 'You halfwit,' I said. 'I'd better do it.' A slightly less contented second hour passed, with me barking instructions while she jabbed in the stakes. Finally done, we headed indoors for a well-earned cup of tea. Shutting the gate, we looked back at our handiwork, only to find that, in the moment our backs were turned, somehow all the stakes had moved again. Nothing was in line at all. Grids, of course, work only so long as a site is flat. In a rhomboid field, where no side is at right angles to any other, on a steep gradient with a pronounced bulge along the contour, all kinds of unscheduled mathematical hiccups interpose themselves.

In the end, after averaging from all sides, we simply adjusted by eye. Even this process might have continued indefinitely, had I not announced I was going to dig the first 'soil profile pit'. Tony had been most insistent about these. At his lecture, he'd impressed on us the importance of getting to know our land, as the Victorians did by walking behind their ploughs for sixteen miles a day. Mechanisation, he said, had meant we'd lost this vital intimacy with our soil and the soil profile pit was a way of reacquainting ourselves. Each pit had to be a metre square and 'at least' one metre deep. Essential, said Tony's report, 'to observe water movement in or through them and to assess the soil drainage characteristics'. I started with gusto, rejoicing in the exercise, the spring air, the honest, manly toil. But the ground was hard and stony. After thirty minutes of vigorous hacking with spade and mattock, during which I shed three layers and was mopping sweat from my eyes, I'd made a scarcely discernible peck in the hillside. After another hour, my enthusiasm had turned to sick dread at the scale of the undertaking ahead. A hole 1m x 1m x 1m? Had Tony ever done this himself? It was like digging a grave. He had specified three such pits, one at the top, one in the middle and one at the bottom of the hill. Worse, I was presumably also going to have to dig holes not dissimilar twenty-five more times in which to plant the rest of the bloody trees. The task might take months. Twenty-eight trees? What were we thinking of?

As I finished the first pit, however, it struck me that, whatever conclusions the soil pits revealed, good or bad, it wasn't going to make the slightest difference. This was the place the orchard was going; it was the only place available. Tony had already, effectively, signed it off. The pit digging was optional. I threw down the mattock and banished tree-planting to the back of my mind.

It refused to stay there however. Those twenty-eight stakes stood as a disagreeable daily reminder of the immensity of the task ahead. How was the planting to be accomplished? By December, I was almost considering canning the orchard altogether, when I bumped into Phil, a forester I'd met when he was planting some trees nearby. Phil knew all about trees. 'We'll put them in for you,' he said. 'Collect them too if you like. We're up near that nursery next week.' My relief was tempered by a fascination to see how his two lads would cope with the twenty-eight holes. When the day arrived, I handed them my plan and gave them half an hour to get started. By the time I emerged, spade at the ready, thirty-five minutes later, the trees were planted. Every one of them.

———•◆•———

The following April was one of the sunniest I remember, and within weeks the buds were swelling and the first delicate pink blossom was appearing. By mid-summer, the growth was so prodigious I was worried we'd chosen too vigorous a rooting stock. We knew how trees grew like weeds in the red Monmouthshire soil (we only had to look across the valley to the sheep-free lower slopes of Sugar Loaf or Bryn Arw to observe their relentless colonisation). What hadn't occurred to me was how different they'd all look, how somehow motley the orchard would appear, as each tree took its different shape. Some drooped like weeping willows. Some accelerated skyward like beanstalks. Some had big, broad, matt-green leaves, others—the pears, especially—thin, curly, shiny ones. They all came into blossom and leaf at different times. The quince appeared first, bursting with life, and within three weeks the leaves had turned brown and it looked as if someone had discreetly poured weedkiller over it. The trees that looked best were the plums along the base of the slope, the Victoria, the Shropshire Prune and the Opal, which produced bushy canopies of luxurious light green leaves.

None of this, however, could match the delight of seeing tiny apples and pears swelling on our very own trees, and in the first year, too. By midsummer, the fruit was so heavy it was bowing the green stalks and I forced myself to prune half of them in the approved manner. In the autumn, we had our first harvest: misshapen, blighted and, when we tasted them, hard, bitter and revolting. No fruit was sweeter, of course.

Perhaps such a triumphant first year skewed my expectations. I looked forward to mounting yields, to a larder lined with bottled pears and gages, demijohns of ruby-coloured damson and plum gin, freezers of juice pressed from iron-cranked juicers, dark chutneys, jellies and jams with linen tops. Mentally, I prepared myself for the moment when, inundated, we'd have to adapt the collapsing tin shed into an Apple House lined with slatted beechwood shelves. Year Two's yield corrected this expectation. It was ... zero. It was only then that I remembered: some trees were alternate-year croppers, 'resting' every other year ready for the next bumper crop. Clearly we'd planted such 'bi-annual burners', though it seemed a remarkable coincidence. Still, there it was. Year Three would be the proof.

Alas, Year Three never came. Because Year Two-and-Three-Quarters brought, in February, heavy snow. For three weeks we were snowed in. Revelling in the shoulder-high drifts that blocked the track, we tobogganed under starry moonlit skies, stoked the stove and built snow holes with the children. Meanwhile, savvier members of the animal kingdom were putting the situation to useful purpose. With a foot of snow compacted into a hard, wind-flayed crust, it was at just the right height to allow rabbits to reach above the fourteen-inch rabbit guards around the trees and nibble the bark. Within days, fourteen of the trees bore such tell-tale gnaw marks, six stretching right round the trunk. The damage looked pretty trivial to me. (It was only a bit of bark; how much harm could a few nibble-marks do?) But having posted my situation on the Marcher Apple Network blog, I was bluntly apprised of the facts: 'All ring-barked trees will die.'

That checked their progress alright. On advice, I cut the damaged trees back to below the ring-barking, but above the original graft, so half the orchard is now back to square one. Oh, and I bought a gun. My sympathies, as I read Maya and Storm *The Tale of Peter Rabbit*, have shifted entirely from the eponymous hero to poor, longsuffering Mr MacGregor – an important turning point, I presume, in any gardener's education.

11

Bees

Beekeeper. It's a very disturbing term, I find.
BARRY THE BEE, *Bee Movie*, 2008

Obviously, we needed bees. What properly rendered Nirvana would be complete without the little chaps, pottering around, doing whatever it was bees did?* The buzz of bees was as intrinsic and integral to the garden as the trickle of running water—their hum, no doubt, in Henry James's ears when he pronounced the words 'summer afternoon' the most beautiful in the English language. On a practical level, too, a beehive was obviously an asset. Bees were necessary to pollinate the flowers in the wild flower meadows, the fruit trees in the new orchard

---

* These events, it should be said, all occurred before the world was alerted to the worrying and yet-to-be-explained plight of the honey bee.

and, from the place I had in mind for them at the top of the hill behind the house, they'd also have ready access to the heather on the moor.

I knew nothing about honey bees. I wasn't at all sure I'd even recognise one. My mother enjoyed telling us she was a *qualified* beekeeper and had kept bees as a teenager during the war, though the experience appeared to have brought her little pleasure. Certainly, if my impression of the activity were anything to go by, it would be hard to imagine a person less temperamentally suited. 'They were a menace,' she'd tell us. 'They'd swarm just as we were sitting down to Sunday lunch.'

'They always seemed to need attention when there was clinker to be raked out of the Rayburn,' said my mother's younger sister, Aunty Ann, when I asked her about it. 'I certainly remember that.'

For all the ambrosial associations, however, there was no getting away from the fact that, when all was said and done, bees were still stinging insects. And I'd always been freaked out by stinging insects. Whether or not I'd have got over this mental block unaided, I don't know, but as it happened, I didn't have to. Shortly after we bought Tair-Ffynnon, one Sunday morning, a man's voice hailed us from the track below the house. It turned out to belong to Ray. He and his wife, Meryl, owned a cottage, Ty Bach, on the opposite side of the valley. Ray was in his seventies, a former company director. He had the slight stoop of many tall people, and there was something about this, combined with the regal set of his mouth, that suggested the Frog Footman from *Alice in Wonderland*. There was also a hint of CJ from *The Rise and Fall of Reginald Perrin*, in his grave, almost pantomime formality, in the way he said 'Ty Bach' when he answered the phone, as if it were 'Downing Street' or 'The Treasury'. We subsequently dropped in on them for a cup of tea during a rainy walk, whereupon two further facts emerged. One was that Meryl, a former teacher, was better at handling our children than we were. The other was that they kept bees.

That summer, I bumped into Ray at the Llanthony Show, of which I saw, by the gold-embossed cardboard disc on his lapel, he was a 'Vice

President'. He steered us to the local beekeeping association stall. I was still sufficiently disconcerted by the possibility of being stung not to have made any further steps towards beekeeping. But in the blazing sunshine, under the white canvas, with an old beehive giving off a heady aroma, simultaneously sweet, resinous and woody, thoughts of stings were banished and I found myself signing up for a course of evening classes early the following year. A fortnight later a brusque email arrived from Ray. He and Meryl would be 'taking the honey off' the following weekend, an opportunity to observe the most interesting moment in the beekeeping year. If I wished to join them, I should present myself at Ty Bach Saturday afternoon, 3.30 p.m. sharp.

'The first thing to do,' said Ray in a business-like voice, 'is to get you stung.'

Ray plainly enjoyed the role of apiarian mentor; none of his children had taken to beekeeping, and I got the impression he'd been awaiting this opportunity for some time. Warming cheerfully to his theme, he looked at me severely. 'Have you been stung by a bee before?'

'No, thank goodness. I was stung by a wasp last year, so hopefully—'

'Quite irrelevant. A wasp's sting is completely different. You're sure you've never been stung by a bee?'

'Don't think so. But—'

'Then we must try to get you stung this afternoon.' I'm sure there wasn't really any relish in his voice. 'We need to know what happens when you are. If you're allergic, you may not be able to keep bees at all. Even if you're alright, it may change. Meryl got stung last year after keeping bees for fifteen years and suddenly she started swelling up everywhere. We only just got her to A & E in time. Now she can't go near the bees again, which is why she isn't coming with us. In bee-keeping'—he fixed me with a stern glare—'you can very easily get yourself killed.' He produced a sheaf of laminated cards: diagrams of

153

prostrate humans with arrows and instructions, like airline safety cards. 'See these?' He flicked through them. They outlined summary symptoms of histamine reactions, steps for injecting noradrenaline, emergency resuscitation procedures, directions to be read by emergency services should one's twitching body be discovered in the hedgerow by a passerby. The last card, smaller, simply bore his name, address and telephone number on a loop of chain.

'God—a dog tag. Like soldiers have.'

'By the time you reach hospital you may be unable to speak. It's just a sensible precaution.' There was no doubt about it. Ray was enjoying himself.

I'd arrived punctually at the agreed time, to find Ray already in his bee suit and impatience in the air. The cottage had been stripped for action. Newspapers covered every square inch of the stone flags. The kitchen resembled an expertly dressed film set of Edwardian England. A big cylindrical metal drum the size of an upended garden roller sat on a wooden stand. It had an iron hand crank on the top. A narrower, taller metal tank, like a caterer's tea urn, stood on the kitchen worktop. Above a heavy brass tap at its base was taped a note saying 'TURN OFF' in big letters. Ray noticed me looking at it. 'Honey is SILENT,' he said, as if I'd just contradicted him. 'You don't hear it. It's not like a dripping tap. It's very easy to fail to close a tap fully. Next thing you know, honey's all over the floor.'

The room was almost unbearably hot and stuffy, as if the central heating had stuck on despite it being late-August. All the windows were hermetically sealed.

'You may notice something about this room?' Ray demanded.

'Er ... it's all set up ready? You're expecting to make a lot of mess?' It seemed rude to mention the stuffiness.

'The TEMPERATURE. Can't you feel how warm it is? Hmm, you're not very observant. Bad sign. Beekeepers need to be *very* observant. The radiators are on. The windows are shut. We've turned up the stove. Why? Because for honey to flow, it must be warm.'

Despite the severity of my tutor, I was beginning to enjoy myself. The kit was better than I'd dared hope. In that whitewashed stone room, with its deep-set windows looking onto the green, sheep-dotted slopes of the Black Mountains, it was a beguiling scene. Apart from Ray's mobile and the fridge there was no evidence of the twenty-first century at all. I'd been ordered to wear long trousers and a long-sleeved shirt ('not too thick. You'll be hot inside a bee suit') and to bring a pair of washing-up gloves and wellington boots. Ray looked me up and down. 'You're taller than I remember. How tall are you?'

'About six one.'

'Hmmm.' I waited for Ray to comment further, half-expecting this problem to require a solution. 'Come on. Come on,' he snapped. 'Get your suit on.' He indicated a beekeeper's suit draped over the sofa back. The material felt soft and pliable from countless washes, and disarmingly thin. Once, clearly, it had been white, but now it was almost brown, it was so rubbed and stained. There were a worrying number of gaps: holes, small tears, wrenched zips, through which, it seemed to me, a determined bee would have little difficulty in finding its way. Ray was also correct in his concern about my height. As I pulled the suit over my shoulders, a two-inch stretch of bare calf appeared between the top of my socks and the elasticated bottoms of the bee suit, while the elasticated cuffs ended two inches above my wrists. These expanses widened as I pulled the masked hood over my head.

'There's a bit of a gap.' I didn't want to seem alarmist, but this seemed to write off any trip to the bees.

'Don't worry about that. Bees go upwards, remember.' This, apparently, was meant to reassure me. I slid my foot—and gaping stretch of bare leg—into my wellingtons, while Meryl zipped round the head of the suit with its characteristic gauze mask. She hovered round me, tugging and tucking, zipping and adjusting. Meanwhile, Ray, having pulled on rubber Marigolds, was securing the ends with elastic bands, making loud snapping noises.

'Have you had a pee? We may be some time.'

There's nothing like being sealed into an unwieldy suit with endless finicky poppers and fasteners to make you want a pee.

'Come on. *Come on.*' Ray grasped a wooden box of miscellaneous items: a blowtorch, coils of baler twine, a squeezy houseplant sprayer, odd-shaped tools and packets. It looked like a wine box, a suspicion confirmed by the words 'Avery's of Bristol' stencilled down the side. 'No smoker?' I asked. This was a disappointment. I'd hoped for the full authentic beekeeping experience. Ray's face fell. 'Meryl! The smoker! I've forgotten the smoker!' Dropping the kit box, he groped behind the sofa and produced a device shaped like an old-fashioned oil jug, attached to a bellows mechanism. Peeling off his Marigolds, he opened the woodburner and held a coil of baler twine from his kit box in the flames. When it caught, still flaming, he stuffed it into the smoker, closed the tin lid with a click, and started pumping the bellows mechanism. A plume of smoke issued from the spout. After several more brisk squeezes, the smoke thickened.

'What's the smoke actually for?'

The authority returned. 'Well, what do you think?'

'Calms them down?'

'Correct. Makes them think there's a forest fire. So what do they do? They make straight for their honey reserves and gorge themselves ready to flee the hive. Eating honey makes them docile.'

I was entrusted with the smoker ('Squeeze it now and then to make sure it's still going'). Then, resembling a pair of extras from *28 Days Later*, we proceeded to the car. The back was lined with newspaper, just like the kitchen, and contained what looked like two bottomless wooden wine boxes. 'Put the smoker in there.' He indicated a lidless cake tin. 'Many a car's been set on fire by one of those.' As we set off, I was already overheating, so I opened the window. 'Close the window, please.'

'Why? Will bees get in?'

'You'll just forget to do so otherwise.'

Ray's metamorphosis to a martinet made him curiously relaxing company. I just had to do as I was told. We bumped the few hundred yards across an adjoining field of sloping pasture. Tucked into the top corner, in the shade of an overgrown hazel hedge, surrounded by clumps of nettles, was a wired-off enclosure. Some cattle harrumphed out of our away as we parked, but as we got out their curiosity got the better of them and they turned back towards us, craning their necks and exhaling loudly through wet nostrils. There was the rich summer smell of fresh cow pats, the whirr of orange dung flies. Ray checked all the windows were shut, then fiddled with the gate into the bee enclosure, where I could see, in a row, five tall, old-fashioned-looking hives in peeling white paint. 'There, did you see that?' His voice acquired a note of urgency. There was an angry whining around my face and an insect cannoned into the gauze of my bee suit. 'That's a guard bee. Probably he can smell me from yesterday. And he doesn't like it a bit.'

'What do they do? Tell everyone else we're here?'

'Correct.'

Between the hives, on sections of railway sleepers, sat jars with holes in the lids.

'What are those?'

'Wasp traps.' Wasps and bees, apparently, were sworn enemies.

Halfway down the row, Ray lifted a roof off one of the hives. I craned forwards to peek in. It turned out not to contain bees at all. It was a store cupboard full of miscellaneous packets, Tupperware boxes, jam jars with labels, plastic milk bottles labelled 'SUGAR SYRUP, WINTER FEED', cloths, tools and other bits and pieces. I half-expected to see a bottle of whisky.

Ray lifted off the bricks weighing down the shallow pitched roofs of each hive, then lifted off one of the roofs. 'Out of my way, please.' He swivelled through 180 degrees and perched it on the opposite side of the path. 'You're constantly in the way. Could you stand over there, please?' He then lifted off the rest of the outer walls or 'lifts' of the double-walled hive, revealing an inner case. He cupped his hands under the whole of this and tilted it back a couple of inches. 'There ... now go on ... you try.' I mimicked his action.

'Heavy.'

'Correct. Just as it should be. That's called *hefting* the hive. Seeing how heavy it is. If it's heavy it means there's plenty of honey. I'd say there's twenty to thirty pounds in here.' He produced a small metal tool, chisel one end, jemmy the other, about nine inches long. He brandished it under my nose. 'This is a "hive tool". You use it for every-thing—opening the lid, separating the supers, unsticking the frames. The bees gum everything together with stuff called propolis.' He inserted the blade under the plywood inner lid of the hive and prised it upwards. There was a sharp crack as it came away. 'That's the propolis seal breaking. Now, yesterday I put in a "clearing board". That's a sort of bee valve. It allows bees out, but not in, so there'll be hardly any bees in here. Usually, of course, it would be teeming with them.' He lifted the lid up. It was teeming with bees.

'Err ... hmm ... hmmph ... how odd.'

Inside the 'super', which was essentially four sides of a wooden box, without the base or top, twelve wooden frames of honeycomb hung from wooden lugs like suspension files, bees crawling all over them. Ray inserted his hive tool beneath this super and the next one down. There was another loud crack as it was freed from the one beneath. Then he lifted the whole super up, frames of honeycomb, bees and all, and banged it on the top of a nearby fence post. It seemed a lunatic action. Cascades of bees dropped out of the bottom, and took furiously to the air. The place swarmed with apoplectic insects. Not yet used to the idea that I was protected, I recoiled into my bee suit. 'Is that wise?'

'Nothing else for it,' he said. There was a new tension in Ray's voice, but it was hard to gauge how serious a setback this was. On the hillside opposite, the lattice of hedges and walls was acquiring shadows as the afternoon glare began to soften into the glow of early evening. With his hive tool, Ray prised one of the frames from the super. 'Look at that. Capped honey.' Most of the little hexagonal chambers, apart from round the edges, were sealed over with wax.

'That's good?'

'You won't see a better frame than that. Why, there must be two pounds in this frame alone.'

After shaking most of the bees off the frame, he handed it to me and rummaged in his kit box. He reappeared with a large feather. 'Know what this is?'

'A feather?'

'A *goose* feather. Vital beekeeping equipment.'

Ray brushed and chivvied the remaining bees off the frame with the feather as if it were a highly technical operation; then he placed the frame in the empty box we'd brought from the car. 'Right. You do the next one.' He handed me the hive tool. I prised out the next frame and so we went on, until the hive was finished. By now, bees were buzzing around us in clouds. Great clusters, I noticed, covered Ray's back and arms.

'Ow!' he said.

'What happened?'

'Nothing.'

'You got stung? Where?' He was examining his finger.

'There it is. See? The tip of my finger. That's the sting just there.' He pointed out a tiny black barb sticking out of the finger of his glove, and brushed it away. 'Stinging releases a pheromone which tells the bees they're under attack, so now there'll be more.' I was far too busy digesting the implications of the first sting, however, to think about subsequent ones.

'What ... they can sting *through the gloves?*'

'Yes, of course. Ow!' He rubbed his chin with his arm. 'The important thing is to get the sting out.' There was now an unsettling sense of being in the midst of insects on the war path. 'Where's the smoker?' He sprayed a puff of smoke into his face, then into mine, then a layer of smoke into the top of the hive. What had until moments before been an Elysian scene, now took on a different and sinister complexion. I no longer felt safe at all. Fortunately, as Ray moved to the second and third hives, the 'clearing boards' had been more successful, and it was the work of moments to reassemble the much-reduced hives, and carry the honey-laden supers to the car. A few persistent bees were ushered away, and Ray slammed the boot. 'That's the hard work done,' said Ray. 'Now we can relax a bit.'

In Ty Bach's stone kitchen, a quarter of an hour later, divested of gloves, wellies and bee suits, mug of tea in hand, we succumbed to an expectant hush as Ray took a sample frame of the honeycomb and ritually sawed the wax capping off with a carving knife. Then, like a Master of Wine, he bent down until his nose was practically touching the sticky amber goo dribbling onto the worktop. He closed his eyes and inhaled deeply. 'Is it?' whispered Meryl. The atmosphere was suddenly so pregnant with expectation I was reminded of the Man from Del Monte ads.

'It's heather honey,' whispered Ray. ('The man from Del Monte—he say "Yes!"')

Heather flowered in August, and gave honey an especially charac-teristic flavour, Meryl explained. Tomorrow they'd extract it with the big old centrifuge (the drum with the iron crank), strain it into the metal tank (the 'ripener'), then once it had 'settled', bottle it in one-pound glass jars. There was an intoxicating old-world charm to it all, to the baler twine and smoker, the old wine boxes and Ray's goose feather and Ty Bach's stone-flagged kitchen, even to Ray and Meryl themselves, Ray now haranguing me benignly from beneath a battered panama. It didn't occur to me for a moment that this scene was as artfully propped as a Sunday night detective series, that the honey might more easily have been collected using an electric centrifuge of polythene and stainless steel. So with my illusions intact, I got up to leave, convinced that bee-keeping was just as it was supposed to be.

'If you take up beekeeping, of course, you'll need a gurrer,' said Ray.

'A gurrer?'

'Yes, a gurrer.'

Doubtless it was some specialist item of beekeeping equipment. I'd learn about it soon enough on my course in the spring. For the moment,

I felt I'd learnt quite enough for one afternoon. 'Sorry we didn't get you stung,' said Ray. 'Still', he said, brightening slightly, 'plenty of time for that.'

———— ‹•›‹•›‹•› ————

The surroundings for my beekeeping course the following February, in Pontypool, could hardly have been in starker contrast to Ray and Meryl's pitch-perfect idyll. The Torfaen People's Centre in Trosnant House was as municipal as it sounds, a brick hall and tarmac car park, kerbed and planted with berberis and other tough-looking, charmless plants, reached by a series of bypasses and roundabouts.

Sixteen of us, mainly men, mostly between forty and sixty, sat at tables in a ragged semi-circle around an overhead projector. Two or three had the weatherbeaten complexions of those used to working outdoors. Our first talk ('Life in the Beehive') was by a woman, but it soon became clear that our presiding spirit was a mysterious figure called John. His name continually cropped up as the supreme authority on bee matters, whether on questions of currency of data, prevailing agronomic theory, Defra directives, or matters of apiarian history and law. 'You'd have to ask John'; 'John would know that'; 'We'll check with John.' Yet for the first three lectures we saw not a glimpse of this hallowed mortal. On our third evening ('The Beekeeper's Year'), a question that prompted the lecturer to respond: 'Well, I don't know. What d'you think John?' indicated that the great man was in our midst. However, as the room was in darkness, by Week Four I still hadn't an inkling who he was.

All was revealed, however, in Week Five ('Things That Can Go Wrong'), when John took the lectern himself, He had the lugubrious physiognomy of a bloodhound, as if his head had been moulded in beeswax and then inadvertently left a little too long in the sun. In his mid-sixties, he was (it was now revealed) no less than the ex-County Bee Inspector. In fact his recent enforced retirement from this exalted government office, due to statutory age limits, was, we soon learnt, one of the greater iniquities of our time, prompting regular swipes about imbecilic new procedures and declining Ministry standards. John was, it went without saying, a towering figure within the Gwent Beekeepers Association.

As for the theoretical side, there was a good deal more to the working of a colony of bees than I'd realised. The gist (and there was no shortage of jokes about the matter) was that the females (the 'workers') did all the work, while the larger males (the 'drones') did little except hang around waiting to fertilise the Queen. Given the endless British cultural claims on honey and bees, from Rupert Brooke to Winnie-the-Pooh, I'd rather assumed that the British invented modern beekeeping, so it was a surprise to learn this couldn't be further from the truth. America, Germany, Austria and France all had made their mark, but the sole British contribution, when it came down to it, was the 'beehive-shaped' beehive that every Brit associates with the word, and which Ray had, but which hardly anyone else now used.*

Little was made of stings. Indeed, for the first five weeks of the course you might have thought that getting stung wasn't even a hazard connected to the activity. In a short film (with an appropriately crackly soundtrack and lurid 1970s colours), we watched beekeepers not using any gloves at all. It transpired that many beekeepers didn't. Only after

---

* The American Reverend L. L. Langstroth came up with the first re-usable beehive (patented in 1852), allegedly adapted from an empty case of champagne, improving the ideas of a Swiss and a German. It was another German who introduced the moulded wax 'foundation' that helps bees make comb. A French abbot invented the wire mesh 'Queen Excluder' that separates the egg-laying from the honey storage area. An Austrian devised centrifugal honey extraction. Another American made the first smoker, and a third invented the 'bee valves' like those on Ray's 'clearing boards'. A German collected the 1973 Nobel Prize for elucidating the dances by which bees communicate with each other. The Englishman William Broughton Carr's double-walled hive (plans published 1890) didn't catch on elsewhere, and is now confined to diehard romantics, because its double wall means twice as much lifting and handling.

lengthy discussion of hive diseases and other problems did John make a cursory mention of severe allergic reactions to stings.

At the end of his talk, John announced that he knew of two hives of bees that had become available. Was anyone interested? I expected a forest of hands. But it was still March, and I remember reflecting, as I picked my way between the puddles of the car park afterwards, through the sodium-lit night, how very far I still was from being able to take up such an offer. Clutching my collection of desultory notes, plus a wad of stupefying Defra handouts about bee diseases, the very idea of a colony of bees under my charge seemed absurd. It had become clear from the first week's gallop through the lifecycle of the honey bee that some extra-curricular reading was crucial. But despite my best intentions (I definitely enjoyed flicking through the catalogues of beekeeping equipment), there never seemed time to fit it in between one week and the next.

At a practical day, a fortnight later, John repeated his offer of bees. In the intervening two weeks, the clocks had gone forwards, the days were lighter and longer and there were signs of spring in the fields and hedges. Somehow, having my own buzzing colony no longer seemed quite so unthinkable, and it struck me that it must be far easier getting someone else's hives, complete with bees, than having to order a flat-pack and start from scratch. John didn't know how much was wanted for them, but thought £100 sounded about right, which he said would be remarkable value for two hives and two colonies. I said I'd have them. 'Well done,' he said, noticing me properly for the first time. 'Only way to learn is by doing it. I'll help you get them.'

——◆——

On the designated day, I got up early to prepare for the bees' arrival. John had said he'd call to confirm our meeting time, and, as he was being so kind, it seemed only right to be ready. Initially, I'd selected a spot at the top of the Top Field, so the bees would be out of harm's way and have easy access to the moor for heather. But Ray had pronounced this unsatisfactory: too exposed in winter, too hot in summer. 'You're not yet thinking like a bee,' he said. 'What books have you read? Hamilton? De Bruyn? Waring? Have you subscribed to *Beecraft*? You won't learn by *osmosis* you know. And have you got a gurrer yet?'

That word again. I scoured my memory but, inattentive as I'd been, I felt sure I'd have remembered it if it had been mentioned. 'I haven't bought any kit yet,' I explained. 'I thought I'd get the bees first, then—'

'No, no, a *gurrer*,' he said impatiently. 'Someone you can call for help, someone to help you.'

The penny dropped. 'Oh, a *guru* ... No. Well, in fact, come to think of it, yes—you.'

'I can't possibly be. I'm not here enough,' said Ray. But I think he secretly quite liked the idea.

Ray had eventually specified somewhere for the hives lower down, in the lee of a row of thorns growing on a stone bank. It seemed a slightly odd place to me—until, standing back, I realised the hives would be pleasingly framed by Sugar Loaf behind.

There I'd dug beehive-sized steps into the rising ground and laid some broken concrete lintels for the hives to sit on. By ten o'clock I was ready for John's call as to where we should meet. By lunchtime, having tried him twice more, I began to wonder if he'd forgotten our assignment. When four o'clock came and I'd still heard nothing, I rang again. No answer. At six o'clock, I tried again, then again at seven. By this point it was evident our rendezvous was off, and I couldn't help feeling mildly frustrated. At 7.45, John finally called. 'Where shall we meet then?' No apology or even a word of explanation. 'Shall we say half past eight?' The man either kept curious hours or had a very relaxed attitude to time.

'Shouldn't we have met a bit sooner?' I said. I didn't want to sound ungracious, but daylight was running out. 'It'll be dark if we don't get a move on.'

'Yes, that's the idea.'

'But ... wouldn't it be easier in daylight?' I tried to keep the sarcasm out of my voice.

'You mean collect the hives while the bees are all out in the fields?'

Well, really. How was I supposed to know?

A few days later, the bees safely installed at Tair-Ffynnon, I was sunning myself at the Hay Festival with Gerry, a friend from our previous London existence who was staying for the weekend, when I received an agitated call from Vez. 'Something weird's happening round the new hive near the house,' she said. 'There are bees everywhere.'

'Which new hive?' There weren't any new hives. There was just a heap of empty hive parts I'd dumped by the front door and not yet put away.

'The one by the front door.'

'That's not a hive.'

'Well, I don't care what it is. There are bees all over it and more arriving every second. They're everywhere, and they seem pretty pissed off if we go anywhere near. We can't use the front door. The only way we can get in or out is through the kitchen window. What do we do?'

What indeed? Obviously my new bees—I assumed they must be my bees—had discovered the spare hive parts with disconcerting efficiency. But what could they be up to? Had they swarmed and moved into one of the spare brood boxes or supers? My knowledge of swarming was virtually non-existent. Ray had quizzed me on the subject a couple of times, but always cut any answer short with one of his complicated analogies. 'Listen. The peasants are rising; they're fed up with the old Queen. She gets wind of it and decides to leave. She takes with her a number of her courtiers. The Lord Chancellor, the Lord Chamberlain, the Gentlemen of the Bedchamber, the Lord Privy Seal ... who does she leave? *All the rest.* Her subjects. The commoners. The *plebeians.* But the plebeians are crafty. They know she is leaving. They've made Queen cells, six or seven of them.' At this point Ray leant closer, tapping my arm at the looming denouement. 'And, like royalty throughout history, what does the first-born new Queen do? Well? What does she do?'

'Er ...' History was never my strong point.

'She kills her rivals, that's what she does. How? She stings them. The Queen is the only bee which can sting and survive.'

I always struggled with Ray's Royal Household analogies. 'Who goes and who stays?' I'd ask. 'The Queen takes the Prime Minister ...?'

'No, no, you don't listen ...' and round we'd go again.

But short of a swarm, what could it be? I tried John, and then Ray, but neither answered. One thing was certain, however: there was no point hurrying back until I'd found out from them what to do. So I congratulated Vez on her cool handling of the situation and went in to another of the festival's talks.

By the time Gerry and I got back, around midnight, things seemed to have quietened down. We were able to enter through the front door, but Vez made it clear she was not impressed with my beekeeping, her indignation stoked by Gerry, who enthusiastically imagined the horrors that might have befallen her and the children. 'You might very well have all been killed,' he said with relish.

Warily I approached the various hive casings outside the front door with a torch, prodding at them with a stick. There was no sign of life. Probably my bees—were they my bees? Surely they must be?—had smelt the honey and wax on the spare hives and told their friends about it, who'd dropped by to check it out. It had no doubt looked a bit alarming to Vez and the children but, so long as I moved the stuff first thing in the morning, all would be well.

After breakfast, when the day was still cool, I put on the bee suit John had lent me. Already bees were buzzing around the heap outside the front door. 'Goodness, d'you have to wear a safety suit like that?' said Gerry. 'These creatures are that dangerous?'

Carefully I lifted away the various hive parts. Then I raised the lid of the deeper brood box that seemed to be at the centre of the trouble. Inside was a strange and terrifying sight. The box was alive with thousands of insects. I don't know *why* it was so freaky, given that I'd seen something similar in a beehive numerous times now. But there was something unnerving in the thought that these insects were not in a controlled situation. They were feral creatures following their own agenda. As for the speed with which they'd discovered their new home, that was even creepier. I felt the primal, clammy fear I recalled experiencing as a child while watching my father remove a big wasps' nest, with its sinister cocoon shape. But at least one thing was cleared up. There was no doubt it was a swarm. 'God,' said a voice behind me. 'It's like *The Naked Jungle*.' Gerry, I discovered, was peering over my shoulder. We climbed back through the kitchen window, shutting it tightly behind us. 'Someone should have warned you about this,' he said. 'These things are clearly very dangerous.' Gerry was not someone to waste a drama.

Finally, I got through to John.

'Yes, that's a swarm,' he said laconically. 'That'll teach you not to put things away properly.'

The day was saved by Mervyn. It so happened he was up that morning to look over the Fergie's bar mower and baler for me.

'Where are they, Antney?'

I pointed to the danger zone. Mervyn walked over and lifted the lid.
'Careful, Mervyn.'

'Don't worry, Antney. Used to keep a few bees myself.' Of course he did. And in the same moment a neat solution occurred.

'Mervyn, you wouldn't like these bees would you?'

'Well, that's very kind of you, Antney. But don't you want them?'

'No ... no. They're yours for the taking.' I might be losing a few of my new bees, but frankly I had more than enough to be going on with.

'That'd be grand, Antney. Why don't you bring 'em down this evening?' This was less satisfactory.

'Er ... bring them down? How?'

'Aw, just wrap 'em in a sheet. Wrap 'em in a sheet good an' tidy.'

'Wrap them in a sheet?'

'That's right. Put a sheet round 'em, knot it up, bring 'em down an' we'll go from there.'

'Well, Antony, there you are,' said Gerry delightedly when Mervyn had left. 'That's all you have to do. Just knot them up in a sheet and drop them round to Mervyn tonight. What a shame I won't be here to watch you do it.'

Somehow, as the sun set—with the children in bed, Gerry returned to London, and Vez snoozing in front of the television, without Ray or John to give advice—my bee suit felt scant protection as I tiptoed up to the swarm. With a feather touch born of undiluted fear, I delicately removed the first section from the pile of hives. As I wasn't sure how far the 'infestation' extended, the only thing seemed to be to reduce the heap bit by bit, disturbing them as little as possible in the process, like a live game of Jenga, where one false move would release a lethal cloud of killer insects. Carefully I lifted away supers, brood boxes, hive lids and nameless other items until just the one rogue brood box remained. I stopped up the entrance with a tea towel as I'd watched John do a few nights earlier, laid out the sheet, then backed up the Land Rover.

The hive relied on gravity alone to keep it together, with nothing to prevent the base and top from sliding apart. Lifting it as if it were a primed thermonuclear device, I got it onto the sheet, pulled it up and knotted it securely. This boosted my confidence, so a little more boldly I picked up the bundle, placed it on the tailgate of the Land Rover and slid it inside. At least, that's what I intended to do. Unfortunately, in the process, I snagged the base on the uneven surface between the tailgate and the interior. The base and brood box separated, and my attempts to reunite them produced the unmistakeable sound of crunching insects. A dynamo hum started to issue from the bundle. Ignoring it, I set off down the track. With every jolt of the Land Rover's suspension—and there were many—there was an accompanying rise in the note emitted from the box behind me, as if someone were gradually turning up the dial of a power station.

Was Mervyn wearing shorts? I can't now be absolutely sure. But I remember thinking he wasn't wearing anything like enough clothing. His sleeves were rolled up, his shirt was open at least three buttons and there was certainly no sign of hat, veil, boots or gloves. 'Well done Antney, well done,' he said, unhitching the tailgate and picking up the bundle. Feeling like the only person at the party in fancy dress, I followed him into the darkness behind a tractor shed, clutching my torch and smoker. In front of an ancient hive, Mervyn had put down a ply-wood ramp up to the entrance. 'We'll just drop 'em onto the grass there,' said Mervyn. 'Shine the torch in front of the ramp there, Antney.' Then he undid the sheet, picked the box up and shook it over the pool of light. Thousands of testy bees fell onto the grass. Thousands more rose in a furious cloud around us.

'What now?' I shouted above the roar of the insects.

'They go up the ramp. We get ourselves a cup of coffee. Doesn't always work, but usually does.'

And he was right. By the time we returned fifteen minutes later, the bees had almost all settled onto the ground, formed a wide column and were marching like a moving carpet up the ramp into their new home. It was an extraordinary sight.

'You've got to say it,' said Mervyn, and I knew his greatest term of approval was about to follow. 'Fair play to 'em.'

———◆———

The main event of Llanthony Valley and District Show, for which people travel from well beyond the show's nominal catchment area, is not the cattle or sheep classes, or the sheep-shearing or the fell-running or the horse stuff, or even the stalls and produce tents. Nor is it the imaginative and artfully mounted floats. No, the main event of the day—which nobody can ever believe has survived another year—is the justly celebrated pony rodeo. Heralded by a thunderous clatter of hooves, followed by the sound of splintering wood as the high-sided 'crate', a sort of stock crush, is called into commission on one side of the main showring, the rodeo pitches wild ponies herded off the hill against anyone courageous, foolish or drunk enough to risk their necks.* Most contestants are unceremoniously disposed of in less than two seconds. To witness this amiable raspberry to Health and Safety, people come miles.

This year, however, it was not the pony rodeo that attracted me to the Llanthony Show; it was a section I usually gave a wide berth to: the produce tent. Because alongside the prizes for flowers and vegetables and homemade cakes was a category I'd quietly had my eye on since the bees had first arrived: 'Class 66—one pound of honey'.

I'd designated the preceding Monday afternoon for collecting the honey-filled frames from the hives, Tuesday for 'extracting', Wednesday and Thursday for letting it 'ripen' (strain and settle), Friday for bottling the stuff, and on the Saturday morning planned to get up early to apply the 'Secret Tips' I'd been given by Kath, from whom I'd rented the Gwent Beekeepers' centrifugal extractor. Two cases of new glass jars sat

---

* 'Each competitor will be asked to perform a co-ordination test to make sure he/she is not inebriated'—from the Programme rules.

ready. The fine weather continued and on the Tuesday, on schedule, I collected five honey-laden supers from the two hives.

These now sat on the draining board, leaking silently. With all external doors and windows now sealed according to Ray's instructions, the Aga going full blast and the sun blazing outside, the heat was suffocating. But the house was suffused with that incomparable scent. The floor was lined with newspaper. The centrifugal 'spinner' was set up on blocks in the middle of the room. The polythene 'ripener', with its double strainer and plastic tap, was on the draining board (not so charming as Ray's tin version but, Kath assured me, more in line with prevailing food hygiene standards).

With a bread knife, I tentatively started sawing the wax capping off the first frame. In seconds it was gummed into a hopeless morass of gooey gunk. Honey ran down the knife handle over my fingers and down my wrist. I scraped the blade on the side of a bowl. Honey dribbled down the side of it, collecting in little pools on the table while I turned over the frame, now haemorrhaging honey freely, and repeated the action on the opposite side. The thus uncapped frame could now be transferred to the spinner. I tried to do this quickly, but it still left little trails of honey across the table and floor. The spinner took two frames, so I now repeated the operation, by the end of which I realised I'd never felt a greater desire to wash my hands. This I did, but having turned the tap on with my sticky fingers, and having to turn it off again afterwards, I finished only slightly less sticky than before.

Transferring my attentions to the spinner, I cranked vigorously for thirty seconds, before opening the lid to reverse each frame. Returning to the crank (hands back up to full stickiness), I did another thirty seconds' vigorous cranking. In this way, the uncapped honey in the comb was hurled out by centrifugal force, splattered against the side of the drum, whence it dripped down to collect in the base, there to be drained off with a tap. The cranking was surprisingly hard work, enough to generate beads of perspiration in the hothouse atmosphere. These I wiped with kitchen towel, only to find that in the process I'd transferred

honey onto my forehead. I removed the two 'harvested' but still unbelievably sticky frames and placed them in an empty super, so they
could continue oozing onto a new part of the kitchen. Meanwhile I
seized the bread knife to uncap the next two frames, and so the whole
process began again.

Vez, who'd been observing this procedure for a quarter of an hour,
pointed out that, with sixty frames to do, unless I speeded up considerably the operation was going to take seven hours. Obviously, some
kind of production line was required. Vez decided she'd work the spinner, while I removed the cappings. After twenty minutes of this, honey
had somehow transferred itself from the direct zones of operation—
knife, table, spinner, draining board—to many other surfaces. In fact,
every incidental action, such as scratching an itch, boiling the kettle or
opening the door spread the sticky zone ever wider. Attempts to move
around the room became accompanied by the sound of tearing newspaper, as sections of our carefully laid floor covering came up with the
soles of our shoes.

This was the stage we were at when the phone rang. It was Jonny,
announcing his intention of coming over to put the mower on the Fergie
ready for cutting the hay. 'Not ideal,' I said.

'Why not? It's a lovely evening. What could be more ideal?' Jonny
was not someone to be put off by the casual whims of others.

'We're trying to extract the honey from our new bees.'

'Bees? When did you get bees?'

'A few weeks ago.'

'What does extracting the honey involve?'

'We're not sure. But it's messy.'

'How long does it take?'

'We don't know that either.'

Vez was mouthing 'No. No. No way. Absolutely not' and waving
her hands around.

'Why don't I come over? You'll finish quicker if I help. Then we
can get on with the Fergie.'

'Hmm ...' It was far from clear how useful Jonny's help was likely to be in our present circumstances. 'How about tomorrow?'

'Hmm ... tomorrow, tomorrow,' he said. 'I'm in the mood tonight. It's lovely weather. It might not be tomorrow.'

'Well, the day after, then. Anytime—just not tonight.'

'We'll see.'

'He's not coming, is he?' said Vez, as I put the phone down.

'You heard what I said.' At that moment I was more concerned with trying to get honey off the phone keypad. Her short spell on the spinner had convinced Vez that uncapping was what she really wished to do, so she demanded to hand back to me. Certainly working the spinner in the heat was arduous, sweaty and back-aching. The heavy frames had to be spun slowly to start with, to avoid damage, first one way, then the other, then the operation repeated at greater speed. We'd also hopelessly underestimated the quantity of scraped cappings and were constantly having to go in search of larger dishes, each expedition to another room leaving another sticky trail behind us.

Jonny arrived around seven. At that moment, I was involved in the intricate task of decanting honey from the bottom of the spinner into the double strainer at the top of the ripener. 'What an incredible mess,' he said. 'You need to open a window. It's like an oven in here.'

It has to be said, our spirits were flagging. There were still twenty frames to go. We pressed Jonny into service on the spinner. 'I can't believe honey in the shops is got this way,' he said. 'It wouldn't be worth it. You must be doing something wrong.'

Our one solace was the steadily filling ripener. The level of the clear brown fluid, filtered free of the particles of wax and bees' wings that floated at the base of the spinner, was now nearly two feet deep, with plenty more still in the sieves above it. Twice Jonny threw open the windows, and had to be ordered to shut them. 'Why?'

'Because the honey's got to be kept warm, so it's runny. And because otherwise the bees will smell it and mount a recovery raid.' In truth, however, those blasts of cool air were life-saving.

'Christmas,' said Jonny. 'I'm going to look at the Fergie.'

By now we were almost drunk on the rich, heavy scent of honey and five hours of moving around the house, of putting the children to bed, of visiting the loo and getting periodic gulps of air, meant that every surface had an adhesive tape tackiness to it—handles of all kinds, light switches, taps, floors and stairs, banisters, even towels.

But at last it was done. The final frame was taken from the spinner and returned to a sticky super. We drained the spinner into the honey ripener. We collected up the newspapers on the floor and burnt them, wiping every surface, and washing our hands for the hundredth time. The ripener was now almost full: six and a half gallons. Even Jonny was impressed. It was the colour of pale straw, and had a slightly tea-like aftertaste. We all agreed it was by far the best honey there had ever been.

Next morning, we were upstairs getting the children dressed when Jonny, who'd slept in the brake van, arrived in the kitchen for breakfast. When I came downstairs, to my surprise, all the windows were open. Jonny, sprinkling toast crumbs and honey, waved his knife cheerfully. 'This waxy honey, the stuff you cut off with the knife, is delicious. I might take a jar or two.'

'Who opened all these windows?'

'I did. I assumed it was alright now you've done the honey.' He glanced at his watch. 'I must be off.'

We can't have been outside more than a few minutes saying goodbye, but it was enough. When we came back into the kitchen, it was to an almost biblical scene. The air was dense with airborne bees. They were settled on every surface, waggling their bottoms in every nook and cranny. Hundreds more covered the sticky supers of empty, extracted frames. They lined the rim of the honey ripener, to which we'd forgotten to attach the lid, floating drunkenly in its contents. They were

crawling over the table and draining board.
Worse, more were arriving so fast that, as
we rushed to shut the windows, there were
loud thuds against the glass. Much had
been made on our course of the remarkable
communications skills of bees, the little
dances that told each other where the nectar was,
but I hadn't ever expected to witness quite such dramatic proof.

'Who opened the windows?' said Vez.

The window glass was now dark with crawling insects desperate to
get in. Where the window frames had rotted, leaving gaps, bees welled
out from every crevice. Opening the cupboard under the sink released
a cloud of bees where they'd found a gap round the cold water inlet.
Pulling on my bee suit, for half an hour I hectically plugged gaps with
wet dishcloths and scooped up dustpans of bees to release outside.
Gradually, the word seemed to get round: free honey was no longer
available. The numbers arriving slowed. The windows began to clear.
Vez finally deemed it safe to enter. 'D'you think this happens to Ray
and Meryl?' she said.

———◦⊶⊷◦———

As the morning of Llanthony Show dawned, I shook off the horrors of
the preceding days. All that remained was to put into practice Kath's
Secret Tips for competition victory:

1 Remove any scum with a teaspoon.
2. Holding a finger over the end of a straw, remove all tiny air bubbles.
3. Wash the jar with detergent to remove any stickiness.
4. Take a clean lid to replace the lid sticky from transit.

As I wasn't due at the show for gate duty until midday, and the
produce category had to be in place for judging by nine o'clock, I drove

175

my precious cargo down to the farm at the bottom of the hill to give to Liz, Mark's wife, who had to be there early. It went severely against the grain to hand it over to a third party, and I made Liz repeat back to me exactly what she was to do with the spare lid I'd supplied, hoping this would impress upon her the importance of her mission.

Judging was still underway, with the entrance roped off, when I took over on the gate, after which I didn't have time to give the matter another thought. Gate duty was a hectic business once the noon rush commenced. There wasn't a moment's respite until, in the mid-afternoon, Vez came to find me. 'Heard the news from the produce tent?'

'What? *What?*'

'Well, the children came third with their garden on a plate.'

'Yes, yes …'

'My floral centrepiece was disqualified, unbelievably.'

'*And …?*'

'And what?'

'What about the bloody honey?'

'Oh babe … *we won!*'

She flung her arms round me and gave me one of her thousand-watt grins. And sure enough, when I made my way to the main tent, there was my unmarked jar of honey, alongside a red FIRST PRIZE certificate.

Honesty compels me to admit that the class only consisted of two. (The other entrant was Ray.) And I also have to admit to feeling more than a little fraudulent taking the credit: the truth was that the well-managed colonies I'd inherited, 'unharvested', the previous year, probably had most of their honey in them before they came up the hill in the back of John's car.

Still. First prize is first prize.

12

How not to mow
a meadow

Many gardeners like the concept of an area devoted to
meadow ... If you do the right things at the right time,
it is all very simple.

CHRISTOPHER LLOYD, *Guardian*, 2 August 2003

In retrospect, I don't think my desire to make hay with old machines
was half as odd as everyone tried to make out. Hay-making has been
part of nostalgic fantasies of pastoral bliss since Theocritus came up with
his *Idylls* in Ancient Greece, and the idea has been ripped off and
rehashed by any number of romantics since—from Roman poets to
English composers. There's hardly a British country memoir which
doesn't involve some lyrical passage about hay-making, generally
including salt-of-the-earth farmhands and parched throats relieved by
life-giving jugs of cider. The most celebrated is probably Hilaire Belloc's
essay 'The Mowing of a Field', written in 1921, where with shameless

177

sentimentality he wallows in the delights of dawn and birdsong, and locals who say 'Ar', the ring of a sharpened blade and the skills involved in an ancient activity. ('When I got out into the long grass the sun was not yet risen, but there were already many colors in the eastern sky, and I made haste to sharpen my scythe, so that I might get to the cutting before the dew should dry.') Yet Belloc, with his two Sussex acres (plus windmill), was the archetypal hobby farmer, had not the slightest need for hay, and could far more sensibly have paid someone to do his mowing for him. He was doing it for every reason except that he needed a decent crop of hay—principally a kind of consummation of his love of England, summertime, landscape and the old ways that he feared were disappearing as mechanisation swept the countryside.

My motives were far more plausible. I had a genuine reason for making hay: flowers. As the only flowers in our garden were to be those growing in wild flower meadows, it was reasonably important some appeared. With meadows the height of fashion, books on the subject had started popping up like dandelions. From these I'd learnt that the first crucial step in meadow-making is to reduce the nutrients in the soil, to deter the aggressive agricultural rye grasses thereby giving the flowers a chance. Taking off regular crops of hay was an excellent way to do this.

The one small qualification to this otherwise ruthlessly pragmatic operation was that my hay had to be made using old machines—of the kind I remembered working in the fields when I was a child. I had no idea why this was so important, but it was. The presence around Tair-Ffynnon of rusting machinery from precisely this era seemed to lend validity to the idea. And, besides, it felt appropriate for our marginal mountain situation, especially as working versions of such machines were still available at farm sales for a few pounds.

I felt at least a nodding acquaintance with hay. I'd watched it being made in the fields around home as a child. My 'Britains' farm toys had included a blue Ford 5000 tractor, a drum mower, a rotary tedder and baler, complete with six yellow plastic hay bales so detailed you could see the baler twine. I was familiar, too, with handling bales. Every year my mother ordered a load of hay and straw for her horses from the farmer at the end of our lane. 'I think a ton and a half, Ken,' she'd sigh, as if he, as a fellow hunt member, would appreciate the iniquitous demands of horse-keeping. A few days later his tractor would back a laden trailer up to the stables and Ken's sidekick, Ginger, would hurl bales down from the great square stack. Later, I got used to 'humping' bales around the bale store, feeling their dead weight as the twine cut into my hands, the dull pop as it was cut, the annoyance of a loose bale falling apart at the wrong moment, and the sweet, dusty smell as I collected a few 'leaves'—the six-inch thick sections into which bales naturally divide—to stuff into a hay net. So, all in all, when it came to hay, I'd done pretty much everything except make the stuff. How hard could it be?

The hay-making year began straightforwardly enough. In the early spring, before the grass started growing, the fields had to be chain-harrowed. A chain harrow is a net of wide, interlocked steel links, each bearing spikes a few inches long. As these are pulled along behind a tractor they act like a sturdy comb, pulling out dead grass or 'thatch', levelling and spreading molehills and animal droppings, collecting up sticks and twigs. 'Both ways. Across and down,' was the rule, my researches told me, and a most satisfactory injunction it was. Mark, from down the hill, sold me a set of chain harrows for £30.

It was the first time I'd entered a field with a sense of proper agricultural purpose, and it surprised me how different it felt to my usual hapless potterings. Trundling round the field on the Fergie, the chain harrows chinking and clinking behind, I discovered dry patches and boggy patches, bumps and dips. As I hopped on and off the tractor to chuck sticks and stones to the perimeter (away from fragile mower blades), I felt I was getting to know my ground like the Victorian ploughmen Tony had told us about. The views changed with each circuit, I had the breeze in my face and the burble of the engine made a friendly companion, its note changing as it chugged on the uphill sections and clattered down the downhill ones. Having looked out over fields for half my life, there was an inexpressible satisfaction to at last be using one for what it was intended. The finished field looked tended and cared for and ready for spring.

The easy bit, I was aware, was now over. From here on, the implements involved were nothing like so fool-proof; starting with the ancient bar mower I'd acquired with the Fergie. This consisted of a cutting bar with scissor blades like a big garden hedge-trimmer, which extended out to the right-hand side of the tractor. It attached to the lifting arms at the back and was driven by the tractor's engine via a breathtakingly Heath Robinson arrangement of rods, levers, cams, belts and sprockets. You didn't need to be a mechanic to see that this was a device dying to go wrong.

Here I was banking on Jonny. He loved tinkering with old machines. On a visit in May, he'd mounted the mower on the back of the Fergie in readiness, and had agreed to keep every possible weekend free through the summer. By June, the muddy turf left by the chain-harrowing three months earlier had become a shaggy mop of mowing grass, tall enough to ripple in the wind. But when the fine weather came, inevitably Jonny was abroad working, testing for Le Mans. For weeks I stalled, waiting, but every time the weather forecast looked promising, it coincided with his work, making him unavailable. 'I don't see what the problem is,' said Vez, as another cloudless day came to a close. 'Jonny's put the thing on the tractor for you. Just get on with it.'

Which, in the end, is what I did. Or at least, what I tried to do. Following Jonny's instructions, I drove into the field, lowered the mowing bar and set off through the long grass. After my first row, I climbed off the tractor and gave the thick grass a good boot to inspect the closeness of the cut, only to find it hadn't been cut at all. It was just lying flat. I pressed on. Maybe it would cut better going the other way. However, I was soon distracted by a burning smell. Moments later, there was a screech followed by a slapping sound. One of the two drive belts had snapped. I removed the broken belt. A few yards further on, there was a second casualty. On the far side of the mower was a wooden 'swarf board', intended (I think) to direct the cut grass into a tidy heap. Despite the absence of any cut grass to direct, it had broken off. It appeared to have woodworm. I concluded I could get along without it. Scarcely was I back on the tractor when there was a more fundamental failure: the mower refused to lift clear of the ground. A lengthy inspection revealed this to be due to a missing bolt which must have worked itself free. I found a replacement bolt back at the house, which I fitted and, feeling quite pleased with myself, resumed. I'd not quite completed my first circuit of the field, when the chattering of the blades stopped, this despite all the complicated mechanisms still whirring and pumping. Eventually I located the trouble: a metal bar to which the blades were riveted had sheared in two.

I sank onto the grass. Really, this was ridiculous. How many more bits were going to fall off this rattletrap? And where was I going to get spares for a machine half a century old? Even if I found them, what would I do with them? I had no handy book of instructions. It was impossible without someone familiar with Fergies and bar mowers, someone who knew their tricks and foibles. Someone, moreover, who could show me, once the mower was working, how to mow a field. But no-one used mowers like this any more—presumably for exactly the reasons I was discovering. I'd got as far as wondering if I should just junk the whole silly project and get Mervyn to come and make the hay ... when it struck me: Mervyn! He was the perfect age. He might only use huge, shiny machines these days, but he loved the old ones and had grown up working with them. He'd know all about Fergies and their infuriating mowers. I'd ask Mervyn to teach me.

I was, however, nervous about asking. This was Mervyn and Martin's busiest time of year. Whenever the weather was fine, there was hay and silage to be cut and baled. Dozens of farmers, *real* farmers, depended on them. I would be trying to borrow Mervyn, to make hay I didn't strictly need, just when everyone else wanted him. I was also aware that whenever Martin and Mervyn appeared, I seemed to be doing something imbecilic. When they came to dig the base for the carriage and I'd tried to move the Fergie out of their way, I discovered it had frozen solid because I'd failed to put anti-freeze in. When they came to do the fencing I'd got the chain-saw blade pinched immoveably in a tree trunk and couldn't extricate it. And, on one especially ignominious occasion, when they were laying the armoured electricity cable to the carriage, I measured it, told them briskly where to cut, only to find I'd ordered them to make it a foot too short to reach the junction box. ('Just glad it was the boss who did it, an' not me, Antney, that's all,' said Mervyn.) Still, if my dream of a wildflower meadow was ever to come off, I needed help.

I caught them both in the yard around eight in the evening. Martin was supervising the fitting of a spare part to one of the mowers, punctuated by calls on his mobile as other requests and reports of progress came in. The yard had the smell and feel of action. "Ow're the little ones?' said Martin.

'Exhausting,' I said. 'I'm half the man I was.'

'Why, Antney, there must be almost nothing left at all.'

I put my proposal, explaining that I wanted to make hay, but it had to be made using my old machines. It sounded eccentric, even to me. I knew there was nothing in it for them: the last thing they wanted was more work at such a time. But they took it as a perfectly natural request. 'Don't you worry, Antney. We'll fit you in,' said Martin. There was not so much as a raised eyebrow. Mervyn said he'd come up and look over the machines at the weekend.

And, sure enough, he did. On Sunday morning, Mervyn hoisted a battered metal tool box and socket set out of his old pick-up and started going over the Fergie. He topped up the oil and checked the water and fan belt. Moving onto the mower, he hooked two fingers round the single remaining belt and tugged to check its tautness. 'Oho, what about that belt, Antney? Doesn't look so good.' He fitted two new belts, then went over every moving part, assessing, greasing, spraying rusty nuts with diesel from a plastic houseplant sprayer. ('Like the ladies use, Antney,' he said. 'I've found nothing to beat 'em.') He straightened the fingers on the cutter bar, heating them with a blow torch, then hammering them against a tiny anvil. 'That's where the grass gets caught, right in there,' he curled his finger round the crook of the tooth. Idly, I tried to pick up the anvil. It was heavier than I was expecting, and so caked with grime my fingers just slid off. 'Forty pounds, she weighs,' said Mervyn. I tried again, with even less effect. Mervyn (twenty years older than me) reached over with his left hand, pinched the anvil between thumb and finger as I had, flicked the metal lump into the air, caught it and handed it back with a smile. Finally, having sharpened every blade and adjusted various wheels and bars for height and angle of cut, he stood back. 'I think we're there, Antney.'

He started the Fergie and gently set the mower going. The blades set up their noisy chatter. Heading out into the Hang-Glider Field, he cut an experimental swathe. It was clean-cut, close as a lawn mower, quite unlike my earlier botch. I asked him how to mow a field. Every one was different, he said, but in general the first circuit should be anti-clockwise, the 'back swath', so the right-mounted mower reached to the edge. 'After that, go clockwise for a couple of circuits. Grass is very thick in here. On the slope he'll tend to fall into the mower. I'd cut 'im just by coming towards you'—he motioned across the slope of the hill—'then reverse back. Usually you'd do half a dozen times round, then up and down. But here, I'd stick to the one direction.'

I started mowing that afternoon about four o'clock—the time, Mervyn said, when the sugars in the grass were richest, so the hay would be best. At first, there seemed a lot to concentrate on, keeping the tractor straight while looking backwards over my shoulder to check the blades weren't clogging, but gradually I began to get the hang of it. The raising of the mower and reversing back after each pass gave the activity a pleasant rhythm (if inducing, by the fifth swath, a mildly cricked neck). The sun was hot. The mown grass smelt damp and fresh; if the colour

183

green had a scent, then surely this was it. Pottering up and down, the Fergie chugging placidly, a strange contentment crept over me: a sense of knowing there was nothing in the world I would rather be doing at that moment. When I paused for a drink, I noticed the finger bar had lost its dry rustiness. It was dark with sprayed oil and crushed grass, the moving parts shone and it radiated an evocative harvest smell of chlorophyll, old iron and diesel. When a row of heads—walkers on Offa's Dyke—appeared over the dry-stone wall, followed, a moment later, by cameras, it became clear the appeal of the scene was not only in my own imagination. I nearly went to pieces. Uncertain of the correct response, but feeling I should take seriously my elevation to the farming community, I did what I trusted a farmer would have done. I ignored them.

In fine weather, for an average crop, I knew I should wait at least two to three days after mowing for the hay to dry before gathering. Traditionally, this would have been turned several times with rakes, but the modern equivalent (familiar, again, from my 1960s Britains toy set) was a gadget called a hay bob. Using big springs mounted on two rotating drums powered by the tractor, this ingenious device not only turns the hay but, once it's dry enough, can be adjusted to collect it into neat rows for baling. Attending a farm sale in search of a hay bob, looking suitably clueless—I didn't even know if a hay bob would fit on the Fergie, let alone how to judge a good one—a farmer took pity on me ('Just starting out are you? How much ground you got?'). Inspecting the hay bobs on offer he'd pronounced both very poor examples, showing me where they'd been damaged and re-sprayed. He said, if I really wanted one, he probably had one he could sell me. And so I'd bought it from him. Mervyn, when he came to sort the mower, had noted it with approval. 'Revolutionised hay-making,' he said. 'Transformed it overnight. Suddenly you could turn hay at ten miles an hour, three times faster than before. You could turn corners. The hay didn't roll into a "rope" like with an Acrobat. Changed everything. Just one thing, Antney. Tie a loop of baler twine round each of those,' he said, indicating the ten heavy, sprung prongs or 'tines' mounted on each drum which picked up the grass. 'They have a habit of breaking off and that way you don't lose 'em. Lose one in the field and it's a great way to break a baler.'

I'd nodded sagely at this advice—such precautions were doubtless important for professionals like him—but my mind was already on the enjoyable task ahead. Just as he'd promised, using the hay bob was a breeze. Those spinning tines picked up every wisp of grass and flung it neatly over, damp side uppermost. The job delivered the satisfaction of executing a tedious, laborious chore with no effort at all. My only worry was the weather: would it hold until Wednesday afternoon, when Mervyn had said he'd do the baling? There was a perverse pleasure in this novel concern. Usually, fine days or wet days, it made no difference. I relished my new dependence on the elements.

Wednesday was overcast, but the rain held off. Before lunch I did a final circuit of the fields with the hay bob, 'rowing up' the hay ready for the baler. Mervyn arrived after lunch, having that morning, he told me, baled his ten thousandth bale of the summer. He immediately spotted two tines were missing from the hay bob. 'Now, that's not so good, Antney. If they're not on here, it means they're somewhere out there.' He nodded towards the field. 'Great way to break the baler.' His words came back. I felt ashamed. How could I have been so foolish? The fact that he uttered not a word of rebuke made it worse. I looked sheepishly across the field of which, until that moment, I'd been so proud, with its snaking rows of hay. Somewhere there lurked those metal springs, but where? Never had similes about needles and haystacks seemed more apposite.

It was hardly as if the baling weren't already fraught enough. I'd bought the baler for £70 at a local auction and towed it back to Tair-Ffynnon with the Land Rover (earning a few quizzical looks and a couple of nodded 'fair plays'). But having identified that the machine in

185

question was, indeed, a baler—an identical twin, in fact, to one of the rusting relics lying around Tair-Ffynnon—there my knowledge was exhausted. Of all farm machinery ever invented, the baler must rank as one of the most brilliantly ingenious. It picks up hay off the ground, compresses it tightly into bales of a pre-set and regular size, which, before ejecting, it ties with string. And therein lies the downside. Need more be said than that here is a machine that can *tie a knot*? Grasp that astonishing capability and you grasp the baler's potential for mischief. Consequently, for nearly two years, my baler had sat in the barn, aloof, untouchable, a talisman to my fraudulent ownership.

As Mervyn hadn't had time to service the baler, the high-jinks began immediately. An hour was spent freeing the clutch, which had seized. Then the gearbox was found to be wobbly. 'We'll just see if she can make a bale before we look at that,' said Mervyn. And, when she made a bale, 'She's made a few bales like that. She can make a few more.' It was now five o'clock and the first few bales kept falling apart. After exhaustive scrutiny, Mervyn concluded the needle brake appeared to be seized. A few more bales, then the shear pin sheared. This, according to Mervyn, showed that something was wrong elsewhere in the machine. But before we could figure out what, we had to replace the shear pin— a part which, needless to say, I didn't have. A fruitless forty-five minutes was spent trying to extricate a shear pin from the remains of the baler's twin in the yard, requiring the undoing of numerous rusted bolts, until this was abandoned as too big a task. In the end Mervyn tried a spare shear pin from a modern baler, it worked, and we pressed on. Then the shear pin sheared a second time. Mervyn glanced at his watch. I think the thought was in both our minds that the reason the pin had sheared was a broken hay bob tine in the works. Bill the Shepherd walked by with his dogs. He and Mervyn greeted each other. Bill asked if he'd nearly finished baling for the summer. 'Just about,' said Mervyn. 'Some people still got hay to bale, mind,' he said, smiling at me.

'Aye,' said Bill.

My role in the afternoon's proceedings thus far, it may be imagined, was a passive one, mainly consisting of talking to Mervyn's feet as he lay on his back under the baler, while piles of spanners accumulated on the grass. Watching him patiently working there, sorting problem after problem, I marvelled at the sheer multiplicity of tasks a farmer has to be able to turn his hand to.* In due course, Mervyn got the baler going again, the rhythmic whirring and ker-thunking resumed, and I, useful at last, started collecting the bales in the Land Rover and stacking them in the Dutch barn. Soon, part of the field at least was clear and swept of hay. 'I think we're winning, Antney.'

And so the evening wore on. And on. By nine, when I'd probably have packed up, we were barely halfway through. By the time the last bale was heaved safely under cover, by the light of the Land Rover's headlamps, it was after eleven. As we surveyed the stack—about a ton and a half, Mervyn said—there was the satisfaction of hearing the slow, irregular thumps of fat rain drops hitting the tin roof. Parched and aching, I couldn't remember when I'd felt so tired. My palms, sore and cut from the baler twine, were polished to a grimy shine. My skin felt tight from sunburn, dust and dried sweat. But the fields looked shorn and harvested and we had a barn warm with delicious, sweet-smelling hay.

I wondered what on earth we'd do with it.

———•◦•———

I felt different after the hay-making. More settled and complete, as though some solemn, vital and long overdue rite had finally been enacted. I might make hay again, but it would no longer, of necessity, have to be with crummy old machines. As the nights lengthened, I still

---

* In addition to shepherd, dairyman, veterinary surgeon, market gardener, meteorologist, roofer, hedger, ditcher, tractor-driver, carpenter, fencer, welder, sheep-shearer, entrepreneur, salesman, secretary and small businessman, the job, of course, included being a capable mechanic.

hadn't an inkling what it had all been about, though a possible clue arrived four months later. We were back at my father's for Sunday lunch. Combing the shelf of children's books for Maya and Storm, next to the Thomas the Tank Engine and Little Grey Rabbit stories, I spotted a clutch of Ladybird books. Among them were the four seasonal volumes of the 'What to Look for in ...' series. I hadn't looked at these for decades, but turning the pages of *What to Look for in Winter* I remembered how beautifully illustrated they were by the artist Charles Tunnicliffe, with their country calendar scenes, capped craftsmen and old farm machines. For a few minutes, I was engulfed by nostalgia. How much lovelier Britain was then, how much less spoiled. How much smaller the fields were—and the machines working in them. I had to remind myself that these were illustrations, not photographs. When I came to *What to Look for in Summer*, there was something oddly familiar about the cover. It depicted a hay-making scene—but not any old scene. The field was on a hill, with wide views across a distant vale. In the foreground was a dry-stone wall. Swallows flitted about. The tractor was a little grey Fergie, cutting the hay with an old-fashioned bar

mower. And there, sitting on the tractor—cloth cap, red overalls and air of competence notwithstanding—was … well, I could only suppose it was me.

I gazed at the image. Was it significant? It did seem uncanny that it was *quite* so similar. As a vignette representing rural Britain at its summertime best it was hard to beat (evidently the publishers agreed, or why was it on the cover?). I flicked through the books again. Undoubtedly the scenes were artfully contrived and highly romanticised. There was not a pylon, not a grain silo, not a brick bungalow. But there was also something else. The machines: they looked dated, even given the age of the book. I checked the publication date: the series had come out between 1959 and 1961. Yet many of the images in the illustrations might have been pre-First World War. There was a belt-driven threshing machine, unbaled hay being cut from a rick with a knife, two men felling a beech tree with a hand-saw. Tunnicliffe was plainly as sentimental and determinedly nostalgic as Hilaire Belloc. Were Jonny and I just suffering from the same thing? Though it seemed odd, to say the least, that we should both be afflicted by our specialised affection for old machines while being so different in every other way. And why should we be so nostalgic for an era we could barely remember? It was all very confusing.

My father was in the kitchen making tea. 'Do you yearn for the countryside and farm machinery that was around when you were little? About the time when your conscious memory kicked in?' I said.

'Not really, no.' He considered for a moment. 'No, not in the least.' I showed him the cover of *What to Look for in Summer*, explaining how a large part of my summer had been devoted to re-enacting, effectively, that very scene.

'D'you think it's pretty normal, though, that kind of nostalgia?'

'No. I think it's most peculiar.'

'So you can't explain it?'

'No.' He paused, kettle mid-air. 'But I think there can be no doubt your mother's accident had a profound effect on you both.'

189

13

The Accident

There had been an accident, my father was told. It was Aunty Ann, my mother's sister, who called, at around six in the evening on the last Saturday of October 1967. My mother and Jonny had gone to stay with her in Hampshire, so Ma could compete in the Tweseldown Horse Trials. She'd fallen riding the cross-country course. They'd called an ambulance to take her to a hospital called Stoke Mandeville in Buckinghamshire. She was comfortable and in good hands, Aunty Ann said. There'd be more news tomorrow.

Next day we drove to Stoke Mandeville to meet Jonny and Aunty Ann. I remember a labyrinth of corridors and double doors, until we eventually arrived at a brightly lit ward containing Ma. She looked alright, though I'd seldom seen her lying in bed before. More details emerged. She'd been the last rider of the day (she often was, with a surname beginning with 'W') and it was dusk by the time she'd set off. In the half-light, her horse Sally May had tripped as she jumped a big fence of parallel bars, throwing Ma, then falling on top of her. When she couldn't get up, a couple of soldiers had put her in the back of a Land Rover and driven her to the First Aid tent. Was she coming home? No, not now. Not today. When was she coming home? No-one was sure, but soon.

Someone called Pam, whom I couldn't remember having met before, appeared out of nowhere. Pam was no-nonsense, deadpan jokes, smiling eyes—clearly a member of the collective of formidable women to which my mother belonged. She scooped me and Jonny up and took us to live with her four children on the other side of Somerset. 'Just 'til Ma's better,' my father said. Pam lived on a farm—a real farm, with a dairy herd and tractors and a silage clamp and barns full of hay and straw. We collected eggs from the hen house and milk arrived each morning, warm and frothy from the milking parlour, in little aluminium churns with wire handles. On Saturdays, my father would arrive to collect us and drive us to Stoke Mandeville, a name that now entered our lives like a new sibling's. We'd stay with a great uncle and aunt who happened to live nearby. It soon seemed as if my mother was going to live at Stoke Mandeville for good.

My memory of all this, aged between four and five is hazy. All I really remember about Stoke Mandeville is how very surprised I was to be told that this grotty place, with its tunnel-shaped sheds, was the best hospital in the world for whatever was wrong with Ma. I became adept at running along the endless corridors to find her, ahead of everyone else. But it wasn't difficult. She was always in the same ward, in the same bed.

Initially the consultant was positive. Backs were obviously tricky. You never quite knew where you were until the bones had 'knitted'. The only course was to lie still and see what happened, because amazing things did. All in all, my father was told, we should look on the bright side. By Christmas, however, the situation that everyone had suspected, but no-one dared acknowledge, was becoming accepted as the reality. It could be a lot worse, said the consultant. It was a low break, hardly above the waist. 'T4', it was called. This translated simply: she was not going to walk again.

***

Having a mother on wheels was a novelty, certainly. But it also meant we needed somewhere step-free to live, and urgently. Fortunately, Granny, who'd just moved to Bath from Rookwoods, had a flat beneath her house. It had the advantage of being all on one level, the disadvantage that it was in the basement, sixteen steps below street level. Here we regrouped when my mother discharged herself from hospital the following spring, six months after the accident, to adjust ourselves to her new world: one circumscribed by boundaries previously invisible. Once innocent phrases like 'upstairs', 'downstairs', 'in the garden' or even just 'over here' now acquired a loaded significance, representing forbidden lands. Even on the level there were substantial no-go areas. Indeed, Granny's flat sometimes seemed to have been designed deliberately to thwart a wheelchair. The doors weren't really wide enough, so my mother gashed her knuckles every time she tried to move rooms. The corners were too sharp: the bathroom led off a narrow corridor, requiring two heaves of the wheelchair's back wheels by an adult; first into the corridor, then into the bathroom. Not, in the event, that this mattered much, as once inside the loo was too low, the basin miles out of reach, and the bath an impossibility. She washed in bed.

The physical side-effects of her injury, apart from the loss of all movement and feeling below her waist, were that she felt perpetually chilly from the poorer circulation engendered by her newly sedentary lifestyle. She was constantly asking for extra clothing, rugs and heaters to be brought to her. She couldn't cough properly, either, if something tickled her throat, offering up instead a pitiful '*Aheftu ... Aheftu ...*' At random moments her legs might be seized by involuntary muscle contractions. By far the most significant consequence, however, was the loss of bladder and bowel control.

Accordingly our life now centred mainly around the loo, which temporarily meant a dangerously unstable Elsan portable—essentially a deep metal bucket filled with evil-smelling blue chemicals and a plastic seat. Getting her on and off this, changing her, encouraging her body to perform the functions that used to be controlled by her brain, watching her beating the front of her pelvis with her cupped hand, now became the rituals of our newly complicated existence. The alarm call 'Quick, I'm in a flood!' prompted urgent relays bearing disposable paper sheets or 'pads', clean clothing and wheelchair cushions. Mopping up and the continual smell of 'penny' (as Jonny and I called it)—gradually we adjusted to the consequences of paraplegia.

We didn't go out much. Leaving the flat was a major expedition, partly because of the long flight of steps to street level, partly because, once there, the streets themselves presented a whole new range of obstacles. Britain in the late sixties was not so wheelchair-friendly as it is today. The vast majority of shops, streets, cafés, restaurants, hotels or public spaces and buildings had no provision at all for wheelchairs. It's amazing how many steps and bumps the world has, once you have a heavy load to wheel over them. And of all British cities, Bath was possibly the least suited to a wheelchair. Everywhere was on a gradient, usually a steep one. There were countless steps. My father was five foot six inches tall and lightly built. My mother was strongly built, a shade under six foot in her socks, weighing (I'd guess) at least eleven stone. On those handsome Pennant stone pavements, we discovered a whole Lilliputian geography of hazard lying in wait to snag the little wheels on the front of her chair. My father was continually almost tipping her out.

The main incentive for these effortful missions to the outside world was the arrival of a new car with hand controls, a modification which had only just become available. My parents, for reasons known only to themselves, opted for a car with a manual rather than automatic gearbox. This meant that my mother, who'd learnt to drive before driving tests were introduced and, I suspect, had never gained even the most basic skills needed to pass, had to learn to change gear via two stiff, spring-operated levers by the steering wheel. This required the simultaneous release of the clutch lever with the first two fingers of her right hand while her third and fourth fingers pulled up on the accelerator, all the while directing the steering wheel with the thumb and shifting the gear stick with her left hand. A separate brake lever was fitted near the gear stick. The controls were crudely made, early prototypes, plainly designed by someone who'd never been near a wheelchair. They required, at T-junctions, at least three hands (one to work the brake, one to turn the wheel, one to work the clutch and accelerator). In Bath, where many junctions were at the top of steep gradients and required switchback turns and handbrake starts, they needed four hands. It was hopeless. We stalled. We kangaroo-hopped. We slid backwards out of control. As the queues built up in all directions, in the back, Jonny and I buried our heads in embarrassment.

Things culminated one Saturday morning. My mother was driving (she nearly always did as she was trying to practise). Bath was jammed with shopping traffic. By some madness we found ourselves in the middle of a box junction on the busy London Road, on a pronounced gradient, as the lights changed to red. Hill-starts in traffic were always the trickiest manoeuvre with the finger-tip clutch. As the lights turned green, Ma stalled for what seemed the ten thousandth time. We were blocking traffic from four directions. Again and again, as the lights changed, she stalled. After four or five changes the traffic had backed up as far as we could see. Horns were sounding. People were shouting. Inside our car, something approaching hysteria was setting in. My father was saying, 'For goodness sake, woman … *concentrate.*' Ma was yelling, 'I'd like to see you do it,' and stalling again. My brother and I, horrified at the scene we were causing, were screaming at them both to do something. All the accumulated frustrations of our new life seemed to converge in that moment: the limitations, the shrunken world, the fact that everything took so long, that mundanities now dominated our whole existence. It felt as if we were going to be stuck in that box junction for ever. Until at last my father clicked: she was never going to do it. He had to get her out of the driving seat so he could move the car using conventional controls. This meant he had to extricate the wheelchair from the boot, assemble it, get her into it and wheel her round to the passenger side to get her back in before putting the chair away again.

In the mêlée, as she was getting out, one nearby driver leant on his horn. To my mother, perhaps, that single action summarised the world's attitude to her new condition. As my father started pushing her round to the passenger side, she broke away, wheeling herself in short bursts up the hill. He attempted to pull her back towards our car— 'Come on, Liza,' he said softly. 'It won't do any good'—but then he let her go. Awkward as it was to propel herself, she bumped unsteadily up over the lumpy, much-patched surface. Twice, one of the little front wheels caught against something, nearly tipping her out of the chair, but she recovered and wheeled on, bump-bumping over the cross-hatchings and the mended holes, against the background of horns and engines and muffled shouts until she reached the door of the driver, still honking. He didn't lower his window. He released the horn, but he wouldn't look at her. 'You,' she shouted through the window. 'Yes, you. I'm talking to *you*.' He looked dead ahead. 'Yes, you can pretend you can't hear. But perhaps one day *you'll* end up in a wheelchair. Perhaps then *you'll* find out what it's like.' Then she swung herself round and bumped back to the passenger side of our car. It was the only time I ever heard her complain.

———•◆•———

After two months in Bath, the situation was hardly improving. If we were to recover any quality of life, we needed somewhere easier to live. After looking at countless flats and bungalows, it became clear that the most practical solution would be an extension to our existing house designed around a wheelchair. To this end, my father was already working. In his rigorous, academic way he set his mind to discovering what life was like in a wheelchair. Sitting in my mother's chair after he'd got her to bed, he spent hours wheeling, turning, seeing where he could reach, where he couldn't, what bumps he could get over, how steep a ramp he could negotiate, what surfaces were easiest to wheel on. He tried getting onto the loo, in and out of bed, in and out of the bath, washing, brushing his teeth, filling a kettle, filling a vase, unhooking coats, making tea, cooking, plugging things into sockets, writing, loading the washing machine, hanging laundry onto a clothes horse.*

And so, gradually, Phase Two of the Great Modernist Experiment came into being. The addition had to be affordable on a mortgage raised on my father's university salary and built fast, ideally prefabricated. It would be single-storey, flat-roofed, timber-framed and cedar-clad, plugged onto the existing glass sitting room. The kitchen would be round because that, my father had concluded, was the easiest shape for a wheelchair to navigate.** The walls would be all glass, because my mother had said she wished to feel as if she were in the garden. Apart from its modernity, the house must feel like an ordinary home, not a home for someone disabled (my mother was adamant about that). Yet almost every ordinary detail would be slightly adjusted: doors would be wider; sockets and WCs higher; switches, basins, shelves, window handles, worktops, cupboards and racks lower. The attached stone cottage, twenty-eight steps below, would provide free accommodation in return for someone to help Ma. The only drawback was that it wouldn't be ready for months, maybe years. Until then, Granny's flat would have to do.

As autumn arrived and the academic year began, Jonny went away

---

* 'The difficulty,' he later told me, 'was not to cheat. Like pretending to be blind, it's too easy to open your eyes and take a quick look when things get awkward, to use your legs, to reach a little bit further than really you can.'

** Technically, tetradecahedral—fourteen-sided.

to school and my father returned to work in Bristol. To look after my mother, until we'd worked things out, it was decided I would stay in the flat with her and she would teach me there. I became her companion, messenger, factotum, nurse and alarm system—her legs. Much as she loathed having to ask for help, a half-hour seldom passed in which, say, papers or a pen didn't slide off her lap and need to be recovered. This, combined with her natural propensity to demand, every time I left a room, 'Where are you going?', had the effect of convincing me that her life was now entirely dependent on mine. How true this was, really, I have no way of knowing, but there no longer seemed room for defiance, disobedience or irresponsibility of any kind, nor did I seek it. My days were spent in an exclusively adult world. While most children were out at school, I was with my mother almost every minute of every day, relieved only by odd errands to the shop or dog walks with my grandmother. My mother's universe had contracted dramatically. But so, by extension, had mine.

Phase Two of the Great Modernist Experiment was an immediate and resounding success. From the moment she wheeled herself into the new space, my mother was mobile again. No greater tribute could be paid to my father's loving determination to understand every aspect of her situation than that, within days, she was almost completely independent. Modernism, with its clean, uncluttered, flowing space, suited the requirements of a wheelchair perfectly. We got used to the sound of squeaking tyres on the polished Ilminster paving, the chink of her rings on the rear metal wheelgrips, the whirring of the tyres rubbing the chair's arms as she sped from room to room. She could, without assistance, do almost everything she wanted in a warm house full of sunshine. With second-generation hand controls in a new automatic car, she could leave and return unaided from the open garage we were determinedly learning (it was the 1970s now after all) to call the 'car port'.

As proof of her new freedom, she once again disappeared. With her car now her second home, she resumed a schedule as hectic as before. She became Chairman of Bristol Community Health Council, sat on committees for Somerset County Council and Cheshire Homes, gave riding lessons and taught 'A' Level biology as a supply teacher. She qualified as a dressage judge and at weekends began to travel the country, adjudicating the events in which she'd previously competed. Her life was soon so full, so back to normal, that, for most people, her disability went almost unnoticed. For me, though, the sense of responsibility never quite went away.

In the summer of 1970 we took our first family holiday since the accident. After a major research project, my father had found a hotel on the west coast of Scotland with a lift (a rarity at the time) which was free in July. The air was cool and midgeless, and the sun shone hard and bright every day. It was my first experience of mountain scenery and I was appropriately open-mouthed. The size and emptiness of it all, the combination of rocky, heather-clad Highlands and dark blue lochs, the whitewashed granite farms and cottages gleaming in the sunshine combined with the fenceless roads so narrow they had passing places added up to a beauty unlike anything I'd ever imagined. The sense of tantalising wilderness was accentuated by our car-bound status, never straying more than a few yards from it, compounded when my father and brother were released to walk up Ben Nevis, an expedition for which I was declared too young. Every year after that holiday, I pleaded to return to Scotland.

Eight years later we finally did, though this time just my parents and I (Jonny now being too old for family holidays). I was fifteen and toting a new camera. On this occasion the skies were less obliging. The clouds over the east coast and the Central Highlands were grey and low, and released a steady, set-in rain, day after day. The place I'd been dying to revisit for so long was dull, miserable and largely hidden. The hotels, selected as usual according to the presence, size and specification of their lifts, were gloomy and dispiriting. For a week that August we motored disconsolately around in a suffocating fug (the car heater roaring away at the default MAX setting specified by my mother), every mountain and view buried. Rain streamed down the outside of the car, condensation down the inside. After four days peering through the arc cleared by the windscreen wipers at the strip of road ahead, I had cabin fever as I've never known it before or since.

Late morning of Day Five found us in dense mist on Ben Lawers in the Central Grampians. Needing a pee, at a convenient moment I was let out of the car. Clutching my new camera, I followed a burn a little way up the hillside into the murk, gratefully gulping the saturated air. It felt marvellous to be stretching my legs. Sprinkled among the sodden tussocks were tiny blue flowers, just a few inches tall, their bell heads suspended on

hair-like stalks, flashes of pure colour in that grey-green landscape. Their heads never rested, nodding and quivering with every breath of wind. They seemed too delicate, somehow, for this bleak place.

With the car out-of-sight in the mist, its gravitational pull lessened. I decided to follow the burn a bit further up. As I plodded through the mist, feet now soaking, it grew rockier underfoot, slabs of dark, shining stone appearing through the springy turf. I'd gone about as far as I thought I should when, unexpectedly, the mist swept back, revealing, in front of me, a shallow pool. Here, after negotiating a step in the rock, the brown waters of the rushing burn were momentarily checked. It was a perfect natural rockery. Delicate ferns sprouted amongst the clumps of heather, laden with purple flowers. In the brightness, beads of rainwater gleamed on the heads of the harebells. Here, finally, was the Scotland I'd come to see. It was my first close encounter, alone, with a truly wild place, and the intimacy and secrecy of the moment took me by surprise. Though there was more to it than that. The experience also had the thrill of being stolen, of rebellion against and truancy from the car and all it stood for—spiked, obviously, with a generous measure of guilt. I just had time to snap a photograph before the mist closed back in and, at the same moment, a series of impatient blasts of the horn indicated that my mother felt more than enough time had elapsed for even the longest of pees.

The image of that rocky pool was destined to stay with me. Of all forbidden places, after that, mountains and moorland became the most exotic and alluring, simply by being the most off-limits. Implicit in them seemed to be all the possibilities of unfettered wanderlust— escape, freedom, the opportunity to stride out and stretch my legs. Not, of course, that the reason struck me until years later, when an old friend and I were quizzing each other about where our ideal country hideaways would be. By the sea? On a river? In the woods? In the hills? Sometimes your body knows something before your head. My answer slipped out, reflex and unthinking. 'My place? That's easy,' I said. 'Walking country.'

14

The pond

My own pleasure in finding water in a garden has so often led me into the wildest errors that I have learnt to stop and reflect very carefully before starting work.

RUSSELL PAGE, *The Education of a Gardener*, 1962

The moment I saw the grassy bowl beneath the spring in the Top Field, I knew it had to be my Scottish rock pool. A marshy, turf basin about thirty feet across, hollowed out by centuries of water trickling out of the spring that emerged directly above it, it looked almost as if it might once have been a pond. Now, though, it was a boggy mess of sedges and tufty grasses, muddy from sheep's feet, invaded by gorse and bracken through the broken fence that bordered the hill. I was so pleased on discovering it that I went straight to dig out my old photograph albums. It was years since I'd last looked at them, but, flicking through the protective cellophane flapping away from the once self-adhesive pages, I found the photograph almost at once. Presaged by several pages of dreary grey-green Scottish landscapes, suddenly—bang—there it was. The colours had faded, it had yellowed, and there was no sign of the rowan tree laden with orange berries which I could have sworn overhung the pool. But, there it was, just the same. I'd even, which I'd forgotten, had the picture enlarged.

It all came flooding back: my sodden trudge, coming upon it out of nowhere, the dense mist suddenly clearing. We could certainly match those aspects, feature for feature. And the size and general form of the two sites were really not dissimilar at all. The Scottish one, admittedly, had the edge: clumps of heather and tiny, delicate ferns rather than the coarse five-foot bracken we offered. It was a good bit rockier, too. And, of course, it had water in it. Our boggy patch would have to be built up a good deal on the downhill side before it could do that. But apart from these details, they were twins. It was just a matter of a bit of digging and damming.

The first thing to do was to consult Ness. Our neighbour had been an invaluable source of information and advice on all matters since our arrival, be it finding a competent plumber or some arcane detail of local history. The procedure was always the same. A question would be posited, then, gradually, the information surge would begin: first would come phone messages with initial thoughts and suggestions, invariably so long she'd be cut off by the machine.* Cuttings and leaflets would follow, with covering notes on one of her elegantly printed compliments slips, always, like all her written communications, filling whatever space was available, front, back, up the sides and frequently along the top too, so that never a square inch was 'wasted'; invariably these were finished 'In haste', or with an apology for her unavoidable brevity. Then, in due course, these were followed in turn by relevant

---

* Whenever a mobile message was flagged by the automaton's voice: 'THE ... NEXT ... MESSAGE ... IS ... ELEVEN ... MINUTES ... LONG', prompting a presumption that someone had dialled us by mistake, we got used to hearing Ness's familiar tones: 'Ah, Anto, justaquickthought...'

books or samples, in stamp-less packages marked 'By Les', meaning they were collected by Les the Post, via a sort of internal mail system for the hill instigated by Ness. Despite this sometimes intimidating onslaught, something helpful always emerged; it was unthinkable to do anything without consulting Ness first.

Raising the idea of a pond by the spring, Ness said we must do nothing until we'd spoken to her friend Phil, the country's greatest living authority on the Holy Wells of Wales. Photographs and booklets of Phil's published photographs started arriving with Les. The immensity of the cultural baggage attached to natural water sources, from pre-Christian Celtic wells to eighteenth-century spas, had not even occurred to me. Now Phil's photographs showed rubble-stone springheads like tiny chapels, high on bracken-strewn hillsides, or dank, mossy chambers in forgotten woods, with niches and stone gargoyles, formal as tombs. Many had adjacent, placid, stone-edged pools. It opened up a whole range of new possibilities.

Thus encouraged, I'd taken to consulting each and every visitor to Tair-Ffynnon who might conceivably have useful advice to offer. Standing by the spring, I'd ply them with questions. Did they think it would work? Would the basin hold water? Mervyn thought there was a good chance. 'The ground's soft. Means the water's not getting away. Good sign. If the ground's holding water, you're on the way to a pond, aren't you?' Improvements were suggested: lanterns hanging from the thorn trees; stocking with brown trout. Maya and Vez got it into their heads it could be a swimming pool. No-one seemed quite certain about the actual mechanics, but the overwhelming consensus was: it was a splendid idea. The place was made to be a pond.

The only dissenting voices came from Tony and Liz, the orchard experts, who during their visit had offered supplementary advice (free) on every aspect of the property. 'It would be disastrous to make a pond here,' they agreed, as one. 'Don't change a thing.' We stood by the stunted thorns surveying the grassy bowl. 'Besides, it would look awful,' added Tony. 'The water would be cloudy and never clear.' Now this *was* news. 'It's not deep enough. Water needs to be at least two-feet deep to clear.' I plainly looked unconvinced, because he launched into further explanation. 'D'you know what a colloid is?'

'No.'

'Well, clay is a colloid. And colloids turn into suspension when disturbed, making the water cloudy ...' Colloids ... suspensions ... Tony evidently noticed I was glazing over. 'Every time it rains,' he said, 'it'll look like a muddy puddle.'

<hr />

Tony's colloids, frankly, were the least of my worries. My concern was the spring. For, at Tair-Ffynnon, the spring was everything. That was the reason the smallholding was here, in this particular fold of this particular hill. It was how the place got its name. Should anything happen to the spring, that would be that: the place would be uninhabitable. There was something magnificently primeval about it. It trickled steadily and unstintingly, swelling to a bucket-emptying gush in very wet weather (when our baths turned a peaty brown), reducing to an apologetic dribble in droughts, but never quite stopping. It emerged from our taps at an unvarying, icy 6°C, so cold we could only drink it in sips. As for the taste, it made mains water undrinkable. Apart from the initial *E. coli* scare (remedied by replacing the manhole cover on the collection tank), it had never failed.

Only once had I glimpsed its source, discretely hidden behind a paving stone leaning against the steep bank where it emerged. The occasion had been a crisis brought on by a prolonged dry spell one August, after which our water supply had faltered. Dreading that the spring had run dry, and unsure where to turn, I'd called the company that supplied our water filters. In response, Trevor had arrived in overalls and a plumber's van, and I'd led him up to springhead. I'd previously only dared take the briefest peek into this holy of holies— meddling with something so vital, on which my family and home were entirely dependent, even looking at it without good reason, seemed not so much tempting Providence as prodding her with a sharp stick.

Trevor suffered no such hang-ups. He heaved the paving stone aside, got down on his knees, reached into the bank and started scrabbling about amongst the stones, speaking, as he did so, of the dark art of spring-catching. 'Sometimes they move,' he said, just before his head disappeared into the bank. 'But we can usually find them again.' By this time he was stretched out on his stomach and, with only his headless torso visible, conversation was less easy. He seemed still to be talking, but his tone-of-voice had altered. Gone was the practical overalled technician who'd stepped out of the plumber's van, replaced by some more nebulous practitioner—dowser, trout tickler, witch doctor? Soft, wheedling murmurings had begun to emerge from the bank. 'Oh yes, we'll find her ... we'll find you ... won't we, my pretty.' Did he say that? I can't be absolutely sure, but not being able to see his head or face, it was hard to tell. In any case, it was no longer clear whether he was addressing me, himself, the hill, the spring, or an obscure watery god. I half-wondered if he was entering a sort of trance. I monitored his body carefully in case it started vibrating or should begin to levitate. In the end, however, he'd merely withdrawn his head, straightened up, and said: 'The pipe to the header tank is blocked.'

With an expert present, curiosity banished superstitious diffidence and I bent down to peer at the spring myself. Inside the small entrance into the hillside was a triangular rocky niche about the size of a kitchen wall cupboard, wider and deeper at its base and tapering towards the top. It smelt of clean, stony dampness. The sides were streaked orange-yellow, presumably from mineral deposits, and shone with moisture. In the gravelly base was a pool of water. It looked the coldest, cleanest, clearest water I'd ever seen. This bewitching impression was only slightly marred by dark insects skating about on the surface. 'Should those be there?'

'Sign of clean water,' said Trevor, as his head arrived alongside mine. 'See the spring?'

'No, where?'

'Over there, on the right.'

'Where? I can't see anything.'

'There. Right there. At the back. Look at the surface by that darker rock.'

I'm not sure what I'd been expecting: something like a drinking fountain, I suppose, or, at the very least, the trickle of a tap left half on. Instead, there was, over one surface of the stone he indicated, just the tiniest, most infinitesimal bulge in the wetness on one side. 'What? That's it?'

'That's it.'

It was only detectable at all because the moving water reflected the light from the entrance, in tiny flickering ripples. It looked so gentle, so fragile—yet somehow all the more precious for that. Was this how great rivers like the Severn and the Thames began, with such tiny relentless flows?

'That's enough to produce all the water that comes through our yard?'

'More than enough. That's a strong spring, even if it's at its weakest moment after a dry spell like this. Though in fact you've got four springs coming out there.' The other springs, fainter still, were on the other side. Was this the explanation of Tair-Ffynnon's name at last? We'd been wondering about the three missing ones.

Grit in the copper pipe leading from the rocky niche to the adjacent tank was the problem, it turned out. In a matter of moments Trevor had unblocked it, replaced the paving stone, and was packing up his kit. But before he left, I questioned him about the possible risks to the spring that might be posed by digging out the pond. 'Well ... water always finds the easiest point of escape from the ground, so you've got to be careful. You might divert the flow.' This sounded bad. 'If you do, we can usually catch it again,' he said airily.

'Usually?'

'There's always a risk, of course. Sometimes you lose 'em. They change course. They find another way. Then there's nothing you can do.'

My experience watching Trevor had impressed me. How right I'd been to be reticent about inspecting the spring before! Clearly one meddled with these things at one's peril. On the other hand, I wanted my goddam pond. The Scottish rock pool was one of the reasons we were at Tair-Ffynnon. And whoever built all the wells and springheads that littered the hills presumably faced the same dilemma. We weren't doing anything major: just enough to see if the bowl would hold water. Sod it, if anything happened to the spring, Trevor was bound to be able to coax it back.

◆ ◆ ◆

Martin dug the pond one September evening. As the JCB tore the springy turf, and the big wheels churned the soft ground to a soggy morass, it seemed insanely heavy-handed treatment for a place that had been untouched for so long. The hole was too big. Tony and Liz were right. We shouldn't be doing this. The machine was too aggressive and worked too fast. Suddenly I could see, with agonising clarity, all the arguments against the project.

Martin worked as fast as ever, with only one brief, rather endearing break, when he shouted to us to rescue a frog. He skimmed off the top layer of wet mud into a pile, scooped out the clay beneath and packed it into the bank. So the pond would be lined with waterproof clay, he said, rather than porous soil.

Then a tooth on the JCB caught the buried pipe that connected the spring to the polythene collection tank feeding the house. A feeble arc of water emerged from what looked like a garden hose. Our water supply was now interrupted, requiring, whatever happened, an emergency visit from Trevor. It was a tedious extra expense, but not disastrous. The pipe lay there, trickling forlornly. As Martin dug deeper into the upstream side of the basin, ever closer to the springhead, I watched it closely. It was hard to believe that this unspectacular piece of black hose, and the dribble emerging from it, was all that made Tair-Ffynnon's existence possible.

It was getting late. Martin was busily scooping, scraping, repositioning the digger to transfer the earth to the dam. He kept wanting to know how far to dig, which it was now impossible to know, as the lines I'd pegged out were long gone. I became distracted. Mervyn came up. He'd been to inspect the bees on the other side of the field: was I thinking of taking the honey off soon? When I next looked at the pipe, the flow had faltered and become irregular. Even as I watched, it gushed, then stopped. There was the sound of hollow gurgling, followed by a sort of hiccupping burp. Another brief gush. Another gurgle. Then a few pitiful, unnervingly valedictory dribbles.

Then nothing.

I stared at the torn pipe, waiting for the flow to resume. It did not. After a wretched pause, I looked up. Martin was still digging away, engine roaring. Mervyn was saying something about having a centrifugal extractor we could borrow. The swallows skimmed and circled in the distance round the roof ridge and chimneys of the house, just visible over the lip of the hill. Sounds and images began to interfere with each other in a grotesque, warped montage, the way film-makers convey catastrophe—the arrival of the four horsemen of the Apocalypse, say, or the opening of the Ark of the Covenant. I found it hard to concentrate. It seemed pointless to tell Martin he could stop now, as his services were now irrelevant, that Tair-Ffynnon's days were over. The spring had stopped. And why? For some footling vanity project? I tried to remain calm.

━━━◆◆━━━

I slept poorly that night. Or rather, I slept not a wink. My thoughts were filled with *Jean de Florette* and holy wells run dry. After Martin had departed (with a carefree 'We'll let the spring sort itself out'), I'd said nothing to Vez. The tanks in the loft still contained water, so there seemed no need to panic everyone. But as I slowly filled the kettle, flushed the lavatory, washed, and brushed my teeth that evening, I felt mocked. Was this the last time I'd enjoy these simple rituals at Tair-Ffynnon? *Tair*-Ffynnon? *Dim*-Ffynnon, more like. *No* springs. How long before it was just another roofless ruin like so many others in the Welsh mountains?

It was still night time, that deep quiet before the first streaks of dawn, as I crept out of bed, pulled on my clothes and let myself silently out of the house. Not a creature moved as I made urgently for the spring. If it were even just a bit wet, everything was alright.

I reached the saucer-shaped excavations by the springhead. And ... oh, the relief, the joy. The earth was wet. Puddles gleamed in the moonlight. The spring had returned. I sploshed happily in the mud for a few minutes, making sucking noises with my wellington boots. I was midway through my celebratory breakfast fry-up, when Vez put her head round the kitchen door. 'You're up early. What's going on?' I looked at the clock. It wasn't yet five.

The pond filled steadily. I'm not sure how like my Scottish rock pool it's ever going to be. It leaks badly. Following heavy rain, when the spring runs faster than the leaks and overflow can carry the water away, it looks at its best. The level rises two feet. It appears as a placid upland pool of clear spring water, with Skirrid framed between the thorn trees. The beauty of this scene is partially offset by the sense of impending disaster as water courses over the earth dam and we wonder if it will wash away, carrying the hay barn below with it. After such bursts, the water level gradually recedes, leaving a muddy shoreline. The depth dips to less than eighteen inches and at the slightest disturbance—wind, a spot of rain, a falling leaf—the water becomes cloudy. Most of the time, say ninety-nine per cent, Tony's prediction is correct. It looks exactly like a muddy puddle.

15

Stoning

I am a dry stone waller,
All day I dry stone wall,
Of all appalling callings,
Dry stone walling's worst of all.
PAM AYRES, 'I am a Dry Stone Waller',
Some More of Me Poetry, 1976

Even by his own Eeyore-ish standards, Don looked grumpy. It was 8.30 on a Monday morning in late August, and the long-awaited moment had finally arrived: he was going to start building the two stretches of wall down the eastern side of the yard. But as he plodded towards me, past the huge heaps of stone we'd had delivered in preparation, it was clear something was up. 'Ah'm disappointed. Ah see ye're not ready for us.'

I'd clearly misheard him. For a second it sounded as if he'd said we weren't ready for him. I beamed.

'Morning, Don. How are you?'

'Ah said, ah'm disappointed. With yer preparations. As ah say, ye're not ready for us.' I eyed him narrowly: he was joking. He had to be joking. Was he joking? He didn't look as if he was, but then with Don—never exactly Mr Sunshine—it was hard to be sure. And if he wasn't joking ... I began to feel slightly queasy.

I'd been thinking about dry-stone walls pretty much since the day we got Tair-Ffynnon. 'Stone wall country' had been one of the prerequisites for my rural idyll. Dry-stone walls were part of what characterised the open hills and were instrumental to the Yellow Book plan. 'Have you got some walls?' had been the County Organiser's first comment when I told her where we lived. Rebuilt walls promised transformative visual payback while simultaneously converting useless open pastureland into usable fields. Most important of all, they were one of the few tasks realistically accomplishable in the five months before the County Organiser's return in September. Or so we'd thought.

It had always been my intention to rebuild our walls myself, but as this might take years, decades even, we'd decided to splurge on some professional help to get us started. So our first task, obviously, was to find a waller. At the Royal Welsh Show (the same event where I'd picked up my book on gates and been press-ganged into the Marcher Apple Network), I'd also collected a sheaf of leaflets at the Dry Stone Walling Association's stand, from *Notes on Building a Cairn,* via *Geology for Wallers,* to specifications for building everything from bee boles to grouse butts. (The impression was that if you wished to reconstruct Machu Picchu or an Egyptian pyramid, the DSWA would have a concise leaflet explaining how.) Every one of these documents contained, somewhere, the same sentence: 'In dry-stone walling there is an enormous difference between the best and the worst workmanship, probably greater than with any other skill.' I had no reason to doubt this. Walls, anyone could see, varied vastly in quality, and although I couldn't say exactly why some looked so much better than others, they clearly did. The best ones had an effortlessness to them, a casual grace as they flowed over the hills and nimbly vaulted streams that somehow defied the varying quality of the stone and the hours of back-aching toil that must have been involved. I wanted walls like those.

But in Border Country, it turned out, finding a waller of any description was an achievement. Being a lowland area as much as an upland one, it only just qualified as stone wall country: most farms were in the valleys, where the fields were divided by hedges, not walls. It was only on the high ground, where the soil was too thin and the weather too bleak for hedges to thrive, that walls took over. Most of these tended not to be repaired, but left, instead, to collapse while wire stock fencing maintained the boundary. So the sad fact was there wasn't much call for wallers. The DSWA's 'Register of Certificated Professional Members' listed a mere handful for the whole of Wales, and of these only two or three could be classed as local.

The most local was Don. When I called him the first time, he chuckled (though knowing him better now, I realise he couldn't conceivably have chuckled) at the notion that I could just ring up, out of the blue, and book a waller, just like that. He wasn't available for *months* he explained, probably *years*. Then there was his forthcoming world cruise. And soon after that he was retiring, because he'd been thinking of retiring for a while now. Whatever happened, he'd have to visit to see if it was the kind of job he was interested in. He was so obviously reluctant it seemed foolish to try to persuade him, so I pressed on down the directory's list. The next waller I called said he was, these days, fully employed by a building company so was no longer available. The third—by now a good deal less local—sounded more amenable. Yes, he was available: fortunately for me a large job had just fallen through. He came to visit. Yes, it all looked fine. He'd consult his diary when he got home and get back to me with a date when he could start. Alas, in the brief period between visiting us and getting home, his cancelled job was reinstated, a big garden job, too, he said, at least nine months to complete. And that, it became clear, was the problem. As few farmers built or maintained walls any more, garden work had become the waller's stock-in-trade. They could find plenty of cushy work closer to home.

As I'd now run through all the local DSWA-qualified wallers, I tried a couple of people whose cards I'd seen in newsagents. Despite promising-sounding claims ('STONE MASON—DRY-STONE WALLING A SPECIALITY'), inspection of their efforts invariably confirmed their work didn't match up. Whenever I saw a recently built or repaired wall I liked, I tried to find who'd done it. There was always some reason why they weren't available. One widow informed me, tearfully, that her husband had died suddenly the previous year; another waller had emigrated to New Zealand. All the other decent walls were by Don.

Reluctantly, I called him again.

Evidently I caught him on a good day, because this time he seemed positively compliant, agreeing to drop by later that week. He turned out to be a small, wiry man of few words, in his early fifties, who, I later learnt, had been a soldier. Certainly he looked tough. However, he brought with him some books on dry-stone walling which he lent me. He even agreed, in principle, to include us in his schedule.

From Don's books, I acquainted myself with the arcane world of walling and its charming vocabulary of 'smoots' and 'lunky holes', 'stoops' and 'clonks'.* I discovered that dry-stone walls can last more than 5,000 years (because, unlike mortared walls, they move as the frost heaves them or the ground subsides, each shift making them settle ever tighter). Reading of the different kinds of wall, from the granite boulder

---

* A clonk is Galloway dialect for a large single stone below the cope: 'a good expressive word but it cannot be found in a Scottish dictionary'—Colonel F. Rainsford-Hannay, *Dry Stone Walling*, 1972. Smoots and lunky holes are the same thing: small rectangular openings at ground level to allow through water or sheep (often built in the absence of timber for a gate, they were quick to block or unblock with stones). Stoops are upright monoliths set into the ground against the wall head of a gate or stile.

'Galloway dykes' to the vertically set slates of a 'Cornish hedge', I wondered if Black Mountain walls, too, had their own peculiarities. The answer was yes. They were taller than most—at least five foot six, meaning you often had to stand on tiptoes to see over them—topped off with over-sized vertical coping stones, deliberately set to overhang: all in a largely unsuccessful attempt to foil their most truculent customer, the Welsh Mountain ewe.

Thus informed, I'd re-contacted Don after the County Organiser's visit in April and tried to introduce the notion that we now had a deadline by which our walls had to be built: September, at the latest. That ought to be possible, he said, making a second visit to re-inspect the course of the prospective walls. The work wouldn't take much more than a week, he said, though obviously he couldn't commit to a date now. In the meantime we ordered stone from Tony—a mix to include big, flat 'copers', general rubble for the body of the wall, some longer 'through-stones' and plenty of small rocks for the 'hearting' in the centre—all to be delivered and carefully tipped in regular piles along the course of the wall.

May passed into June. The stone gateposts (or stoops as I now called them) went in, while grass began to grow up through the piles of stone. Periodically I'd call Don, gently reminding him of our existence, trying not to sound desperate, tactfully enquiring how his schedule was proceeding. Aye, he'd grunt, it looked alright—for the moment. June became July, and July August. Then, out of the blue, in mid-August, Don had rung to announce he'd be starting on Monday. That's marvellous, I said (trying not to sob with gratitude). If the walls took a week to build, as he said, that still left us a fortnight's grace before the County Organiser's visit.

Then, on the Sunday night, Don had called again. 'How are the footings?'

'The footings? How d'you mean, the footings, Don?' What the hell was he on about? Did he mean the ground on which the wall sat?

'Ah mean the footings. What's the surface?'

'Well ... they're ... like you saw ... I've taken down the old fence and cleared the junk away.'

'Ah asked about the footings.'

'Well ... earth and grass I suppose. The same as for any wall.'

'Ah'm used to concrete.'

'Concrete? For a field wall? But surely ... I mean ... surely most field walls don't have a base of concrete, not in the middle of the countryside?' I knew for a fact they didn't.

'Well, that's what ah'm used to.' I'd put the phone down perplexed.

And now, today ... the day he was actually, finally, here and due to start, he was still like Eeyore without his tail. 'What's up, Don?' I said.

'The footings aren't ready.'

'But we discussed that. You know they're not concrete.'

'Ah'm not talking about that. They're not cleared.'

'How d'you mean?'

Don's response was to grab his mattock and set about hacking the turf away along the course of the planned wall. When he'd removed a five-foot section, he raked the soil beneath level, then leant the mattock up against a tree. The operation took about two minutes. 'There. That's how it should have been. An' that's what ah expected.' I tried not to be disconcerted by his ominous shift of tense—from a potentially negotiable 'should be' to a settled, irreversible 'should have been'.

'OK ... fair enough ... well, I'm sure we can get round this. Why don't you go inside and have a cup of coffee and I'll do it now. By the time you come out, I'll have the first section ready, then I'll keep ahead of you as you go.'

'That's not the point. It should have been ready.' He opened the back of his Land Rover, picked up his mattock and other tools and started putting them in.

'But ... er ... you're surely not ... I mean, you're not going to ... just ... *go* ... rather than wait the time it takes to have a cup of coffee?'

'It should have been ready.'

This was no time for pride. 'Look Don, the reason I've waited so

217

long for you is because I think your walls are so beautiful. They're by far the best walls I've ever seen. They're the reason ...'

'Don't flatter me.' Unfortunately, I was light on alternative strategies. 'No, really. Your walls are in a different league ...'

'*Don't flatter me.*'

He slammed the back door of his Land Rover. There was no doubt about it; he really was going. And with that, something in me snapped; the waiting, the not knowing, the grovelling, our looming deadline. He was dead right. The moment for flattery had passed. 'What is it with you, Don? D'you ever get out of bed the right side? I've dialled your wretched phone number until my fingers bled. I've removed the fence. I've got the right stone and put it in the right place. I've waited months on the off-chance the great Don might deign to show up. Then, out of the blue, you announce you're coming today, with about a minute's notice, and what do I get?' Here I put on my finest toddler's impression of the way he spoke: '*Antony, ah'm disappointed. Ah see ye're not ready for us.*'

Don froze. For a moment I thought I'd gone too far. He was an ex-soldier, I belatedly remembered. In silence, he got into his Land Rover, started the engine and bumped off down the track.

Vez emerged from the house with coffee, cheerful and smiling. She looked around. 'Where's Don?' she said.

———•◦•———

I'd built walls with my father. The construction of Phase Two of the Great Modernist Experiment was delayed by months when (despite repeated warnings from my father) the builders discovered that four inches beneath the Mendip topsoil lay bedrock. Bigger diggers were brought, then bigger still. The birdsong was drowned by pneumatic drills, each eternity of drilling yielding a few more shards of splintered rock. The saltpetre smell of rock dust ground by tungsten steel filled the air. By the time the house was finished, the place still resembled a quarry. My father, faced with tons of rock to clear, did what everyone in his situation has always done: he built walls. Walls for raised beds on the downhill side. Retaining walls against the uphill cliff face. Freestanding walls in between.

I helped. From the age of ten to twelve, living in the middle of nowhere, there was, frankly, little else to do. As a family, apart from eating and sleeping, we shared no interests. My mother, I think it's fair to say, found young children a bore. She seemed to be away most weekends, during daylight hours anyway, pursuing her various equestrian capers. Jonny was at a boarding school in Bristol. So with no-one else around on Saturdays and Sundays, my father looked after me. His preferred occupations were solitary, involving things rather than people: reading (*The Times*, Jane Austen, Pevsner), visiting churches, playing the piano, gardening. While he adored his children, most of a young boy's interests, such as football, pop music, guns, television, films, induced a sort of horrified despair at the human condition, making it hard to find any common ground. But walling—walling was the one thing we could do together.

Saturday was walling day. Once the tons of pulverised rock had been heaped according to size, we started nearest the house. My father would specify what we needed and I'd fetch the appropriate stones in the wheelbarrow. 'Goodness, I don't know how you carry so many,' he'd say every time, as, with a marathon heave, I tipped another load at his feet. Then there was a blissful break while he picked amongst the stones. Trying one, bedding it in by jiggling it this way then that, his trowel in constant use, digging, scooping, nudging stones into position.*

* Mendip's carboniferous limestone being famously difficult to build with: lacking any grain to yield to the walling hammer and almost as hard as granite. Every stone is a 'dog's head' or 'highway man's hat', as wallers call the really impossible ones.

I can see him now, stepping back to inspect a newly placed stone, cocking his head to check its level, scratching his nose, returning to make some slight adjustment, mopping his brow with the back of his gardening glove, blowing his nose into a large white handkerchief (the full trombone roar).

We'd stop once mid-morning (Treetops orange squash and Club biscuits), then at one for lunch (fish pie left by my mother, followed by tinned pears and butterscotch Angel Delight). Then it was back to work until we heard my mother's car coming up the lane, heralded by long blasts of the horn. The best bit came once we'd got Ma into the house and had tea: going back outside to admire what we'd done as, bit by bit, almost imperceptibly, the walls grew and the stone piles shrank. The pleasure of walling, my father enjoyed saying, was one of the great pleasures: making order out of chaos.

Over the week following Don's departure, as I related the incident to anyone who'd listen, it emerged that I wasn't alone in my tribulations with wallers; that, in fact, if there were a leaflet missing from the Dry Stone Walling Association's otherwise comprehensive series, it was the one entitled *Dealing with Wallers Who are Miserable Old Sods.* 'It's hardly surprising they're misanthropes,' said one acquaintance. 'Think about it. Alone all day, bending and lifting, heaving stone in all weathers. They feel under-appreciated. Everyone thinks part of their job is to lug the stone to the right place, and regards them as horny-handed labour rather than the craftsmen or artists which, let's face it, the decent ones are. And if you want perfection, you're bound to get a few prima donnas. Chuck in the permanent backache. Do you wonder they're sociopaths?'

By this point the prospect of finding a waller, any waller, at such short notice seemed non-existent. Briefly, wildly, I wondered if I shouldn't build the damn things myself. Time was the problem. Even if I turned out to be a skilled waller and worked night and day until Mrs Kerr's return, I knew there was no way that, single-handed, I could transform seventy tons of rubble into two tidy five foot six walls in three weeks. In any case, as the sole extant 'feature' in the garden, this was no time for experimentation.

Gloomily combing the Register of Certificated Professional Members for the hundredth time, I bemoaned the fact that we didn't live in proper stone wall country. If only we lived in Derbyshire, or Yorkshire, or Lancashire! They had pages of wallers to choose from. I'd even heard that walling up there was half the price. Which was when my narrow-mindedness struck me. I'd been working on a false premise. I wanted the walls to be made of local stone, yes. But who said the wallers themselves had to be local? I turned to the Pennine counties, the nearest in the Register to us. Qualified wallers were divided into 'Intermediate' (clearly the novices), 'Advanced' (Don's standard) and 'Master'. I dialled the number of a Master Waller at random. Aye, said a cheery Midlands voice, he was available. Aye, he was happy to travel if the job was worth it. I emailed pictures. Aye, it would take about four days. He'd bring his walling partner with him. And the rumours were right: he was less than half Don's price.

So the following Monday, shortly before 8 a.m., Shaun and Gaz pitched up. They were in their early thirties, bristling with bumptious energy. They were more than happy with my preparations, especially the way I'd cleared the turf and dug out the course of the wall ('Don't normally see that,' said Gaz). They were both farmers, it turned out, who supplemented their income with walling. The first course was down in minutes. Thereafter they worked as fast as they could pick up stones. Apart from odd snatches of conversation, there was just the click and clock of stone on stone, and the periodic sound of tumbling rubble as the rock pile rapidly diminished.

Shaun and Gaz finished the walls in three-and-a-half days. The messy tangle of wire was but a memory. The yard was transformed. 'Did you build these walls?' said my father on his next visit.

'Er ... no. But I might as well have done.'

'You *employed* somebody, I suppose?'

'Yes ... but I'll definitely build the next one myself. It must be easier.'

'I shall believe it when I see it.'

He was impressed though, I knew. In any case, the important thing was that, finally, one small corner of Tair-Ffynnon, from one view, looked exactly right. We were on our way. We even had something to show Mrs Kerr.

16

Return of the County Organiser

The descriptions of the gardens are written by their owners, and have to be brief. This concentrates the mind and, reading the brief notes on each garden, you learn what each gardener thinks is most important and interesting about his garden, and gain an insight into the aspirations of the present generation of garden makers, even if these are not always successfully realised.

JANE FEARNLEY-WHITTINGSTALL, on Yellow Book gardens,
The Garden: An English Love Affair, 2003

With care, I adjusted the last axe-head and stepped back to admire my handiwork. Immediately in front of the house was a small walled area with a rickety metal gate. It was a lousy wall, bodged together with broken bricks and breezeblocks and any other rubble to hand. Sheep hopped in when they felt like it (for instance to eat Uncle William's trees when we'd naively placed them here for safekeeping) and, after blundering about for a while, usually decided not to waste the effort of hopping out again, barging the gate down instead. Its aesthetic and practical failings aside, however, the top of the wall was at least more or less flat. And it was along this that I'd arranged my treasure trove.

I'd been much taken, when I first saw his garden, with the way Derek Jarman used beachcombings as garden features.* Shingle flints, buoys, fenders, sea-corroded iron, bleached driftwood, lobster claws, boat hooks, propped every square foot. Keen to borrow this idea, I was always on the hunt for such found art. But life on a hill was different from life by the sea, where the stuff just came to you. At Tair-Ffynnon, the wind brought nothing but low cloud and fallen trees, and the hill delivered little but sheep skeletons. However we did, it turned out, have treasure of our own—*buried* treasure. As we cleared and dug over the place, we'd unearthed an ever-increasing mountain of rusting ironmongery: hooks and chains and engine parts, gate hinges and latches, plough shares and cutter bars and weird crooked spanners. Pride of place so far went to an old single-barrelled twelve-bore shotgun. All these items had three things in common. They were heavy, they were rusty, and they were (to me at least) too precious to throw away. So we'd kept them, adding gradually to the collection until we had, literally, tons. And it was this, these *objets trouvés* and 'hill-combings', that I had now sorted, separated, categorised, and artfully arranged along the wall. There was no doubt, as I now stood back to admire my handiwork, it was worth it. They looked terrific.

This burst of organisation had been brought on by panic. It was now

---

* That, in fact, was how he'd started. 'One day, walking on the beach at low tide, I noticed a magnificent flint. I brought it back and pulled out one of the bricks. Soon I had replaced all the rubble with flints. They were hard to find, but after a storm a few more would appear. The bed looked great, like dragon's teeth—white and grey. My journey to the sea each morning had purpose. I decided to stop there; after all, the bleakness of Prospect Cottage was what had made me fall in love with it. At the back I planted a dog rose. Then I found a curious piece of driftwood and used this, and one of the necklaces of holey stones that I hung on the wall, to stake the rose. The garden had begun.' *Derek Jarman's Garden*, 1991.

September. With three days to go before Mrs Kerr returned to decide whether or not we'd made it into the Yellow Book, the question was: had we done enough? A few days previously, in a fit of clear-sightedness, I'd suddenly seen Tair-Ffynnon as most others seemed to see it: in short, a dump. There was no doubt that we were making progress, but most of our endeavours—gates, bees, pond, walls—had only reached their gruelling climax in the last few days.

It wasn't that we were short of ideas. The Infinity Vegetable Patch, we felt sure, would be a winning novelty. The old vegetable patch had been in a sensible and obvious spot in front of the house, sloping south on a collapsing terrace. Our plan was to raise the lower southern end of the terrace by five feet or so on a new (as yet unbuilt) retaining wall. This, in theory, would be just enough to hide the foreground field across the track, thereby leaving the vegetable patch hanging dramatically over an 'infinity view' across the distant valley. How well, or even whether, this would work, we hadn't the faintest idea, for our future vegetable garden presently consisted of 150 tons of unlevelled spoil excavated from the foundations for the railway carriage.

This was merely the first of the various, still unrealised stages of our plan. Having removed the wire fences and the leggy remains of a hedge that formed the only surviving boundaries to the plot, there remained the problem of how to protect the patch from our friends in the sheepskin coats. We couldn't rely on our main yard gate remaining shut. It would take only one person to leave it open once for all to be lost. Besides, trying to keep Welsh Mountain sheep out of our yard was like trying to keep dung flies off a cow pat. So, what? Fences looked ugly. Hedges? For the first ten years that just meant a fence. And dry-stone walls would neatly block the one really good view from the house. Solving this simple problem had vexed me for months until, somewhere, I saw a picture of the garden Gertrude Jekyll designed for Edward Hudson, the founder of *Country Life*, during the 1911 restoration of Lindisfarne Castle on Holy Island off the Northumberland coast.

Lindisfarne occupies an almost absurdly picturesque setting, perched

on a rocky island crag separated from the Northumberland coast by a three-mile tidal causeway. Any conventional garden in such a majestically bleak setting would have looked hopelessly out of place. But someone—Jekyll, or Lutyens, who was restoring the castle—had the brainwave of converting the old stone-walled vegetable patch, half a mile away below the castle, into a cheerful flower garden. Thus it was effectively separated from the sheep-grazed landscape around it, yet was visible from the castle windows above. In order to facilitate this, I noticed, the wall on the castle side was slightly lower so as not to obstruct the view.

Why couldn't we do something similar? If we created a vegetable garden as a separate walled enclosure, like an island, the sheep could roam freely around it, keeping the turf nibbled. It employed the pleasing and fitting hill aesthetic of the sheepfold, gave an excuse for more dry-stone walls (impossible to have too many of those), and it followed and accentuated the lie of the land. And it would do what every book I'd read on the subject insisted was the first commandment of good garden design: it would prevent the view and the garden being seen all at once.

As a bonus, on the west side of the vegetable patch where it bordered the orchard, the fall of the ground meant the wall would have to be significantly higher than on the yard side. This would allow for a garden feature I'd always coveted: a 'low door in a wall'. Of the many garden tropes this, for me, has always been the one that packs maximum romance and excitement, mainlining directly into childhood literary fantasy. Anyone brought up on *Alice's Adventures in Wonderland** or

* Alice's low door, hidden behind a curtain and which she opens with the golden key on the glass table (with the 'Eat Me' cake on), leads to 'the loveliest garden you ever saw'.

The Secret Garden* is fully briefed on low doors. My appreciation came late, after reading *Brideshead Revisited* aged eighteen. In the celebrated passage where Waugh recounts Charles's thoughts the first time he goes to lunch with Sebastian Flyte, he uses a 'low door in the wall' opening onto 'an enclosed and enchanted garden' as the captivating metaphor for Charles's admission into the charmed world that Sebastian's set represents. To my adolescent self, just becoming aware of such worlds within worlds, it struck a powerful chord.** Later, when I discovered that Waugh's low door actually existed and was the same one that inspired Lewis Carroll, I had to see it. So I visited the Dean's Garden at Christ Church, Oxford (otherwise known as 'Alice's Garden'), and there it was: dark green and, as it happened, not that low. Nevertheless, the low door of low doors—one day I vowed to have one in my garden.

* Mary's low door, buried under ivy trails, and to which she's led by a robin, opens into 'the sweetest, most mysterious-looking place anyone could imagine'. Frances Hodgson Burnett said it was based on the abandoned walled orchard at Great Maytham Hall, Rolvenden, Kent, which, when she rented the house from 1898 to 1907, she turned into a rose garden. This was entered by a wooden door in a low arched gateway.

** 'I went full of curiosity and the faint, unrecognised apprehension that here, at last, I should find that low door in the wall, which others, I knew, had found before me, which opened on an enclosed and enchanted garden, which was somewhere, not overlooked by any window, in the heart of that grey city.'

Then there was the quarry in the Top Field, where the tea tent was scheduled to be. Up there, initially, we'd planned a dry-stone cairn, like those capping hills and high passes the world over. This idea, which had so underwhelmed Mrs Kerr on her first visit, had now inflated into a full-blown Himalayan *chorten*, complete with fluttering strings of prayer flags—but for which, as for the cairn before it, not a stone had so far been laid.

We'd hardly finished congratulating ourselves on the *chorten* idea when our neighbour, Ed, emailed a poem he'd come across by the Anglo-Welsh poet Edward Thomas. The first twelve lines of 'The Lofty Sky', from around 1900, might have been written for me, as I headed up to the trig point with Beetle each morning.

> *To-day I want the sky,*
> *The tops of the high hills,*
> *Above the last man's house,*
> *His hedges, and his cows,*
> *Where, if I will, I look*
> *Down even on sheep and rook,*
> *And of all things that move*
> *See buzzards only above:*
> *Past all trees, past furze*
> *And thorn, where nought deters*
> *The desire of the eye*
> *For sky, nothing but sky.*

It so perfectly said everything our garden was supposed to capture, it was essential to incorporate it somehow. How about sign-writing it onto the blank east wall of the tin barn, facing the hill and Offa's Dyke footpath, where walkers and paragliders would see it catching the morning sun? What better way to put vim in their stride and soaring thoughts in their heads?

The only hitch with all these ideas was that they might or might not happen by the time the garden opened—*if* it opened—next summer. None helped us in the here and now, and on this Mrs Kerr had been most specific. 'What you need are features that people can *see*. It's no good telling people what they *might* see one day.' To a County Organiser, promises were no doubt regarded as so much thistledown on the wind. Meanwhile the other aspects of my gardening venture— splitting logs on frosty mornings, high-jinks with bees, making hay with ancient machinery—while addressing various personal longings, left little tangible spoor apart from the odd wood pile, beehive or rusty tractor. So far as Mrs Kerr was concerned, the only visible improvements would be two stretches of wall and a muddy hole we called a pond. The house was still hideous. The vegetable garden was a slagheap. The flower meadows were thickets of docks and thistles.

In short, two nights before her return, I got the fear. After a burst of tidying and pulling up nettles, and hanging an oak swing in the big ash in the Middle Field, I'd arranged the rusty treasure trove along the top of the garden wall. Even having done this, the discrepancy between us and, say, Great Dixter or Little Sparta, seemed wider than I would have liked. In the time remaining, all I could think of was to draw up a garden plan that included a few pictures of some of our ideas, in the hope this might bring them to life and buy us more time. So I sat up late with Maya's felt tips and glue sticks.

To pre-empt any suggestion we hadn't got the minimum forty-five-minutes'-worth of interest, I also compiled a list of what I hoped sounded like tempting features, from the setting ('views to nine counties') and wildlife ('red grouse, redstarts and red kites') to products for sale ('award-winning honey') and, in case the floral side of things might seem neglected, an optimistic list of meadow flowers copied from a flyer I'd picked up at the High Moorland Centre in Dartmoor. It struck me that it would do no harm, either, to have ready-drafted an entry for the garden as it might appear in the Yellow Book (just supposing we got in). It was already getting late in the day for entries for next year, I knew, so anything that saved time must be welcome.

Besides, this would reconfirm our robust sense of purpose, even, perhaps, lull her into believing our acceptance was inevitable.

Consulting a few entries suggested that descriptions were limited to around fifty words, with new gardens that year clearly flagged. I typed:

NEW! TAIR-FFYNNON.

The first sentence, describing what sort of a garden it was, was plainly critical. Here was our chance to separate ourselves from everyone else, to somehow highlight why Tair-Ffynnon was so special. Obviously we should mention the National Park, the mere phrase instantly conjured wildness and unspoiled beauty. And Mrs Kerr, I remembered, had very much liked the fact we were near Offa's Dyke footpath.

NEW! TAIR-FFYNNON. Six-acre smallholding on
Offa's Dyke footpath in the Brecon Beacons National Park.

That was alright so far as it went, but it didn't seem to be making enough of our position. After reflection, I inserted 'wild mountain setting'.

Six-acre smallholding in wild mountain setting on Offa's Dyke
footpath in the Brecon Beacons National Park.

Yes, that definitely added tone. But still it would be good to include a straightforward, unassailable assertion that ours was the *wildest* garden, or the *most mountainous*. What we really wanted to say, of course—and it still rankled badly that we couldn't—was that Tair-Ffynnon was the highest garden in the Yellow Book. But facts had to be faced. And the brutal truth was that we languished at around 1,200 feet, while two other gardens (even ignoring the imposter we'd exposed last year) appeared to have the edge, alleging they were at 1,300 feet and 1,450 feet respectively. What was needed was some mode of expression that would level the opposition for good. I consulted the OS map. The trig point was marked at 1,554 feet. Perhaps that could be worked in? It was, after all, to all intents and purposes, part of our garden. And 1,554 was practically 1,600 feet. With careful wording, perhaps …

> Six-acre smallholding in wild mountain setting (reaching nearly 1,600 feet)

That was more like it. Even so, would people necessarily take from it that we were the highest garden in the book? Might they not still assume there were other pretenders out there? This kind of thing had to be spelt out. While I was musing, I found I'd typed:

> The highest garden in the Yellow Book.

I looked at the words. They certainly had a ring to them: an effortless, peremptory confidence, baloney or not. Though really, of course, one wanted to go one better:

> The highest garden in Britain.

Now *that* was a fact to be reckoned with. That gave people something to chew on. What a shame it wasn't, strictly speaking, true. I poured myself a glass of wine. On the other hand, who was to say we weren't? It was a grey area. It depended on many things—how you defined 'garden' for one. Perhaps if an element of doubt were introduced:

> **NEW! TAIR-FFYNNON.** The highest garden in Britain?
> Six-acre smallholding in wild mountain setting reaching to
> nearly 1,600 feet on Offa's Dyke footpath in the Brecon
> Beacons National Park.

Finally we were getting somewhere. What else? Mrs Kerr had mentioned last time that people would be disappointed, if they were

231

expecting lawns, shrubs and borders, not to get them. Well, fair enough. In that case

> DO NOT COME if you like manicured lawns and herbaceous borders; COME if you like wind, dry-stone walls, upland meadow pasture, rusty tin, heather, red kites and views of 70 miles. TEAS.

A bit clumsy, perhaps, but the point was made. I checked some more entries in the Yellow Book again. Half the word count for most of them was devoted to directions. Here, too, surely, was an opportunity for pleasing evocation? I cobbled together directions for a hill odyssey that might have ended at Wuthering Heights or Baskerville Hall. Really, what fun all this was. I was still putting the finishing touches the following morning when the sound of a car indicated that our big moment had come.

———◆◆◆———

'So ... are we in?'

The tour had gone better than I'd dared hope. From the moment Mrs Kerr arrived, she'd seemed, dare I think it, more cheerful than before. She'd admired the new fifty-yard section of wall, incorporating the old stone trough my father had given us for a wedding present. Even the foundations of the new shed had received explicit approval. And she'd noticed the work on the carriage, its new clean tongue-and-grooved planks alongside the old grey timber with its peeling paint.

Then I'd shown her the orchard and the new gates, at which she'd 'hmmed' approvingly. I'd reiterated that the hedge would be cut and laid come the winter and outlined the plans for the Lindisfarne-style walled vegetable garden.

'That's a lot to do before next year.'

'We're only a third of our way through the available time, remember.'

'A third? How d'you work that out?' She'd frowned for a moment. 'When did I last come, let me see, April? That's one, two, three … five months ago.'

'So if we opened in August, that gives us another ten months.'

'Hmmm.' She'd ignored the presumption implicit in my suggestion. As we passed the beehives, she'd said, 'Are they your bees?'

'Of course.'

'Did you get any honey?'

'First prize at the Llanthony Show.'

'Were there any other competitors?'

'Really, Joanna'—things were going so much better, Christian names seemed in order—'you don't seem to have much faith.'

'Well, were there?'

'One, as it happens.'

'There you are.'

We'd wandered on. The pond, she'd agreed, was a muddy mess, but also that it was early days. But it was when we got up to the old quarry (where I'd mown a patch to show where the tea tent would go) that she'd seemed to capitulate almost completely. 'My goodness. Look at that view.'

Her demeanour was so warm, it was hard to believe she was the same person who'd been here last time. Accordingly, on the way back down to the house, I'd decided to risk it. I'd put the fateful question: 'So, are we in?'

'Hmm,' she said again. But it was a good 'Hmm', a friendly 'Hmm'.

I opened the garden gate for her. She didn't seem to notice my beautiful arrangement of rusty artefacts. 'I'm being bamboozled,' she said to Vez, as we went into the kitchen. 'Is he always like this?'

'Always,' said Vez.

I produced my garden plan. 'I've done a drawing.'

With my finger I ran her along the track to the Far Field, which was going to be the car park, then guided her through the Monmouthshire gates, along the mown serpentine path through the wild flower

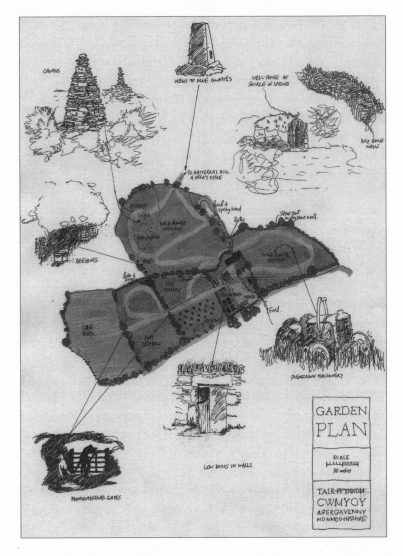

meadows, stopping briefly at the swing ('incredible view of Skirrid'),
then on through the orchard to the yard with the railway carriage, round
the Hang-Glider Field with its overgrown Fordson and old hay rakes,
up the Top Field, via the beehives, to the pond. Then, finally, onto the

cherry on the cake, the quarry with its views and, maybe, its handsome *chorten*. She studied it for a few moments. 'Very pretty,' she said in a don't-think-I'll-be-bought-off-that-easily voice. 'But what still concerns me is whether there's going to be anything for people to *see*. Last week I turned down someone who was as full of promises as you are for what was going to be here and there. She was furious. But I can't allow things just on the basis of promises.'

The crunch was looming, and her mind still sounded by no means made up. I produced my draft for our Yellow Book entry. 'My goodness, you're very certain you're going to get in.'

'No, no. Heavens no. Not at all. Just trying to think ahead. You know, help give an idea how the place might fit in.'

She glanced at the sheet. A red pen appeared and was uncapped with a click. It hovered for a moment over the first sentence, then started moving over the words. It got no further than the first full stop before it reversed, stopped and hovered over the phrase, 'highest garden in Britain'.

'We can't say that.'

'What?' I said. 'Why not?'

'It's not a garden.'

'*What?*'

'It's not a garden.'

'What d'you mean, it's not a garden? Of course it's a garden.'

'Well, it's not most people's idea of a garden. It's a … well … it's a collection of fields. A garden has plants and flowers.'

'Who said gardens have to have flowers?'

'Of course gardens have flowers.' (The don't-mess-with-me tone again.)

'The Garden of Eden didn't. At least there's no mention of them. The original Hebrew means "place of pleasure". The Bible, at least the *New English Bible*, only mentions trees. And most dictionaries have at least one definition which doesn't include flowers.'

235

'Nobody likes a clever clogs, Antony.' Her tone became severer still. I'd hardly begun, I thought. What about Capability Brown, where were his flowers and shrubs? What about Hieronymous Bosch's 'Garden of Earthly Delights'? What about Sir Joshua Reynolds, for whom gardening was merely 'a deviation from Nature'? What *did* constitute a garden? Surely it was entirely subjective? Tair-Ffynnon was a garden if it was a garden to us. 'How about ... "an eccentric arrangement of fields"?' said Joanna.

'An arrangement of fields? Is that what you think it is? But it's appearing in the Yellow Book, a book devoted entirely to gardens.'

'It isn't yet.'

Really, it was extraordinary. After preparing for every kind of objection to our claim to be the highest garden in the land, here we were embroiled in a squabble about the definition of the word 'garden'. The red pen had moved on, however.

'Hmmm ... "Do not come" sounds a bit negative.' A neat line went through the words. 'Goodness, and all these directions. They sound awfully complicated.' More crossing out. '"Follow the yellow signs" would be perfectly adequate. And maybe there should be some warning about the road, something like "very steep and narrow lanes". Also, some idea of what it's like when they get here.' The pen was hovering again.

'"Come if you're fit and intrepid", something like that.' She wrote it down. 'So, where are we? What was it you said?' She looked at my draft again, then wrote: 'Six-acre smallholding at 1,600 feet in wild ...'

'Er ... no, we can't actually say that.'

'Why not?'

'Because we're not that high.'

'That's what you've written here.'

'It's not, in fact. It's what I've implied.'

'So how high are you?'

'Oh ... about 1,300ish.'

'Well, phrase it how you like. No-one's going to check.'

'Really?'

'Of course not. People have got better things to do.' I handed her my list of garden features. 'My goodness. It never stops.'

She scanned the page. '*Award-winning* honey? You've got a nerve. Just because you once won a prize at Llanthony Show, from a class of two? My jams and chutneys have won prizes at Usk Show year in and year out. I wouldn't dream of describing them as "award-winning".'

She went on down the list.

'Foxgloves? In July?'

'Ye-es ...?'

'Foxgloves are well over by the end of July.' That was unfortunate.

'Remember, we're much later up here.'

'Really? That much later?'

Was she ever going to stop? I wasn't sure how much longer I could keep this up.

'So ... are we in?'

'We-e-ell, I was at a Regional Committee meeting yesterday and they said—'

'That they're looking for more offbeat gardens?' I said hopefully.

'No. I said, I was at the Regional Committee meeting all day yesterday and they said—'

'That you should clamp down more on gardens not up to scratch?' I said.

'Will you stop interrupting? They said they're keen to get more *environmental* gardens. I suppose yours just about qualifies.'

'So ... we're in?'

'We-ell.' She gave a sigh of infinite resignation. 'I suppose so.'

———•◆•———

And so it was.

NEW! TAIR-FFYNNON. Highest garden in Britain? 6-acre smallholding in mountain setting (reaching nearly 1,600 feet)

237

on Offa's Dyke footpath in the Brecon Beacons National Park. For anyone fit and intrepid who sees beauty in wild places—in upland hay meadows, dry-stone walls and mountain springs, forgotten farm machinery in field corners and gateways framing 70-mile views. **Adm. £3.50, chd free. Sun. 29 July (11–6).**

It was, unquestionably, a little on the whimsical side. And the pedantic or litigious, having checked their altimeters, might have gone on to quibble about the distance of the framed views. Still, it was the broad brush that counted.

The main thing was—we were in. We'd done it. Tair-Ffynnon was in the Yellow Book. We'd agreed that a late-summer opening date was right. Most gardens had already opened by then, so it filled a useful gap in the garden-visiting calendar. The key thing, Joanna impressed upon us, was not to let up just because we were in. The end of July might be almost a year away, but that was no excuse for slacking. 'There's still an immense amount to do,' she said, the steel briefly returning.

As we left the house, Joanna finally clocked my artful collection along the garden wall. 'Good heavens, what's all this?'

'All stuff we've dug up or found around the place,' I said.

'No! You don't mean it. All this? My goodness, farmers are untidy.' She turned back to me. 'Well, just make sure you clear it all away before the opening.'

17

Life, death and hedge-cutting

The many and varied styles of Welsh hedges seem at first to defy classification, with each area claiming a hedging tradition of its own. On the local level it is often hard to tell if a particular hedge is representative of its area, or is a single craftsman's idiosyncratic blending of styles into a new combination ... There is often fierce argument as to the balance required between protecting and possibly smothering the new growth with deadwood cuttings.

Elizabeth Agate and Alan Brooks,
Hedging: A Practical Handbook, 1998

Despite Joanna's express commands, despite our solemn pledges, the moment we knew we were in the Yellow Book, naturally, we downed tools. From autumn through to spring, we did nothing.*

---

* My father says this is normal for all gardeners; that everyone's bored with gardening by late summer, ready to start again, with possessed enthusiasm, the following spring.

For the winter I'd set myself a solitary goal: to cut and lay the hedge down the west side of the orchard. It was a task I'd been saving up—a prize, if we got in. For hedge-laying is a treat of a job. The hedge was an overgrown, tangled mess, blocking the view without providing any kind of useful barrier. As hedge-laying is pretty severe treatment, it has to happen in winter, when growth is dormant and birds aren't nesting. There's a five-month window between October and February when, theoretically, there isn't much else to do in the country. But still, by the time I'd marshalled the necessary frame of mind, and Mark, who'd said he'd help, had finished lambing, it was almost April. Mark said this didn't matter. Everything up on the hill was later, so really it was still February.

The purpose of this ancient craft is to transform ageing hedgerows into tighter, denser, healthier, more stock-proof field boundaries.* As they grow, hedges become tall and leggy, and get gaps round their base where stock can easily push through. Cutting and laying consists of nearly, but not quite, severing healthy vertical stems at ground level, so that they can then be 'laid' along the length of the hedge to form a much more useful horizontal barrier. These partially severed 'pleachers' (long, straight, healthy branches which can be intertwined like basketwork along the length of the hedge) survive and produce bushy new vertical growth. The process looks brutal to the uninitiated, depending, as it does, on the well-established principle that the harder you cut something back, the more furiously it grows. But a skilfully laid hedge is also a thing of beauty.

It was a perfect early spring morning as Mark and I assembled our kit: a light frost was melting in bright sunshine and the birds were singing lustily. The first rule of hedge-laying is that on a slope you lay uphill—that is, so the branches being cut and laid face up the slope— because sap rises. Keen for Mark to grasp early on that this was one

---

* And wind breaks. Uncle William says a hedge is a much better wind break than a wall because it sieves the air, rather than ricocheting it at full force elsewhere.

activity at which I was not a complete novice, I ferried my chain-saw, cans of petrol and chain oil, funnel, axe, heavy steel post-banger and bill hook down to the downhill end ready to start. Mark was fiddling about at the uphill end, but eventually, as I got the last of these items assembled, he noticed what I was doing. 'We start this end,' he called.

'But you lay uphill,' I said. It was disconcerting to discover he didn't even know this.

'You still have to start at the uphill end, and work backwards,' Mark said. 'Otherwise you're trying to lay into standing timber. "Lay uphill, work downhill." That's how it works.' Duh. I heaved my chainsaw, cans of petrol and chain oil, funnel, axe, post-banger and bill hook back up to the uphill end.

Our first task was to 'clean' the hedge. This meant cutting out the old and dead wood, the brambles and any branches pointing the wrong way; the idea being to leave a filleted, thinned-out hedge, with plenty of potential pleachers for laying. Hacking and sawing enthusiastically, soon I was shedding layers and feeling the colour rise in my cheeks. The orchard hedge was far from ideal for laying. Wide gaps of almost no material alternated with jungle thickets so intertwined that, having severed some gnarly old trunk, I was left panting from the exertion of trying to extricate its tangled branches.

In no time, the first blackthorn ran into my hand. I could see its dark tip beneath the skin.* Cursing my hopeless, cotton gardening gloves, within minutes, I found myself spiked, scratched and gashed a dozen more times. (Mark, I noticed, wore stout leather gauntlets.) And blackthorn was merely one of the potential assailants. Hawthorn also commanded respect. Then there were the brambles snagging my trouser legs, backed up by clumps of nettles, waiting their moment, stinging

---

* Blackthorn, the main constituent of most stock hedges, gets a bad press. A thorn entering the hand, it's said, can work its way up to your elbow before emerging. Endless stories circulate of people dying from blackthorn blood-poisoning.

through denim as if it wasn't there. Worst though was holly, the whippy green branches of which have a habit of evading the most vigorous bill hook swipe, to spring vengefully back across the face.

After half an hour, my face, neck and wrists were striped red, but it couldn't dent my mood. Few uses of a winter day can match laying a hedge. It's good exercise, supplies a grand sense of achievement (impressing those who don't know that it's easier than it looks), while conferring true countryman status. At the same time, it licenses an agreeable self-righteousness by being good for the environment as well as a beauty to behold. On this occasion, besides, the ritual was invested with extra significance.

'I do think Helen's the limit,' my mother announced one weekend the year before we got Tair-Ffynnon. She hunched up her arms and shoulders as she said it, the way she always did when she felt cold. 'She had a very nasty bout of flu earlier this month and came up here before she'd properly got over it. Now I've caught it and just can't seem to shake it off.' Helen was my mother's helper, the best and longest-standing of the numerous occupants of that position over the years. Capable, unflappable, her supreme asset was that she was largely impervious to my mother. Over the following weeks, however, Ma continued to complain of being 'under the weather', canvassing support from whatever quarter she could over the long-suffering Helen's unpardonable behaviour. ('Don't *you* think it was extraordinarily selfish of her? Well? Don't you?')

To start with we didn't take her very seriously. True, she was seldom ill, except for hayfever in the summer or the odd winter cold, which, accordingly, were the only conditions she recognised in others. We assumed her latest complaint was a variant of these. But when it persisted month after month, it finally became time to consult the doctor. It wasn't flu, of course. It was cancer.

In fact she'd had breast cancer for years, but we'd more or less forgotten. Following treatment, she'd settled down to her Tamoxifen pills and expressly forbidden us from mentioning it to anyone. It certainly wasn't allowed to impinge on her hectic schedule. But now she lost her appetite and her sense of taste. She looked pale with deep shadows round her eyes in a way she never had before. After various tests it was confirmed that the cancer had spread, though how far we wouldn't know until the results of a scan on New Year's Eve. So after a trepidatious Christmas (marked by the twin disorientations of my mother for the first time not cooking Christmas lunch and Vez, the same day, discovering she was pregnant with Maya), I met my parents on New Year's Eve at the Oncology Unit of the Bristol Royal Infirmary. I arrived late, as they emerged from their meeting with the consultant. 'The news isn't good,' said my mother with a grimace. The cancer, it seemed, had spread everywhere. Liver. Bones ... How long? The consultant said it was hard to say, but not long. Chemotherapy might conceivably stave off the inevitable for a bit, but it was still weeks rather than months. She opted not to have chemotherapy. I decided to come home for a bit, to be around.

It was strange being back with my parents, buried in the country, after so long away. Sleeping in my old room, I'd be woken each morning by the familiar sound of squeaking and squawking as my father wiped condensation from the plate-glass windows. After breakfast, I'd do some writing, and in the afternoon I'd take a short walk with Da. But in a sedentary household in mid-winter, without my usual London props or friends, in the company of two people in their late seventies, one more or less bed-bound, there wasn't much to do.

It so happened that two men were laying the hedge running up the opposite side of the lane. The land had been let to a new tenant, who was taking it in hand. I found myself drawn to what they were doing, and for a couple of afternoons went to watch them. Two things struck me: first, how much I wanted to lay a hedge; second, that it didn't look that hard. Certainly there seemed precious little finesse to the way this pair were hacking out the old wood with their chainsaws, slicing most of the way through the remaining stems, then flattening them down with a shove. Along the back of the field behind my parents' house there was a hopelessly overgrown hedge. I decided I would lay it. It would get me out of the house, give me something to do.

My mother liked the idea. While the house was my father's domain, the stables and fields had always been hers, but since Jonny and I had left home, they'd been abandoned to their own devices.

There was an obstacle to my plan, however: I lacked the necessary tools. Chainsaw and bill hook were two items signally absent from my father's tool cupboard. This absence was no accident. Da's garden tools were essentially those of an urban mindset, what might broadly be categorised as tidying-up kit: trowel, secateurs, shears, rake, brush, dustpan, mower. To my father, a petrol-driven chainsaw—dangerous, noisy, dirty and brutal—pretty much encapsulated, in a single object, all he most disliked about the country and a particular species within it—establishment, *country*, 'county'—with which he, educated at a grammar school and on a County Scholarship, felt little affinity.*

With my urban existence and a baby due, there was no way I could justify the cost of a chainsaw. Yet to lay the hedge—and I couldn't remember when I'd wanted to do something more—I needed one. To ask my father to buy it was a more loaded request than it might outwardly seem. Da had watched the consequences of my public school

* Buying a first chainsaw, I'm convinced, is a significant rite-of-passage for any hedge-owning country dweller who doesn't actually earn their living from the country: it's a declaration of engagement with the land (one friend described it as like a betrothal to his plot) that separates those who are merely 'in' the country from those who, in their hearts, want more than that. Whether we categorise ourselves as essentially 'urban' or 'rural' (Angus Wilson pointed out in *The Wild Garden*) goes to the heart of who we are, prompting a whole series of unconscious judgments embodying, respectively, progress versus tradition; art versus nature; industry versus the contemplative life; reason versus instinct; sensibility versus common sense; bohemianism versus rootedness, etc. Doubtless the Stihl and Husqvarna marketing departments are only too aware of this.

education (by my mother's choice and cheque book) with mixed feelings. And, certainly, for a time in my teens our values had seemed to diverge ever further, as I threatened to join this most mistrusted class. To ask him for a chainsaw was tantamount to a formal declaration that I'd gone over to the dark side. He rubbed his chin as he always did when he was musing on something.

'You really want … this … this … saw, don't you?'

'I can't lay the hedge without it.'

I steeled myself for the familiar lecture, about always needing fancy kit to do even the simplest job, about how, had I perhaps considered, hedges were laid before chainsaws were invented. It never came. Instead, he said, 'I mean, this is something you want … even after you've done the hedge, isn't it? You're going to have a … a chain sawey kind of life, aren't you?'

'Yes,' I said. 'Yes, I am.'

And so I'd made my first attempt at hedge-laying. For the first hour or two, the delight of trying out my new tools outweighed all other aspects. Some branches I didn't cut enough before trying to lay, leaving me swinging off them to get them to break. Others I cut too deeply, so they snapped. But soon I began to get the hang of it and struck up a sort of rhythm.

It was cathartic work. Hacking at hapless elder trunks, slimy with algae, severing ivy stems choking the ash trees to death to encourage young, vital growth vented many of the complicated feelings churning inside me: fury, fear, relief perhaps, and guilt, not to mention excitement and trepidation about Vez and the baby. It offered a sense of purpose and control, however illusory, at a time when such things were in short supply.

At intervals I would go in to see my mother, sitting on the edge of the bed (she seldom got up now) to give progress reports. She was paler than ever, but in less pain because of the morphine. 'You've scratched yourself,' she would say, noticing a bramble gash on my cheek. 'Do be careful, darling.' It was good, she said, that I was getting the place in order at last, though we both knew she would never see the hedge now. I'd done about two thirds, and her condition seemed to have stabilised, when I returned to London to see Vez.

———◆———

My father called a few days later. Ma had gone into a coma. She'd delivered a short, irritated speech, apparently, to the effect that she was fed up with all this, that if she was going to go, she'd like to get on with it, then just shut her eyes. We should drop everything and come. He'd just called Jonny to say the same.

Screeching to a halt behind Jonny's car I tore through the house to the bedroom, dreading I was too late. I was mildly surprised to find Ma sitting up in bed, holding court. I kissed her hello. 'Her eyes snapped open soon after I called,' my father explained apologetically a few minutes later. 'Then she demanded bacon and eggs.' He sniffed. 'A drama queen to the end, it seems. I'm sorry, it seems I've got you down here on false pretences. But Dr Ashman was very emphatic the end was near.'

So there we all were. Should we talk to the vicar, we wondered, and ask him to perform a simple service? We debated the wisdom of this course. 'We haven't been to church for so long, I'm embarrassed to ask,' said my father. 'And I'm so dreadfully afraid she'll be rude to him. He's such a delightful man.' We were not a religious family. My mother was an atheist of the most impatient kind—or so she'd always led us to believe. However we decided that, on points, it was better to risk it.

The Reverend Clarence Tester was everything a country vicar should be. White-haired, in his seventies, unhurried, charmingly disorganised, kindly, gentle. He arrived on his bicycle, producing from the folds of his surplice a glass phial of water, a starched linen napkin and a small silver bowl, together with a black leather pocket Bible and a Book of Common Prayer. Nervously, we followed him into the bedroom, where he arranged these items on the bedside table. I remember the sound as he poured the water from the glass phial into the silver bowl. He put the Bible in her hand, made the sign of the cross on her forehead and said some prayers. It was so dignified and beautiful, so simple and moving, I wished I believed in it all. My mother appeared to be comatose, but maybe she was just pretending, keeping her options open. Certainly she didn't object or order him from the room.

Time seemed suspended, our lives on hold. Jonny sat reading copies of *Old Glory* and *Tractor and Machinery.* We took it in turns to sit with Ma, who was now lapsing in and out of consciousness. Doing any more of the hedge, now she was no longer aware of it, had somehow lost its point. It was the first time since Jonny and I were teenagers that we'd all lived under the same roof and soon old tensions began to surface. My father was worried about a blocked downpipe at the back of the house, which flowed into a water butt. 'Just take the lid off,' I said.

'I think it's a bit more complicated than that,' said my father. 'Would you mind taking a look at it, darling?' he said to Jonny. They went off to look at the problem together after lunch. Later I went to find them. 'Your brother has brilliantly solved the problem,' said my father.

'That's good. What's he done?'

'He's simply removed the lid to the butt.'

'That's what I said you should do.'

'No you didn't.'

'Yes I did. That's what I said before, at lunch.'

'No you didn't,' they both said.

I went up to the field to look at my hedge, feeling frightened and lonely.

Occasionally we'd talk about arrangements for the funeral, quietly, as Ma's bedroom was off the sitting room. I was to deliver the recollection and had begun making notes in a half-baked way. I drove up to my favourite place on the top of Mendip amongst the dry-stone walls. But I couldn't get out of my head that she was still alive, or that by the time I read the words she'd be dead.

Time waxed and waned, stretched and compressed in that elastic way it has in the presence of death, simultaneously too much and too little. Ma had been only semi-conscious for a couple of days, increasingly rambling and incoherent (but with bursts of disarming lucidity: 'I know you've got it all worked out. I can hear you out there, planning everything'). In the end it happened mid-afternoon. Jonny and I were with her. She was unconscious. All at once there was a heave and her breathing altered completely to a hollow, wheezing rattle. It really was a rattle, just like they say, like a plastic ball in a metal cylinder. It was immediately clear this was it. My father was in the bathroom, doing something. We called him back, urgently. We all held her hand. She was plainly oblivious. Suddenly she stiffened and strained, then was motionless.

We went next door, to the sitting room, my father sat in his favourite chair, Jonny and I knelt either side, each holding one of his hands. We all cried. After several minutes of this, at almost exactly the same moment, we all stopped. We all felt—it was plain—dramatically better than we had done for weeks.

With a body, the well-oiled machinery of death can finally whirr into operation. Everything becomes practical. We went to check the church and meet the vicar to make arrangements for the service. I hadn't been there for years. I stood in the pulpit to see how it would feel delivering my speech. As we left, the tower (Perpendicular, my father had told me any number of times, and a particularly good one) was catching the afternoon sun. We were headed down the path to the village hall where the wake was to be held, but my father was lagging behind, fussing about something. I went back to see what it was. He'd gone back into the church, was counting the steps, seeing if the second of the double doors would open. 'What are you doing?' I said.

'I'm just wondering how we're going to get the chair in ... where the steps are.' Jonny had joined me by this stage. It's OK we said. It's OK. There's no wheelchair this time.

'Oh yes,' he said. 'I forgot.' We all smiled. It was OK.

I never finished the hedge. It remains a landmark to those weeks still.

Mark was turning out to be a sterner taskmaster than the easy-going companion I'd imagined. Instead of my reckless Mendip slashings, before he cut a pleacher, he considered it as carefully as a snooker player gauging angles before a difficult shot. Tilting his 'hacker' (as he said bill hooks were called round here) this way then that, he assessed exactly where he wanted it to fall, before saying decisively: 'Cut there', marking a precise line with his finger for angle and depth. He showed me a 'double pleach' (advanced) and, on a particularly gnarly old blackthorn stump with big gaps either side, a 'backwards pleach' (very advanced).* He showed me how to bury a double pleacher so that it might take root, and other farmers' tricks: 'If you've got long old branches with no shoots, give 'em a few nicks. They'll soon sprout. But don't have too many pleachers; it strains the plant.' Every three feet or so, he tapped in a stake at right angles to the pleacher, knocking it lightly with the head of his axe. These provided the matrix around which the laid pleachers would be woven.

'How far apart are they meant to be?'

'So a drip off one lands at the foot of the next.'

---

* A 'double pleach' is a single pleacher cut twice. A 'backwards pleach' is a pleacher cut in the opposite direction to the lay of the hedge.

As we worked, Mark pulled in dead material from the brushwood we'd cut out. 'All this stuff we've just removed?' I said. 'You're now putting that back in? Just so the hedge looks prettier? We didn't bother with that kind of nonsense in the Mendips.' Hedge-laying seemed to be very different here in Border Country. And, frankly, without wishing to adopt a moral stance, I wasn't convinced it was for the better. On Mendip, the result might not have looked so just-so, but somehow a hedge of living material seemed purer and more honest than one stuffed with dead thorn brush. Mark was having none of it. 'On the Mendips, they don't have sheep to contend with. The dead thorn protects the new young shoots from being eaten. Here we have to produce a stock-proof hedge straight away, not some time in future when it's had time to grow back.' There were dozens of different regional styles, he said, adapted to local stock, land and weather.*

'So what style's this?'

'Somewhere between a Breconshire and a Radnorshire.'

'What's the difference?'

'In the Breconshire, the dead wood goes in after two stakes, in the Radnorshire version after one. Or maybe it's the other way round.'

'Does it matter much?'

'Not really, no.'

Weaving the pleachers round the stakes, pulling brushwood from the tangled heap behind us ('If you'd piled your thinnings in the same direction, as I told you to, you wouldn't find it such hard work pulling them out again'), threading it back into the hedge base, taking a step down the slope, weaving the pleachers, pulling the brushwood … it was endless.

'Coffee?'

---

* At least forty, according to the National Hedgelaying Society. Their booklet, *Hedge-laying Explained*, offers eighty pages of minutely differing diagrams, like a book of knots, so you can distinguish, for example, the 'Glamorgan Hills Version' and the 'Merioneth Version' of the 'flying hedge'.

'Coffee? We've only just had lunch.
You can have a coffee break when
we've got past the holly.' I got the
impression my life had more coffee
breaks than Mark's.

The last bit was the best: the bit I'd
never done before.

'So now we get the stakes lined up, bang them
in, then fit the hethers?'

'Exactly wrong. We find the hethers, put them on. Then we
straighten the stakes and bang them in.'

Hethers are long, straight, young boughs of some flexible hedgerow
tree—generally hazel or willow. Woven along the top of the laid hedge,
they hold the pleachers in place, giving it its neat, tightly plaited feel,
and stop animals pulling the hedge to pieces once it's finished. The idea
is that the cleaning of the hedge produces enough hethers, but ours had
little hazel, so I was despatched to forage for some.

My hunt took me further than I expected and it was nearly an hour
before I was back, laden with hazel boughs. 'Too thick,' said Mark,
inspecting them. 'Not pliable enough. They'll break.' So off I went
again. This time it took me longer as I had to go further. However, in
due course, I reappeared with another substantial bundle. 'Too thin,'
said Mark. 'Too beanstalky. Not strong enough.' I began to wonder
if he just wanted me out of the way, so he could finish the hedge on his
own. In the end, he said he knew a place with some hazel which was
just right. He'd come back tomorrow with the hethers.

The following day, once we'd woven on the hethers, it was just a
matter of nipping and tucking. We walked down the line, beating the
plait down as hard as we could with the shaft of an axe, compressing
the pleachers and brush into a dense shield of thorn about four feet
high. The final task was to take off the tops of the stakes (which all
protruded differing amounts, according to how far stones and roots had
allowed us to drive them in), to an even three inches above the hethers.

Mark pushed the remaining thinnings into a heap with his tractor for burning.

The result was by no means perfect, but it wasn't bad. There's real beauty to a newly cut-and-laid hedge snaking its way through the landscape—partly from its shorn, braided tidiness, partly from the care and love of a place it implies. But on this occasion it inspired other feelings, too. The sense of completing a job left half-finished, and using the chainsaw my father had given me to do so. In no time new shoots were sprouting from our hedge and it was fascinating to see which pleachers had worked, and which had not, whether the chainsaw nicks really did sprout (yes), whether the buried pleacher took root (no). Trying to work out why laying a hedge felt so much more satisfying than cutting one, I finally realised what it was. Cutting a hedge is about the past. Laying a hedge is about the future. In this case, I supposed, my future. A chainsawey sort of future.

Before

After

18

The house

A garden without a house is like a carriage without a horse.

JOSEPH RYKWERT, *On Adam's House in Paradise*, 1981

There was a cow pat in our Elysian Fields. However much we improved the surroundings, however hard we tried to integrate the garden with the landscape, one feature of Tair-Ffynnon continued to raise two stubborn fingers to our efforts: the house. What I wanted was an idealised version of the hill smallholdings that dot much of upland Britain. I imagined a humble, whitewashed house, stone outbuildings with roofs of mossy stone and rusty tin, anchored into a fold of the hills by a clump of broad-leafed trees, at the centre of a network of dry-stone walls. Instead, we had a boxy cement excrescence, of which each view was uglier than the last, plus a vigorous stand of leylandii. As we badly needed to build onto the house, in the process we wanted to prettify this eyesore. The question was how to get a building that so plainly looked wrong to look 'right'.

Since buying Tair-Ffynnon, we'd spoken to a few architects but, somehow, none had said the right things. When I produced my sheaf of reference material showing, say, Tintagel's low, medieval Post Office huddled on the Cornish headland against the Atlantic wind, or cheerfully painted tin buildings in Iceland, or, closer to home, the dormer windows peeping from the mossy roof at Llanthony Abbey, they listened politely, then continued exactly where they'd left off. They seemed to have little enthusiasm for traditional local building styles and looked instantly bored when I brought the subject up. There was talk of viewing galleries and picture windows and covered walkways, all of which felt so out of keeping, our confidence in everything they said drained away. The problem, we decided, was that we wanted something architects were not trained to deliver: something not 'designed', that was the opposite of slick. Something a bit homespun, in keeping with the make-do-and-mend ethos of the place. A house, as that great architect and Welshman Frank Lloyd Wright put it, 'not on the hill, but of the hill'.

We consulted Ness. 'You need to talk to Robin,' she said. 'He lives in the village—the beautiful old stone house by the bridge, you know, the white medieval one, except that half of it's not medieval at all because Robin built it about five years ago. Spent God know's how long researching local houses in every minute detail to make sure the integrity of the original building was maintained. There's nothing Robin doesn't know about buildings and how to get them right. You need to take him with a pinch of salt, of course, because in the nicest possible way he's a kind of deranged perfectionist, to the extent of peeing in bottles and storing it for months…'

'He keeps his own pee?'

'Yes, you remember how in the Regency, Beau Brummell said he mixed champagne into his bootblack to get the best shine? Well, I think it's on the same principle as that. I was admiring some beautiful old flagstones he'd got in his kitchen, and it turned out they were just modern bits of concrete he'd been treating with his own piss. And he won't allow any of his children's toys about the place because they'd ruin the look. And of course…'

I'd passed Robin's house countless times without giving it a thought:

a quietly distinguished but unassertive presence, with knobbly white-washed walls, tiny oak mullioned windows and roofs of coursed stone slates. From Ness's description (I knew she was given to the picturesque) I wasn't sure whether to expect its owner to be a lab-coated technician, a dishevelled crank or Howard Hughes in his final stages. As it happened, the figure who answered the door looked more like an investment banker: clean-cut, blue serge suit trousers, suavely handsome, lightly tanned, in his late forties. After shaking an immaculate hand and being welcomed in, we were conducted on a tour

It was a small medieval hall house. The sitting room had a massive stone fireplace, oak beams and a stud-and-panel screen at one end. It seemed a long way from Tair-Ffynnon. Robin led the way up an ancient oak staircase, the wood so dark it was almost black—Elizabethan, I guessed—with great carved finials. 'What an amazing staircase. Did you have to do much to it?'

'Yes, make it.'

In the main bedroom was a vast Elizabethan four-poster with elaborately turned posts. After admiring it, I enquired if it was contemporary with the house. 'With this bit, yes. Circa 1994.'

'What, you made that, too?'

'Yes.'

And so it went on. Although the main block of the house was, indeed, medieval, the seamless lower addition was all new. When I asked him which builders he'd used, I received what was starting to become his stock reply: 'I did it.'

'Wherever d'you get window mullions like these nowadays?' I asked unthinkingly a few minutes later, admiring the square leaded panes.

'You make them,' said Robin.

It was becoming clear that, impressive as Robin's achievement was, the visit was going to yield little in the way of practical information for improving Tair-Ffynnon. By the time we'd settled in the kitchen for coffee, on the famous flagstone floor (made by Robin), at the table (made by Robin), on chairs (made by Robin), with cups from the corner

255

cupboard (that too), neither Vez nor I knew quite what to say, so overwhelmed were we by our own inadequacy.

I produced some photographs of Tair-Ffynnon and slid them across the table. Robin winced. 'What date was it built?'

'Hard to say. It had a makeover in 1973. It's just a standard, non-descript cottage, really. Nineteenth-century originally, maybe eighteenth.'

'Nothing's nondescript or standard. You need to know this kind of thing. Everything else follows: your windows, your doors, your gutters. What do you want it to be like? You need to look at places which are similar. Drive up through Longtown and look at the houses there. Look at walls. Look at roofs. Look at windows. Look at what looks right and what doesn't.'

It was what I thought I'd been doing, but it was becoming clear my piecemeal observations were pitifully inadequate. He continued: 'Have you read Iorwerth Peate's *The Welsh House*? You've got Fox and Raglan, of course?'

'Fox and Raglan?'

'*Monmouthshire Houses*, in three volumes. That's the crucial starting point. Then there's the Royal Commission on the Ancient and Historic Monuments volume on Glamorgan farmhouses and cottages. Hundreds of drawings and every reference for doors and windows. If I can find it you can borrow my copy. But Fox and Raglan's the place to start.' As we left his eyes alighted on a DVD of Wallace and Gromit's *Chicken Run* lying on the hall table. He picked it up and handed it to me. 'There you are. Excellent smallholding references there.' He showed us out. 'I'll help you where I can,' he said. 'I like doing it. But you've got to work out what you want. No architect will ever care about your place like you do. If it matters to you, there's no alternative but to do it yourselves.'

———— ·•· ————

That afternoon, spurred by Robin's bald assertions, I went to the library to check out *Monmouthshire Houses*. The three volumes were not as vast as they sounded, but the text was largely incomprehensible (discussing comparative distributions of 'tenoned collars' and 'wern-hir stops'). At the back, however, were some instructive black-and-white photographs of domestic buildings. Immediately striking was the absence of formality. Even the houses captioned 'hall' or 'court' bore no relation to the grand piles those words tend to conjure elsewhere. They looked more like farmhouses, with rough rubble-stone walls, randomly placed doors and crooked, unmatching windows. Every building also appeared to be derelict. They sat like so many mouldering lumps of cheese, roofs sagging, swagged with ivy, ferns sprouting from tottering chimney stacks. Geese and poultry pecked about in yards which were seas of mud. This syntax of decay was compounded by the fact that all the photographs appeared to have been taken on a grey February afternoon. Despite the books being published in the 1950s, the impression was of a place forgotten since the English Civil War and visited just once, if the running boards on the cars were anything to go by, in the 1930s.

After that, I began to notice the old stone buildings around us more closely. Strip away the twentieth century's contributions—the steel sheds, housing estates, villas and bungalows, all apparently dropped by helicopter without so much as a nod to local topography, history or materials—and what was left was, still, a collection of buildings just like the ones in Fox and Raglan. They shared a soft, slightly melancholic air, a relaxed sense of imminent collapse, quite distinct from the hard, angular profiles of the later buildings. It was Vez who put her finger on why the newer ones didn't fit in. 'They don't fall down right,' she said. Not that the older buildings necessarily were about to fall down. They just looked that way.

The features I liked, I soon realised, were precisely the ones that modern building techniques had dispensed with: 'battered' walls which started thicker at the ground and tapered in; open eaves with visible rafters, where swallows and house martins could nest; small windows; chimney tops made from two flat stones leaning against each other like a tent. Crucial was the absence of fussy features in modern materials, like porches and conservatories.* My favourite discovery was a kind of cobbling I'd not seen elsewhere, noticeable in old farmyards and outside ancient pubs, whereby the thin Old Red Sandstone was set into the ground vertically (rather than horizontally like a flagstone). This was called 'pitching', Robin said.

'This is not a county of high-quality building stone,' declared the Monmouthshire Pevsner (an opinion reiterated by Alec Clifton-Taylor in *The Pattern of English Building*). And there was no denying it. The stone was clearly unfit for purpose. Walls appeared to have been gnawed by rats. Tombstones around the local churches were mainly blank, where the engraving had fallen away. Whenever old buildings had, say, a chimney rebuilt, it was always in brick, not stone. The venerable Old Red Sandstone of the Welsh borders, it became clear, might account for the characteristic table-topped escarpments of the Beacons, but for durability it ranked somewhere between a wedding cake left out in the rain and a Cadbury's Flake.

And yet, that was the whole point. Rotten it may be, but it's what the hills were made of. So open sheds were supported on stone columns, water troughs were hewn out of great lumps of the stuff, and everywhere

---

* Germaine Greer neatly summarised why farm buildings have ceased to be pretty. Once upon a time, she said (referring to Ireland, but the same goes for Wales), when people were poor, houses were lovely to look at, but 'they were horrible to live in, which is why when EU subsidies kicked in, everyone who lived in a whitewashed grass-roofed cottage, with a dungheap steaming before the door, knocked it down and built himself a hideous villa. Where the old cottage had been almost windowless and dark, what with the smoke of the peat-fire painting the interior brown as it curled its slow way through the thatch, the new villas had lots of glazing, doors, windows, porches and conservatories, and acres of hardstand. Because over the years he had grown sick of wading through mud and manure, the owner concreted all round the grand new house, and threw up balustrades and gate-posts in all directions.' *Guardian*, 28 July 2008.

there was stone underfoot and stone overhead.
The stone roof slates, in particular, were bigger
and thicker than their counterparts elsewhere
—some as much as four feet wide and three
inches thick—presumably because if any
smaller they'd disintegrate too fast. That was
why the roofs, however strong their timbers,
sagged over time. It was why roof pitches were
often less than forty-five degrees, because oak pegs or copper nails
couldn't hold the weight at steeper angles. The size of those stones
explained the simplicity of the roofs, less cut about with gables and
valleys than roofs elsewhere, and why dormer windows were of the
simple 'cat's slide' type. As for its flakiness, it made the roofs the perfect
habitat for every kind of moss and liverwort, lichen and house leek, stone
crop and fern.* That denigrated stone was the soul of the area.

'You think we should knock it down and start again, don't you?' I knew
it was the thought in Robin's mind. From the moment he got out of
his car, his eyes had looked pained by all they saw, until they settled on
the railway carriage ('LMS ... London and Midland ... yes, quite so, it
would have run on this line'), though even there, he couldn't help

---

* 'The church roofs of Monmouthshire are a key bryophyte [mosses and liverworts]
habitat. South-facing Old Red Sandstone tiles, here and in neighbouring Herefordshire,
support *Grimmia decipiens* NS, *G. laevigata* NS, *G. ovalis* RDB(VU) and *Hedwigia
ciliata* RDB(DD). Two of the *Grimmia* spp. are widespread in the county, *G. decipiens*
has been recorded on one roof and *H. ciliata* is known from three. Re-roofing of buildings with slate or artificial tiles continues to destroy colonies of these rare mosses and an
inevitable conclusion is that all four species have undergone catastrophic declines in
recent history, as locally quarried tiles have been replaced as the most readily available
roofing material.' From the British Bryological Society website (www.britishbryological
society.org.uk).

questioning our decision to paint it the cheerful claret colour we had. ('The correct colour is bauxite.') After that, his gaze had roved restlessly again, shying away from the house, searching for—and patently failing to find—something that didn't offend him, continuing until we reached the kitchen. 'Ah, an Aga,' he said, visibly relieved.

'Bit tatty, I'm afraid,' said Vez.

'At least it's the right colour.'

I was surprised by how much the mere idea of demolition shocked me. 'I just think we'd lose all the heart and history,' I said. Somehow it seemed so cold-blooded. We were aware the house was ugly, but there were still signs of a simple stone cottage hiding underneath—in the stonework where the cement render had flaked and the spiral stone staircase we'd found behind the fire. We knew it would be easier, cheaper, and probably make for a prettier, better-scaled, more convenient house to start again, but even so … Robin had picked up a wooden knob which had come off the old pine chest of drawers months ago, for which the hole was now too big for the handle's spindle. He took a wooden kebab stick out of a stash in the drawer and broke it into four. 'Besides, a new house, however traditionally built, is still new. And to make it look old feels bogus,' I said. Robin pursed his lips, put the broken kebab sticks in the hole where the handle belonged, then screwed the wooden knob back on and tried the drawer. It worked perfectly. 'We'd better keep thinking, then,' he said.

So we did. We bought some fancy pointy pens and tracing paper, borrowed a drawing board and started doing drawings. We tried L-shaped extensions breaking forwards, then backwards. We tried lowering the eaves so cat's slide dormers poked up. We tried every permutation of gabling. Always the house looked too big, or too twee or just ungainly and wrong. Periodically, we'd show our sketches to Robin and he'd agree: none was right.

I grew despondent, but Robin was unmoved. 'It takes a lot of careful thought to get a building right,' he'd say.

In the end, it was he who solved the problem. As long as the house was deeper than it was wide, the proportions would be doomed. He suggested widening the house by one bay so the roof ridge ran along the longest side. As soon as he said it, we knew it was the answer. Finally we knew what to draw. It was just a matter of drawing it.

———•◦•———

We tried to do the plans ourselves. But after wasting hours, Tom, an artist friend, said we were fools. A competent computer designer, he pointed out, could do what we were trying to do in minutes. All we had to do was stand over them and say what we wanted. So we found Rob, an architectural technician who also knew building regulations by heart. He said three sessions should be fine. A week later, having dropped the children at a babysitter, with two clear hours ahead, we were settled in his office, coffees in hand.

Rob had measured Tair-Ffynnon and from the screen leered the face we knew so well. 'Lower the eaves to the top of the upstairs windows,' I commanded. *Clickety-click*, a sweep of the mouse. 'Add another bay to the left,' I said. *Clickety-click*, a sweep of the mouse. 'Right, the windows ...'—this was easier than I thought—'... they need to be much smaller.' *Clickety-click*, a sweep of the mouse. 'No, much smaller,' I said.

'Not come across anyone who's wanted to make windows smaller before,' murmured Rob.

Clickety-click. Clickety-click.

'No, much smaller.' *Clickety-click. Clickety-click.* 'No, no, *much* smaller.'

'It'll look pretty weird,' said Rob.

'Smaller.' *Clickety-click. Clickety-click.*

'That's too small,' said Vez.

'Trust me, you won't like it,' said Rob.

'How can I know until I've seen it? Smaller.' *Clickety-click. Clickety-click.* Robin's voice was in my ears: 'Don't compromise. Do it as you want it.'

'That's ridiculous,' said Vez. 'It'll be pitch black.'

'Cottages are dark. That's how they are. You've just got used to having hideous gaping voids.'

'Well, that's too small. Make it bigger, Rob.'

So the windows were made bigger again, then smaller. And so our first session finished without even the windows sorted. We drove home in silence. For days, the window issue hung over us. Vez spoke to Tom again. 'Tom says architects design from the inside out, not the outside in, like you're trying to do.'

'Lucky we're not using an architect, then.'

'He says only prancing aesthetes make windows smaller.'

And so it went on, as we lowered (and raised and lowered) ceilings, eaves, roof ridge, roof pitches. Bit by bit the chatty bonhomie at the start of each session would harden into tense silence, punctuated by relentless *clickety-clicks*. After each meeting, we'd strike an ungracious compromise and, so long as Vez and I were equally pissed off, and all three of us utterly exhausted, we'd know we'd got it about right.

If only we had known the battle had hardly begun. Once the drawings went to the National Park, a whole farrago of re-packaging was required, but eventually the day arrived when Les the Post delivered a set of plans rubber-stamped with that magical word: 'APPROVED'.

———◆———

We'd already found our builders months before, though we didn't know it. Since then, we'd called a few well-known local firms for quotes, but had been vaguely unsettled by the arrival of men in suits carrying clipboards, with safety helmets on the passenger seats of their cars. They issued us with booklets and checklists and smartly printed cards. Uncertain how to assess them, all I could think to ask was 'Can you do pitching?'—a query which in each case elicited a blank look. In turn, they told us the plans we'd drawn up weren't remotely adequate for estimating purposes. 'When you've got proper plans, and you're ready to start, give us a call,' they said. It all felt a bit impersonal and soulless and we had a suspicion that that's how their buildings would turn out. As the last one departed, we remembered a remark we'd heard on an earlier quarry mission. Having itemised the various kinds of stone we were after—building stone, flagstones, possibly stone slates—the quarryman had remarked: 'Sounds like you'll be needing Gerald Morris.'

When I now called Gerald, in response to my pitching enquiry he suggested he pick me up on Sunday morning and show me some of the work his family had done. There was certainly no sign of clipboards or hard hats as I climbed into his battered white van, to find the grinning muzzle of a vast black retriever alongside me, poking through a hole in the plywood partition. 'Don't worry about him. That's Fred,' said Gerald. As we set off round the east of the Black Mountains, windows open, the smell of Gerald's roll-ups mixing with the spring air, his cheerful chat, round, friendly shape and unkempt, frizzled hair made him easy company. He took me up long stony tracks to places I'd never have known existed—a restored barn here, a house there, a pub. As we drove, he told me how stone steps up to granaries customarily had dog kennels beneath to provide canine sentries against rodents. And when I showed him my picture of Tintagel Post Office, with its vastly over-sized stone slates, he told me they were called 'table tiles' and were so heavy they didn't need pegging. Everywhere we went, the emphasis was on stonework. When we arrived at the last property, and he showed me a whole yard of meticulous stone pitching, it was clear Gerald was our man.

The Morris family arrived with a fanfare. Their ancient JCB had no silencer, so could be heard approaching down the Monnow valley, growing steadily in volume, at least half an hour before it charged triumphantly into the yard. The individual members of Morris Builders (established 1974) brought complementary skills. If Gerald was, in all senses, the father figure, supplying confidence, experience and waggish remarks, Glenn, his thoughtful youngest son, was the brains. He looked at plans, did the calculations and issued lists for the builders' merchants.* Wayne, the eldest Morris son, was the all-rounder, who defied the reputation of builders worldwide by his almost obsessive tidiness, continually collecting and burning rubbish and keeping the place swept and clean. Richard, not strictly a member of the family, but who, confusingly, still called Gerald 'Dad', was the mechanical one, the digger driver and general perfectionist, charged with measuring and other precision operations. Finally, there was Ian, also no relation, the plasterer and general gofer, absurdly good-looking and sweet-natured, whom all our female visitors fell in love with.

Nothing seemed to be organised. There were never any checklists or morning meetings, yet somehow everyone always seemed to know what they were doing, and got on with it. Natural recyclers, we'd find them rifling through the sheds and barns and my rusty collection of ironmongery, before adapting a gate hinge as a meat hook, or a railway sleeper as a window lintel. No sooner were timbers from the old roof removed than they were re-employed as floor joists. This approach was fortunate as, since buying Tair-Ffynnon, we'd been amassing from local house clearance auctions and farm sales an array of old church pews, miscellaneous beams and posts, cast iron radiators, ledge-and-brace doors (£8 for five), a cast iron bath (£2.50), sinks, mismatched floorboards, slate slabs, a clanky high-level WC cistern, a box of door handles (50p) and other ill-fitting junk we wanted installed. They didn't seem bothered, nor did they protest when we constantly changed our minds, or handed them the Ladybird book of *The Farm* or Beatrix Potter's

---

* With him came Will, as unlikely a dog as has ever been lifted from a builder's van: his wife's Lhasa apso (some relation of a Shitzu), a toy-poodle-esque kind of creature. Will looked so similar from both ends it was hard to tell in which direction he was headed. He had the knack of always being in the most inconvenient place—in front of car tyres, in doorways, under your feet—though some deep hunting instinct briefly stirred when he saw the chickens. Whenever he chased them, he would be referred to severely as 'William' and locked in the van.

The Tale of Samuel Whiskers and asked for 'steps like that' or 'a chimney like that'.

Sometimes when they were building, we might say, 'Shouldn't there be a window there, Gerald?' And he'd say, 'Oh, you want one here, do you?' and we'd say, 'It is in the plans,' and he'd say absently, 'Right you are, then.' It was regarded—certainly by Gerald—as an admission of the most abject failure, a very last resort, to consult the drawings. They just built as they felt the place should be and nine times out of ten it was exactly as we wanted it. The plans we'd slaved over sat neatly folded, unopened, under a thickening layer of dust and wood shavings, in a corner of the barn.

We couldn't afford stone slates, though we put in massive oak beams to hold them in case we one day win the Lottery. And the windows should be smaller, of course. But what can you do? When we moved back in, we celebrated by cutting down the leylandii.

Before

After

265

19

'Garden Open Today'

Opening one's garden is an event that is attended by a certain amount of drama—the sort of quiet domestic drama in which the tension gradually rises, and reaches a climax on the eve of the great day, when the posters are nailed to the garden gate ... This pre-opening atmosphere of tension is heightened by the behaviour of the garden itself ... There is a terrible temptation to rush into the market, at the last moment, and buy quantities of pot plants in full bloom, to fill the blank spaces.

BEVERLEY NICHOLS, *Garden Open Today*, 1963

'Aha ... so *you're* the people who say your garden's at 1,600 feet, I'm glad to have met you. May I ask exactly what your evidence is for this claim?' A tall man with a prolific beard had buttonholed Vez. I was trying to eavesdrop while simultaneously explaining to a small, slightly scary woman in orange trousers why Joanna Kerr had introduced me as 'Antony, who doesn't have a garden.' From what I could see, Vez seemed to be handling things badly. She was looking shifty, swaying from side to side.

'Hmm,' the beard was saying. 'Hmm … I'll be interested to check that. Joanna said yes to this, did she?'

A month earlier a package had arrived containing an advance copy of the Yellow Book. And there, on page 534, was Tair-Ffynnon. Our entry was not, I couldn't help noticing, strictly as agreed. Joanna had evidently had further thoughts about the word 'garden', which had been replaced with the phrase 'property-opening'. Still, the fact was, there we were, in the great volume, alongside Sissinghurst, Hidcote, Stourhead and everyone else—kindred spirits, whether they liked it or not, with Gertrude Jekyll, Margery Fish, E. A. Bowles, Rosemary Verey, Uncle William, and the rest of the floristocracy.

A few weeks after that, a letter from Joanna arrived, asking us to her house one Thursday evening in late March to 'meet other openers', collect our yellow posters and signs, and be briefed about the forth-coming season. We were invited, if the weather was fine, to come a few minutes early to walk round the garden.

Her house, when we arrived, was a stuccoed Georgian rectory, in the lower reaches of the Usk valley—a far cry from the Black Mountains, which formed a dark ridge behind. Everyone was gathered on a wide, sunken, front lawn, surrounded by borders bursting with spring life, bulbs pushing through every inch of well-mulched soil. This vision of order was another world after the mud, bracken and flapping tin of our hill. Still, Joanna seemed happy enough to see us and we were offered a drink and had name stickers pressed onto us before meeting some of the other garden owners.

Somehow in the subsequent twenty minutes, I'd got myself entangled with the woman in orange, defending a claim I wasn't sure I'd made, that our garden would contain only indigenous plants. 'Why would you want to do a thing like that?' she was saying. 'It sounds unbelievably dull.' Fortunately, just then we were summoned inside to the sitting room. There were about twenty-five of us, amongst whom one elderly figure sitting in the middle of the room in a shapeless tweed jacket, easily marked out by his whiskery, eighteenth-century countenance, looked vaguely familiar. Then it dawned: it was Lord Raglan. I'd seen him at the final two beekeeping sessions, which had been held in his walled garden, where the club's apiary lived. His name was on the Gwent Bee-keepers' Association event cards as president. He appeared to be winking at me, so I went over, interested to meet the human attached to so venerable a name. The great ruin of Raglan Castle was a key Borders landmark, passed every time we drove to or from the M4. I told him I'd seen him at the beekeeping course.

'What?'

I raised my voice several decibels. 'I'VE BEEN TO YOUR HOUSE—BEEKEEPING.'

'Have you?'

'ARE YOU A BEEKEEPER?' I roared. Unable to think of anything else to say, it seemed a safe gambit.

'What?'

'ARE YOU A BEEKEEPER?'

'Me? No! Heavens no!' He made it sound the oddest question. At that moment Joanna called for silence and Lord Raglan leant forwards, narrowed his eyes and tapped the side of his nose. 'Pay attention now. Marching orders.'

Joanna welcomed us with the practised confidence of someone used to being listened to in committee meetings. New openers—there were three of us—were warned to expect larger numbers than we might think. Our attention was drawn to health and safety, the fact that our visitors might be old, or have young children, that a loo was always appreciated, and that more money was generally made from tea than on the gate. We were advised to consult the five-day weather forecast. If sunshine was predicted, strawberries and cream always sold well. If it was going to be chilly, cancel the strawberries and concentrate on scones and cake.

Everyone agreed that it was fundamental to have plenty of places to sit. I'd been expecting a lot of wafty talk about petunias but it all seemed commendably businesslike.

On our way out, Joanna stopped us. 'How's it all up on the hill? Everything going according to plan?' We assured her it was. 'Good, good. Yes ... Well, I'll pop up, just to make sure.'

In the dining room, bags labelled with our names were crammed with NGS signs, postcards, leaflets, and rolls of yellow posters in various sizes printed with our garden's name. Laid out on the table was further stationery: notices reading 'TEAS', 'THIS WAY', 'OWNERS PARK AT THEIR OWN RISK'. Their distribution was being supervised by a tall, jovial Scot in a tweed suit. 'Tek as much as you like,' he was saying to the woman in front of me. 'Go oan, tek two.' His tone implied he wasn't taking the business entirely seriously. 'You don't look as if you've got enough,' he said to me with a smile as I dithered in front of a packet of yellow NGS balloons. 'Tek everything,' he said. 'Go oan, go oan. Tek five.' He scooped up another few packets and popped them into the carrier bag. 'Tek ten.'

'Have you met my husband, Murray?' said Joanna from behind me. 'Ignore what he says.'

'Go oan,' we heard as we headed for the car. 'Tek the lot.'

With the days lengthening and the buds swelling, suitably inspired by the prodigious sums we were going to raise for charity, we were now firmly back in gardening mode. We decided to focus our energies on the only 'gardeny' bit of the garden: the vegetable patch. However we couldn't make a start until the builders had completed its retaining wall. We had a sense that the Morrises had yet to fully grasp that by midsummer the building site had to be a lush and fertile Eden members of the public would pay to see. ('Really, Antony?' Gerald would say politely. 'Sounds interesting. Where's this garden going to go?')

Meanwhile the vegetable garden remained a mound of spoil beginning to sprout weeds.

For six weeks, through April into May, as the lanes exploded with cow parsley, and spring got into fifth gear, we chafed at enforced inactivity. Our frustration was exacerbated by the strides we couldn't help but notice other gardeners were making; least avoidably, two vegetable plots on the hill-side known as Skirrid Pitch on the way up to the village. Our every journey took us past these, sometimes several times a day, and though I never once saw anyone working in them, the rows of regimented seedlings, ridged earth and neatly tied beanpoles told their own story.

In mid-May the retaining wall was finally finished. Martin levelled the excavated earth and, at last, we could gaze upon our 'Infinity Vegetable Patch'. The 'infinity' part worked fine: the raised ground level hid the foreground of the field sloping away beyond, conveying an impression of a garden suspended over the valley below. It was the 'vegetable patch' bit that now became a cause for concern.

Vez had, to my immense relief, made the vegetable garden her department. For weeks, opened gardening books had been accumulating around the house, with slips of paper marking relevant pages. Articles culled from years of weekend papers, featuring close-ups of tomatoes so plump and ripe you could almost smell them, dew-soaked courgettes, trugs laden with freshly pulled carrots and colanders of cheerfully variegated beans, promised how easy it all was. 'Grow your own' was in the ether, and every supplement sported another celebrity gardener in spotless clothes strutting in the morning mist or beneath charming willow arches festooned with sweet peas and exotic gourds. And yet, as the waste-paper baskets filled with discarded garden plans plastered with squiggles and crosses and complex tables of succession, I couldn't help thinking the reality was less straightforward. A word of encouragement seemed in order: 'You seem to be making a terrible meal of this.'

'Well, why don't you do something, rather than pontificating about verticality and the need for architectural structure?'

'Well, it can't be hard. Everyone else seems to manage it.'

'I'd love to know how. I've never come across anything so complicated in my life.'

It seemed best not to get involved, to attend instead to the immediate practical requirements. As it might be years before our walled garden acquired its walls (decades, even, given that I was now building them myself), a robust temporary barrier was required to exclude the sheep. Here was something I could usefully do. I occupied myself with measuring out a generous rectangle, marked cruciform grass paths within, and erected a fence of chestnut paling with two wicket gates. Then we prepared to dig the ground over. In honour of this auspicious moment, I splashed out on some new spades: a large one for me, a slightly smaller one for Vez, and two children's ones for Maya and Storm. Now, when it comes to kit, no-one has to tell me to buy the best: here was the central implement in any gardener's shed, destined to become virtually an extension of the self. I went to Richard's, the local hardware store. Spades had obviously come on a bit since my father bought the dowdy, workaday object in his tool cupboard. The spades in Richard's were like works of sculpture: heads of mirror-bright stainless steel, with 'YD' handles of smooth, white ash. They seemed most propitious symbols for the rite-of-passage we were about to undergo.

Armed accordingly, and burning with an enthusiasm charged by weeks of waiting, we set to work. Only to find that the new spades wouldn't go into the ground. It was as if someone had laid concrete four inches below the surface. The excavated soil, which, as it was spread, had looked like the finest tilth, had somehow transmogrified into rock. Whether the digger had compacted it, or the top soil had somehow got mixed up with the stuff underneath, after two hours I'd managed to dig over just a three-foot square patch. Not once did the spade sink to its full depth. Vez was finding the same in her corner. As I tried to lever a particularly obstinate stone, the strain took its toll. With an undemonstrative click, my spade's burnished blade broke in two. I grabbed Vez's spade, and within an hour had broken the handle of that. I took the spades back to Richard's and demanded replacements. Three hours' more digging and one of those had broken, too. After that, I dispensed with spades and dug only with pickaxe and crowbar. The stones were more numerous than a bumper crop of potatoes. Barrow after barrow we filled, tipping them into a fast-growing pile in the yard. But finally it was done. Then, laboriously, we barrowed muck up from the muck heap. At least digging this in, we told ourselves, would be a doddle now the ground was prepared. But when we started trying to do so, it was as if the ground hadn't been dug at all. The stones had grown back overnight. Halfway through this second mining operation, the rain began.

By now it was June, and the wet set in, cold and unremitting, as only a British June can do it. It was quickly evident, as the water pooled into puddles which refused to drain, that our freshly dug earth, our crumbly, friable tilth, had somehow metamorphosed into dense, sticky clay.

For ten days it rained. It rained on the roofless house. It rained on the docks and thistles in the orchard. It rained on the brushwood coppicings waiting to be burned after the hedge-laying. It rained on the fourth new spade, jabbed irritably into the ground and resentfully abandoned when the heavens re-opened. Occasionally the sky took a brief break, a metaphorical clearing of its throat. During these pauses Vez hurried out to continue adding straw and sand to the soil, according to her latest formula for improving drainage. And when the rain recommenced, the water collected again where we'd been digging, and in the deep footprints that were now all that remained of the paths, lying in shining silver shapes, reflecting the clouds. I returned to the house one day to find Mark leaning contemplatively over the vegetable patch fence. 'The only thing you'll grow in here is rice,' he said.

In the circumstances, we decided, our plans for asparagus beds and borlotti beans, for okra and salsify and raspberry canes, might be overambitious. As this was our first year, perhaps more modest targets were in order. There'd be no staggering. We'd grow potatoes to clear the ground, rhubarb because it used up plenty of room, runner beans because they gave vertical structure. (Whatever Vez might say, it was important.) We were each allowed two favourites: curly kale and purple-

sprouting broccoli for me, broad beans and sweet peas for Vez, strawberries, peas, carrots and sweetcorn for the children, plus some basic
herbs. However, even these required the rain to stop for long enough
to sow them; maddeningly, it never seemed to do so when we were free.

Then, one morning, apparently by magic, two rows of lettuces
appeared. It turned out Richard the builder had brought them from his
own garden. And it wasn't only the builders who were becoming twitchy
on our behalf. Mervyn delivered a vast tray of runner bean seedlings.
Another friend came over from Hay bringing a boot full of rhubarb and
(more) lettuces, and spent a morning in mackintosh and sou'wester helping Vez erect a hazel trellis for the beans. Later that day, Vez got the
potatoes and the rest of the seeds in. Finally the vegetables were underway.

For the next few weeks, as the rain continued, all we could do was
wait. Which would have been fine—enjoyable in fact—were it not for
those two gardens on Skirrid Pitch. However hard I tried not to look
at them, their triumphant progress refused to be ignored. It was the
beans, particularly. While ours were still four-inch seedlings, theirs were
four feet high. By the time our plants had reached a foot, their bean
poles had disappeared, engulfed by rain-forest foliage and smothered
with orange flowers. Those beans began to haunt me. They were like
bar charts of horticultural proficiency. When our first flower appeared,
their bean poles were sagging beneath the weight of the oversized, foot-
long vegetables. Still, our potatoes were doing alright. And the lettuces.
The rhubarb was positively thriving. There were fat green strawberries
in the children's plots. The purple-sprouting broccoli and curly kale,
caterpillars notwithstanding, were in good shape. Really, all in all, sod
the beans.

———— ·◆· ————

Even so, with a week to go, an unimaginable amount remained to be
done. Plaintive reminders attached to the fridge door listed the critical
('Posters', 'Vicar—cups and saucers', 'Tea tent', 'Cakes—Mrs Lumpkin',

'Mow paths', 'Float money', 'Someone to
direct traffic', 'Parking if wet?'); the hopeful
('Stone seats in fields', 'Paint beehives');
and the pitiful ('Finish house', 'Mend
track', 'Build cairns', 'Sort pond').

We'd taken to carrying a stash of
yellow posters in the car, distributing them
wherever we went, a process which had the
effect of leaving us feeling curiously exposed.* However,
with time running out, and most of our journeys taking us in the same
direction, it was clear we weren't covering the ground. It was Ness who
had the brainwave: 'Whydon'tyouaskLesifhe'dtakesomepostersonhis
roundandpinthemupwhereverhecan?' When we put this to Les, always
obliging, he readily agreed. As we handed over the fat roll of yellow
notices, he said: 'So where's the event going to be held? In a garden, is
it?' Vez explained that it was to be held here, at Tair-Fynnon. A pause
followed this information, during which we watched as Les marshalled
his considerable powers of tact and natural courtesy. '*Here?* Oh, I see.
I see. Right. Right. Here.' He nodded vigorously. 'Of course ... of
course. Silly of me. Right here, of course.'

Then the rain started again.

So much cried out to be done—cutting the paths, setting up the tent,
moving machinery, burning the great piles of brushwood—yet we could
do nothing. The one area thriving in the rain was the vegetable patch,
where, in the closely fought contest of Vegetation vs Bare Earth,
vegetation finally seemed to be winning through. Even so, the
Wednesday before our Sunday opening found us in low spirits. The
difference between having a garden and not having a garden was, in our

---

* As Beverley Nichols observed in *Garden Open Today*: 'I often wonder if this sensation
is shared by shopkeepers when they first see their names in bold letters on a busy street.
Certainly, when I see people gathering round the posters I feel like rushing out and
saying to them: "There is certainly no *need* to come in ... it is only a suggestion."'

case, a slender one: a few mown paths, some artfully placed farm machinery, a novelty vegetable patch. It was starting to look as if everything was riding on the vegetables, making it particularly unfortunate when, sometime on Wednesday evening, someone forgot to tie the gate shut.

It was I who found them. Drawing the curtains on Thursday morning and peering out half-drunk with sleep to check the weather, I noticed seven familiar white shapes milling about the fenced enclosure. 'There are sheep in the vegetable patch,' I mumbled—followed, as the horrific implications of this information sank in, by: 'THERE ARE SHEEP IN THE VEGETABLE PATCH.' I opened the window and bawled at them: a fatuous reflex, born of desperation. They munched on. Racing out, wearing nothing but T-shirt and wellies, possessed with fury, I galloped towards the garden, bellowing demonically. The effect of this on the sheep was predictable. In their confusion and desire to escape, they dived for the gate, which opened inwards and had swung almost closed. It slammed shut, effectively closing off their only means of escape. In panic, they ricocheted around, cannoning off each other and the chestnut paling, like a vigorous snooker break. What few plants hadn't been eaten were now flattened, as they charged the gate again and again. Before I could get to it, there was the sound of splintering wood. The gate gave way. '*Baaaaaaa*-ing' loudly, the sheep careered out.

The devastation was complete. The earth was bare, with the exception of the rhubarb, the mint, and a particularly peppery variety of rocket. Of the strawberries, carrots, sweetcorn, peas, sweet peas, broad beans, purple-sprouting broccoli, curly kale, potato plants, runner beans, parsley, dill, fennel, borage and lettuces, nothing remained. The trellis of hazel poles had been levelled.

By this time, Vez and the children had joined me. For a few moments we stood in silence, gazing at the scorched earth. Maya spoke first.

'Those bloody sheep,' she said.

Then Storm twigged. 'My strawbugs,' he said, and began to cry. All we had to show for our two months of effort was a square of trampled mud, some bolting rhubarb and a large pile of stones. My head filled with thoughts of wolves.

'Well, that settles it,' said Vez, expressing something which I knew had been in her head for days. 'We'll have to cancel.'

'I don't think we can,' I said. 'We're in the Yellow Book.'

To compound our woes, the rain returned. I was out that morning, but when I returned, Vez seemed distracted, fiddling about inconsequentially in the kitchen. 'Mummy talked to the Dragon, Daddy,' said Maya.

'What d'you mean, poppet?'

'I called Joanna to tell her it was impossible,' cut in Vez. 'That opening was out of the question.'

'Did you, by George? What did she say?'

'She said no.'

'Yes, but what *exactly* did she say? How did she say it?'

'She said: "Cancel? Oh no ... there's no cancelling. Where would we be if everyone simply changed their minds at the last minute? We all know it's been raining. No, no you're in the Book. You're committed to opening and open you will. I'll see you on Sunday."'

'That's why the Scheme works so well.'

'Well, I tried.'

She continued to look preoccupied, and a few minutes later said: 'You know, it's just a thought, but why don't we borrow Vicks's garden?' Vicks was our green-fingered friend, who seemed able to grow things without any effort at all. 'We wouldn't need everything. Just some beans, lettuces and curly kale. And maybe some purple-sprouting broccoli.' Her encounter with Joanna seemed to have put the iron back in her soul.

'She had some amazing globe artichokes last time I looked.'

'I'm sure she'd let us have a couple.'

'It *is* an emergency ...'

The rain at least narrowed our options. There was now no question of moving heavy bits of machinery around by tractor as it would turn the place into a mudslide. Or of burning the hedge thinnings. Our strategy now had to be one of damage limitation. While Vez went to negotiate with Vicks and borrow the tea tent, I'd been intending to move the pile of stones by the vegetable patch. But as I did so, the rain dripping off my nose, the fatuity of the effort came home to me. Why bother? What difference did it make whether the stones were there or not? Without the mown paths and the vegetable garden, the whole opening was a fiasco. The day towards which we'd worked so hard, when we revealed our garden to the world, was going to be a monumental damp squib.

Then, on the Friday, the rain stopped and the sun came out. It's astonishing how quickly bright sunshine lifts the spirits—and dries everything out. By lunch, it was easy to forget it had been raining for three weeks. The air was clear and fresh. Everything looked washed, clean, and lusher than usual in late July. Contemplating moving the stones again, in a more positive frame of mind, it struck me that as they were much the most impressive items to emerge from the vegetable garden this year it seemed a shame not to take the credit. So I abandoned my efforts and made a sign to this effect instead.

277

Vez arrived back with Vicks's garden and started planting it. I mowed the path to the Swing Field. It looked crisp and purposeful. Out of nowhere, the garden began to materialise. Once one thing falls into place, it's curious how others follow. For three weeks, because of the rain, I hadn't been taking my usual short-cut up through the Top Field with Beetle each day, so I hadn't noticed that changes had been taking place.

One of my most exciting summer discoveries at Tair-Ffynnon, akin to the arrival of the swallows, was prompted by fencing the Top Field. With the sheep excluded, come July, clumps of harebells appeared; a flower, I need hardly say, that occupied a sacred position in my heart following my Scottish rock pool epiphany. That they grew here, on our hill, seemed almost uncanny. Keen to do whatever was necessary to encourage their proliferation, the following year I'd evicted the sheep a month earlier, by the end of April. Result? Half as many harebells. Mark told me it was almost certainly the sheep grazing the aggressive grasses that had allowed the harebells to flourish. So this year I'd left it until June before chucking them out. And, it seemed, it had worked. Now, cutting the path up to the tea tent, I was greeted by an astonishing sight. The field was shot through with a blue haze from thousands and thousands of harebells. We could have opened for them alone.

■▸◆◂■

'Where's the garden, Woodward? That's what I want to know: *where's the bloody garden?*' Gordon, an old university friend, had dropped in with his family on their way home from Pembrokeshire to help on our Big Day. He was now striding up and down in the sunshine, apparently trying to clarify a few details before the 11 a.m. opening. 'What are we supposed to say to people who want to know what they're getting for their £3.50? That here's ...' Gordon's gaze roved around, eventually alighting on the corrugated iron Dutch barn. '... a particularly fine example of a *black barn*? Or have you seen our prize collection of old fertiliser bags?'

How useful Gordon's contribution was going to be remained to be seen, but his wife, Bin, and their three girls were already in the kitchen, turning out egg-and-parsley sandwiches and mixing buckets of elder-flower cordial. Twenty-four hours had passed in frenzied activity. The tea tent was up, with trestle tables and a tea urn in it. Chairs had been collected from one village hall, cups and saucers from another. Change sat in plastic bags in a shoe box. Signs were up on the roads. Thirty cakes were in the kitchen. Vicks's vegetable garden was at least in, if not yet fully art-directed, and the paths were mown, even if some of the clippings remained to be collected. All in all, we were feeling pretty pleased with ourselves, until Gordon's efforts, as he put it, 'to give us a boost'.

Within the last half-hour, a small army had assembled. Vez's mother and stepfather, Gay and Paul, and her Aunt Susie and Uncle Roger, had all arrived, plus assorted babysitters and their boyfriends. At 10.30, two men and a woman turned up in the Longtown Mountain Rescue Team Land Rover, every inch the emergency vehicle, festooned as it was with luminous stripes, flashing lights and stretchers, its windows crammed with ropes, helmets, reflective jackets and medical kit. This had been a late brainchild, when we remembered that a proportion of the tea take could go to a local charity. What better way to underline our mountain credentials? I directed them to park their magnificent machine in front of an unsightly collection of scaffolding poles and the Morrises' cement mixer. Let no-one forget this garden reached to nearly 1,600 feet.

There was an air of nervous expectancy. We issued instructions and 'to do' lists. 'I do think you might have got yourselves a bit more organised,' said Gay, noting all the activity. Roger and Paul set off to distribute garden benches and folding chairs. Maya helped Susie decorate the blackboard advertising food prices for the tea tent. Storm stuck his fingers in the chocolate cakes. Gordon was sent out onto the hill to erect 'TEAS' signs on Offa's Dyke footpath. Gay took charge of the entrance table. I closeted myself in the carriage to draft a leaflet about the garden. ('He's not starting the leaflet *now* is he?' Gay said to Vez.)

Before we knew it, it was eleven o'clock. Gay called that someone was coming up the track. The yard was still blocked by cars, the first draft of the leaflet was jammed in the printer. Just for a few moments, nothing seemed quite so absurd as the idea of opening our garden to the public. Gordon was right: who on earth wanted to see a black barn? Our first visitor turned out to be a middle-aged woman, and, with her opening remark, I realised none of it mattered in the slightest. 'What a beautiful place,' she said. 'How ever did you find it?'

Joanna arrived soon after, with Murray. I handed them a freshly printed leaflet. 'You have been busy,' said Joanna. 'Where are the balloons?' said Murray. People came in more or less steady drifts after that, some faces familiar but most not. Around midday, Ray and Meryl arrived, bringing some of her signature chocolate fridge cake. Mark and Liz made their way straight to the tea tent, guessing that's where their services would be required. Gerald came with his wife, Mary, and was most impressed by the mown paths. 'No, to be fair to you there, Antony, to be fair to you, you've pulled it out of the 'at.' Les the Post brought a carload of friends and relations.

Vez's Uncle Roger stationed himself in the yard as a sort of unofficial guide, helping out visitors he saw twisting their necks in front of the garden plan I'd pinned up. Unfortunately time hadn't permitted re-drawing of the plan prepared almost a year earlier for Joanna's benefit, with the result that nearly all the advertised features were fictional. 'We can't find the tractor in the hay meadow featured on it,' I heard one say.

'I'm afraid it's in the barn.'

'And I'm so sorry, but we couldn't find the wellhouse either.'

'I'm afraid it hasn't been built.'

'How silly of us. But the cairns ...'

'No, I'm afraid they haven't either ...'

'Dear me, this plan isn't very helpful.'

'I think it's more in the nature of a declaration of intent; a mission statement,' said Roger. He was doing sterling work, so I left him to it.

After that, the day seemed to dissolve in a pleasant haze of chatting and sunshine. Vez had implemented a policy of offering a first cup of tea free (our confidence in the £3.50 entrance charge having disappeared with the vegetable patch) and it was proving a winning formula. One old lady, for whom Vez had fetched a chair when it became clear the tea tent, due to its altitude and steep approaches, was going to be off limits, seemed hardly able to believe it. 'Ooh, a free cup of tea,' she kept repeating to the world at large. 'She gave me a free cup of tea. "No charge," she said. "No charge,"' she went on, chuntering contentedly away, like an echo.

Gordon's fears proved unfounded. No-one seemed to mind the lack of a 'garden'. In fact, we were repeatedly congratulated, as if we personally could take credit for the mountains, the long views falling away to the wide green valleys below, the harebells, the distant glimpse of the Severn, the topaz sky. The visitors pottered happily around, inspecting the heaps of coppicings grown through with nettles, the muddy pond, the unfinished house, before assembling on the grass around the tea tent like starlings gathering on a telephone wire, reluctant to leave. Call after call came through for more sandwiches, more water, more cordial, more cakes. The urn stopped working, prompting an exhausting relay of kettle-ferrying up the Top Field. The sheep got in and started greedily munching the harebells—pleased, at last, to have discovered their favourite food.

There wasn't a pause until six o'clock when, finally, just our families and neighbours remained in the Top Field. Flopping onto the warm grass by the tea tent, Vez gave me a cup of tea and a piece of Mrs Lumpkin's lemon drizzle cake. For the first time that day—for the first time in months—I felt completely relaxed. Maya and Storm were roly-polying through the harebells, chased by Mark and Liz's children and Beetle. Sugar Loaf was turning purple as the sun began to sink. The fat, green woodpecker, smug as ever, made his yaffling call as with undulating swoops he flitted from tree to tree. Across the valley I could see Mervyn and Martin baling in a field. How many bales, I wondered, had Mervyn done now? I thought how far we'd come since that first trip down the M4, how much more part of the scene around me I felt than in the countryside of my childhood. I imagined the place with the pond full and clear, the walls rebuilt around the fields, the house finished. How much would be done by next year, I wondered, how much by the year after? Or the year after that?

We had 131 visitors and raised nearly £700. A day or two later, the father of a friend (a Yellow Book garden owner himself) walked past on his way up the hill. He apologised for missing the opening and pressed £10 onto us for the charitable cause 'not, obviously, for your non-existent garden'. Later, someone in the Skirrid garage shop told us they'd overheard him describing the place: 'I don't know how they *dared* open to the public.'

Epilogue

It's a queer experience to go over a bit of country you haven't seen in twenty years. You remember it in great detail, and you remember it all wrong. All the distances are different, and the landmarks seem to have moved about. You keep feeling, surely this hill used to be a lot steeper—surely that turning was on the other side of the road? And on the other hand you'll have memories which are perfectly accurate, but which only belong to one particular occasion. You'll remember, for instance, a corner of a field, on a wet day in winter, with the grass so green that it's almost blue, and a rotten gatepost covered with lichen and a cow standing in the grass and looking at you. And you'll go back after twenty years and be surprised because the cow isn't standing in the same place and looking at you with the same expression.

GEORGE ORWELL, *Coming Up For Air*, 1939

'Everyone has a garden in their head.' That was the idea my hypnotist friend had put into my mind all those years ago, and it had been nagging away as Tair-Ffynnon had been taking shape. For I knew that, despite all our efforts, if asked to close my eyes and imagine myself in my favourite garden, it still wouldn't be the one we'd made. It would be

283

Rookwoods, Granny's garden in the Cotswolds until I was five. Dear, beloved Rookwoods, with its stream across the lawn, its hanging beech-woods and its smell of wood-smoke. There I'd be, sprawled on the lawn in the sunshine, somewhere between the flowering cherry and the old Irish yew. So when I discovered Rookwoods was still in the Yellow Book, I realised I had to go back. I had to square my two gardens.

It's hard to convey the charmed, almost sacred resonance the word 'Rookwoods' had gradually acquired within our family in the almost four decades since I'd last set eyes on the place. It was after my mother's accident that its formal beatification commenced. Its name was soon mentioned only in tones of hushed respect, a mythical Atlantis or Babylon, lost in time. When Granny died and Ernest Dinkel's water-colour of the place came to us, the stand-off that developed over whose room it should hang in, Jonny's or mine, became so unpleasant that my father had the picture copied, so we could each live with Rookwoods immortalised in the watery spring sunshine. Meanwhile, Cyril's bird table beyond the kitchen window, as a holy relic of the Rookwoods era, hinted at the enchanted world we'd once known, and ensured that that capped horticulturalist soon became the divine apogee of the gentle, working countryman, a version of Cecil Beaton's 'Dove' at Ashcombe: patient, kind, devoted and infinitely wise.

I suggested to my father he might like to accompany me on Rook-woods' open day, the last Saturday in June. 'Nothing would induce me. And—if I may say so—you're mad to go yourself. You'll ruin your memories.' The trouble was rumours had reached us. Of housing developments nearby, of makeovers, of garden revamps. Would a return destroy the magic? Certainly the date in question could hardly have dawned less magical: one of those lifeless days of sullen white overcast. Nevertheless, brimming with curiosity and trepidation, with just the Yellow Book and a bootful of emotional baggage for company, I set off up the M4 onto the Cotswold escarpment.

As part of my extensive psychological preparations for the trip I'd looked up the year Granny first opened for the Scheme in the 1960

Yellow Book: 'Small garden, stream running through. Beautiful position in typical Cotswold valley,' read her entry. The contrast between this description and the one in the current Yellow Book lying on the passenger seat beside me had been weighing on my mind:

> 3-acre, well-structured garden with herbaceous borders to colour themes. Pleached whitebeam around pool area. Wide variety of old-fashioned and modern climbing and shrub roses (labelled), water gardens and outstanding views.

Not that I wasn't determined to be open-minded and non-judgmental. But honestly. Well-structured indeed! Colour themes and pleached whitebeams! Perhaps Rookwoods' new owners might have a few improvements for Eden, too?

After crossing the western edge of the Cotswolds, I plunged steeply downhill into unfamiliar terrain, through woodland so dense the midday glare was reduced to a dim half-light. It seemed an unlikely approach and I wondered if I'd made a mistake, if I was in pursuit of the wrong Rookwoods. Then, as the road narrowed, there was a kink through the brick arch of a railway viaduct. That I recognised. By some obscure reflex, it made me think of Cirencester, where Granny went to shop. And that, in turn, made me think of Butter Buns, because Cirencester was the only place that sold them. I hadn't thought of Butter Buns for decades. Granny used to have them for tea, and bring them to us in Somerset: doughy buns that became sweeter and more buttery as you neared the centre. As the Rookwoods myth picked up, my brother and I remembered about Butter Buns and my mother tried to get them again. No-one seemed to have heard of them—and Rookwoods became a notch more remote and unreal.

Another turn brought me to a small junction with yellow signs pointing down a no through road. Then one of the buildings, a farm, sprang into familiarity: *Mr Hunt's farm!* There it was. No question. A big tin barn, heaps of muck, clumps of nettles. Then I was passing through a pair of bright new stone gate piers, and bowling downhill between rows of young apple trees. I remembered the drive opening into a yard of shingle, mostly compacted hard, but loose at the edges where wheels had thrown up tiny Chesil banks, and the crunching sound whenever a car arrived or departed, or as the hooves of my mother's horses stamped and scraped. A friendly figure took my entrance fee and I was directed past the house to park. The front: was that how it used to be? I couldn't be sure. There was a sunken rose garden, yes, I thought I remembered that. But the house seemed wider. I drove through the stable yard past the woodshed. Everywhere seemed to have been glazed: there were no more dusty sheds and barns to explore now. I parked in a big rectangular arena for exercising horses.

The obvious starting point seemed to be to get to Dinkel's view and proceed from there. Following a flagged path round the side of the house—yes, that was definitely a new extension—I rounded the corner towards the lawn and the garden. And there, unmistakeably, was the yew. There was a lot of other planting, but the big old Irish yew, that couldn't be changed: so often imagined, it was weird to see it in all its solid reality. It was fatter and squatter than I remembered. It had clearly lost its top half and had somehow shuffled thirty yards closer to the house. In fact, everything had subtly shifted position. Taking the yew as my datum, I strode across the absurdly shrunken lawn and tried to station myself about where Dinkel must have set up his easel. Then I surveyed the scene.

It was all most disorientating. Every proportion had been tinkered with. On second thoughts, maybe the yew hadn't lost its top. Maybe it had just got fatter, and I'd remembered it as taller. The house was lower, and had definitely sprouted additions to left and right. I tried to focus on specifics. There seemed a lot less stonework. Where had that gone? Closer inspection revealed it was still there, but the wisteria and climbing roses had been allowed to take over, so that just the tops of the gables were visible. Yes, it was laxity with the pruning shears; that was the problem. I felt proprietorial, but prepared to be magnanimous. In my memory (no doubt greatly shaped by Dinkel) the scene was simpler and cleaner: the yew with its soft, dark roundness setting off the harder angles of the lighter-coloured building. Somehow, it was all a lot busier now: too much garden fighting with too much house. But there was no need for panic. There was little here that a day with wrecking ball, chainsaw and bill hook couldn't remedy.

Slightly at a loss what to do next, I decided to make for the pool. Of Rookwoods' many charms, the natural swimming pool, as the years elapsed, had come to seem the most singular. Cut into the hillside somewhere below the main garden, it was fed by the clear waters of the fast-flowing brook, which entered one end and left the other. I recalled balmy summer afternoons splashing in its crystalline waters. When I once described this almost Mediterranean scene to my father, he was fascinated: 'Is that really how you remember it?' The facts, he said, were somewhat different. The temperature of the water never once, in his memory, rose above 58°F. As for clarity, the stream may have been clear, but the pool itself—possibly, he thought, due to the action of algae on the concrete lining—remained a resolute black. The rotted, slime-coated wooden ladder with the crucial rungs missing was the cause of one accident after another, while the absence of changing facilities meant those tempted by a dip had to endure a 200-yard, bare-legged dash to and from the house via a narrow earth path lined with spiky gorse bushes and carpeted with their needles. 'It was,' he said, 'the most awful pool I've ever had anything to do with.'

Plainly a subsequent owner had agreed, because its replacement, a spotless turquoise rectangle in a terraced area (complete with the pleached whitebeams), was unconnected to the stream. Associated buildings, one emitting whirring sounds, indicated that water clarity, quality and temperature were no longer left to nature. From here was the view down the valley of hanging beeches. This too seemed preposterously small. The skyline, I noted, was now interrupted by a plantation of conifers.

It was hard to know what to think. While subsequent owners might have made changes I regarded as retrograde, I could hardly accuse them of shrinking the valley or moving the house about in relation to the lawn and the yew. What was becoming clear was that Rookwoods would be completely different, even if it hadn't changed a bit since I was last here. Because I'd changed.

Which was disconcerting. I'd come prepared for alterations—but not ones made in my head. Climbing the steps back up from the pool, anxious I was not using my visit to best advantage, I decided to try to find the place on the lawn between the cherry and the yew where I always saw myself whenever I thought of Rookwoods. The cherry seemed to have gone, so I picked a spot on an axis between the door in the central gable and a lychgate in the corner, placing me somewhere in the middle of Dinkel's painting. I lay down on the grass, closed my eyes and tried to imagine the sun warming my face. Immediately, a chilly breeze sent goose pimples rippling up my arms. I ransacked my mind for favourite Rookwoods memories: the musical chair in the nursery, the swing seat, the terrace where I first tasted dark, soft brown sugar on my porridge, climbing into Granny's bed before breakfast for a tedious fairy story and a glass of warm rosehip syrup. But it was no good. The discrepancy was too great. Even with my eyes shut, the humdrum ordinariness of the day kept intervening. 'Leave the flowers alone, Kitty ...,' said a voice. '... frankly Marjorie hasn't the faintest idea,' said another. 'D'you think the teas are over there?' I seemed to have chosen a principal thoroughfare across the lawn and the padding of feet was alarmingly close: people were practically stepping over me. Presently a fly settled on my nose. When a small brown dog began investigating my crutch with enthusiastic head-butts and snuffles of delight, I got to my feet.

As I did so a nearby group of adults and children resolved itself into unexpected familiarity. 'Hel-lo,' said a familiar voice. 'Fancy you being here.' It was Aunty Ruth, who has the same slight huskiness as her brother, Uncle William. And, in fact: there was Uncle William. 'Hello Ant,' he said, giving me a cheerful wave. And Aunty Jeanette was there, too; and my cousin Marcus with his family. What were they all doing? They lived miles away, and miles apart. Did they come every year when the place opened for the Yellow Book? 'We've been a couple of times,' said Aunty Ruth. 'We came last year.' Plainly Rookwoods' pulling power within our family had not diminished.

I explained I was on a pilgrimage, trying to see how Rookwoods matched my memories, what the place meant. 'Box,' volunteered Marcus. 'The smell of box. That's what it's always meant to me. Brings me back here the instant I smell it.' Uncle William had set off by himself. Something in the lawn had caught his attention and he was poking at it vigorously with a stick. I caught him up. It looked like an old root, surfacing where the stream emerged to cross the lawn. Whatever it was, he seemed very pleased to have found it. 'There you are,' he said. 'That's the cherry tree.'

After arranging to meet for tea, I hurried off to the kitchen garden to find out what box smelt like. Yes, sure enough, the cat's pee smell *was* familiar—so that's why I always associated Granny with it. Really it was just essence of Rookwoods. I glanced at my watch. The place closed in half an hour and I still didn't feel I'd got what I'd come for—whatever that was. I decided to buttonhole some people at random to find out why they were here. As luck would have it, the first person I tackled, a young woman with a child, told me she'd grown up at Rookwoods. She introduced me to her mother. I asked her, as an ex-owner, what she thought of the place now. 'Ghastly,' the woman said cheerfully.

'Ruined.' After a moment, she added: 'You know at least two other owners are here. Though frankly, they did some pretty dreadful things too.' Her directness was infectious and I joined in an enthusiastic bitching session. We were alongside the extension I'd passed on the way in, so that seemed a good place to start. I spared nothing as I lamented the grotesque disfigurement of a perfectly proportioned jewel. A short pause followed this sally. 'We put that on,' she said.

As I left, I wondered what my trip had achieved. Could I declare that Rookwoods was now deposed as the garden in my head, and that Tair-Ffynnon was installed in its place? The answer, I knew, was no. It was all very muddling. Everything about the place seemed different, yet Rookwoods' throne remained as impregnable as ever. Belatedly, I realised, the trip was an irrelevance. It wasn't the real Rookwoods that Tair-Ffynnon was competing with; it was the Rookwoods in my head. There, the sun always shone (except on Christmas Eve, obviously, when snow fell heavily), the cherry was always in blossom and the fire always burning in the hall. My imaginary Rookwoods was an edited compilation of highlights, forever bubble-wrapped in the cocoon of carefree childhood. 'The true paradises,' Proust tells us, 'are the paradises we have lost', and, of course, that was the whole point; it's precisely the losing that makes us remember the good bits and forget the bad. How could a real garden like Tair-Ffynnon ever compete, with its mud and flies, its grey days and day-to-day domestic mundanities? Obviously it had its moments. They are paraded whenever I pause at my computer keyboard, and the screensaver flashes up photographs we've taken over our time here: of pristine snow in sculptured drifts, of little grey Fergies working, of children frolicking like putti in the hay. Each time I find myself wondering: where is this charmed place? Then I remember— directly outside the door.

By the time I passed Raglan Castle and the Black Mountains loomed ahead, Blorenge's great bulk, Sugar Loaf's cone, Skirrid's slumped summit off to the right, I was ready to get home. Gerald says the Welsh have a word, *hiraeth*, that means a sort of nostalgia, but more place-based, a wistful homesickness that combines happiness for times past with melancholy because they are no more. That was what all this was about. Taking the unsigned turn at the bottom of the hill, I drove up through Mark's farmyard, past Vanessa's reprieved oak, still splodged with its yellow 'C', past the gate framing the view of Sugar Loaf, and on up and up until, after my ears popped on the final straight, I was back in stone-wall country. Despite it being June, the cloud—our cloud—had settled into its usual position at the hill gate.

Proust was wrong about one thing, I decided, as I let the gate clang shut. True paradises don't have to be lost. They can also lie ahead, just around the corner, just out of reach, born of anticipation as much as recollection. What was that French saying? 'The best moment in love is climbing the stairs to your beloved's apartment.' With that fine thought, I let out the clutch, sending loose stones flying as the wheels scrabbled for purchase on the steep gradient, and drove, with the usual feeling of intense satisfaction, into the murk.

291

Acknowledgements

Supreme thanks to Arabella Pike and Annabel Wright at HarperCollins for their dextrous surgery and (every bit as much) for their tact, tolerance and charm. Thanks also to Minna Fry and my agent Felicity Rubinstein. From the National Gardens Scheme, I'm grateful to Julia Grant, who threw open the Scheme's archives at Hatchlands, to Chris Morley and, most of all, to Joanna Kerr for her support throughout. Our lives in the Black Mountains would be unthinkable without Ginny and Paolo Baillie, Corisande and Angus Grahame, Vanessa Horne and Vicks and Rob Penn, all of whom have looked after us, our children and Beetle the dog, as well as helping in any number of other ways. To Angus, I'm also irksomely beholden for the book's title. Tom Hallifax has been an irrepressible fount of drawings, thoughts and ideas, not always appalling. In the making of the garden in the clouds—book and place—we also received help from countless others, beginning with Mary Rose-Richards, who first called to tell me about 'a place in the Black Mountains', but who, sadly, didn't live long enough to see it. Thanks also to Robin Alldred; Stephen Anderton; Clive Aslet; Richard Bower; Ed Buck; Willy Bullough and Whitney Sawmills; the Buxton family, for their patience; Len Cheeseman; Katherine Cooper; Philip and Terina Davies; Russell Davies; Pete Downey; Ronnie Duncan, whose Yorkshire garden made a stunning aperitif for Ian Hamilton Finlay's Little Sparta; Mark and Liz Egerton; Andrew Evans and Black Mountain Sheep's Wool Insulation; John Evans; Jasper and Mari Fforde and Jake Gavin for their artistic eyes and exquisite photographs (see www.gardenin theclouds.com); Gerry Fox; Ricky Gallop of Gallop & Rivers; Tony and Liz Gentil; James Greenwood; Brian Greenow; Revel Guest and Rob Albert; William and

Jeanette Gueterbock; Ben and Jen Hamilton-Baillie; Richard and Pat Harrad; John Holden and the Gwent Beekeepers; Nick and Kate Holmes; Richard Hopton; Stefan Horowskyj; Ann and Owen Inskip; Andrew Jackson; Oliver James; Mark, Bin, Naomi, Serena and Zoë Johnston; William Kendall; Mark and Susan Kidel, for copies of their BBC series *The Architecture of the Imagination* (1994); Bruce MacDougall; Harry Marshall and Icon Films for filming the carriage's progression up the mountain (also viewable on the website); Sue Milward; Guy Monson, for telling me about the garden in our heads; Gerald, Wayne and Glenn Morris and Richard Brymer; Tony Muhl; Ray and Meryl Newbigin; Petra Pinnock; James Powell; Garth Roberts; Merryn Somerset Webb; Jeremy Swift; Barnaby and Camilla Swire; Stephen and Sally Thomas; Roger and Susie Turnbull; Ian Wallace; Molly Watson; Phil Webb; Mervyn and Martin Whistance; Clive Williams of the Brecon Beacons National Park; Stephen Williams; the always helpful conservation officers of the Landmark Trust, National Trust and Cadw; and the longsuffering librarians at the Royal Horticultural Society's Lindley Library for my endlessly overdue books. Finally, thanks to my father, Peter, for his endless generosity, likewise to my mother-in-law Gay Woodley and her husband Paul. Also to my brother, Jonny. To my children Maya, Storm and Ivo, the last of whom arrived too late to feature in these pages but who (once he can read) will no doubt be miffed not to get a mention. Mercifully, they all seem to 'get' the joys of old Land Rovers, grey Fergies and living in gales and snow. May Tair-Ffynnon one day be the garden in their heads. Most of all, of course, thanks to Vez, to whom this windswept, fog-bound, muddy slice-of-life is dedicated with all my love.

All illustrations are by Fred van Deelen. The photographs on pages 37 and 38 appear courtesy of the National Gardens Scheme. The photograph on page 46 of William Ewart Gladstone by Elliott & Fry (1887) appears courtesy of © the National Portrait Gallery, London. The photograph on page 80 of Nanda Devi appears on the cover of *The Nanda Devi Affair* by Bill Aitken (Penguin Books India, 1994). The photographs on pages 98 and 101 appear courtesy of Jasper and Mari Fforde. The photograph on page 226 of Lindisfarne Castle appears courtesy of © NTPL/Joe Cornish. All other images are the author's own.

While every effort has been made to trace the owners of copyright material reproduced herein, the publishers would like to apologise for any omissions and would be pleased to incorporate missing acknowledgements in future editions.

The National Gardens Scheme

Because the National Gardens Scheme, by its nature, is about so much that is ideal, it can be easy to forget its central purpose: to raise funds to help those in the profoundly non-ideal situation of suffering from terminal illness. To me, the support and care of the dying meant little beyond the pictures in charity leaflets—which always seemed to show happy, smiling nurses and patients in brightly lit surroundings—until, at our first 'garden openers' meeting, Joanna Kerr told us a story.

A year or two ago, she said, on a remote farm in mid-Wales, ten miles by road from his nearest neighbour, lived an elderly bachelor farmer. He had terminal cancer, no surviving relations, and only a matter of days to live. He was visited by a nurse from Marie Curie Cancer Care (one of the charities sponsored by the National Gardens Scheme). Having made him comfortable, she could tell he was still somehow unsettled. It took a while to work out why, but gradually it emerged that, although he'd sold the rest of his livestock, he still had a cow. She was in calf, due any moment, and he was worried about her. So, following the farmer's instructions, the nurse put on his overalls, went out to the cow shed, calved the cow, and was soon able to report back that cow and calf were doing well. The farmer visibly relaxed, remaining so until he died a few days later. 'That,' said Joanna, 'is the kind of thing the money you are raising allows to happen.'

In the last ten years, the National Gardens Scheme has raised more than £25 million for its various charities, chief amongst them Macmillan Cancer Support, Marie Curie Cancer Care, Crossroads Care and Help the Hospices.

10% of any author's royalties arising from the sale of this book will go to the National Gardens Scheme.